Published by CGP

From original material by Richard Parsons.

Editors:
Katherine Craig, Ceara Hayden, Helena Hayes, Helen Ronan.

ISBN: 978 1 84146 756 6

With thanks to Hayley Thompson for the proofreading.
With thanks to Jan Greenway for the copyright research.

Data used to draw graph on page 31, source developed by the National Center for Health Statistics in collaboration with the National Center for Chronic Disease Prevention and Health Promotion (2000). http://www.cdc.gov/growthcharts

Data used to construct stopping distance diagram on page 103 from the Highway Code.
© Crown Copyright re-produced under the terms of the Click Use licence.

Every effort has been made to locate copyright holders and obtain permission to reproduce sources. For those sources where it has been difficult to trace the originator of the work, we would be grateful for information. If any copyright holder would like us to make an amendment to the acknowledgements, please notify us and we will gladly update the book at the next reprint. Thank you.

Groovy website: www.cgpbooks.co.uk

Printed by Elanders Ltd, Newcastle upon Tyne.
Jolly bits of clipart from CorelDRAW®

Photocopying — it's dull, grey and sometimes a bit naughty. Luckily, it's dead cheap, easy and quick to order more copies of this book from CGP — just call us on 0870 750 1242. Phew!

How Science Works

The Scientific Process

Before you get started with the really fun stuff, it's a good idea to understand exactly <u>how</u> the world of science <u>works</u>. Investigate these next few pages and you'll be laughing all day long on results day.

Scientists Come Up with <u>Hypotheses</u> — Then Test <u>Them</u>

About 100 years ago, we thought atoms looked like this.

1) Scientists try to <u>explain</u> things. Everything.

2) They start by <u>observing</u> or <u>thinking about</u> something they don't understand — it could be anything, e.g. planets in the sky, a person suffering from an illness, what matter is made of... anything.

3) Then, using what they already know (plus a bit of insight), they come up with a <u>hypothesis</u> — a possible <u>explanation</u> for what they've observed.

4) The next step is to <u>test</u> whether the hypothesis might be <u>right or not</u> — this involves <u>gathering evidence</u> (i.e. <u>data</u> from <u>investigations</u>).

5) To gather evidence the scientist uses the hypothesis to make a <u>prediction</u> — a statement based on the hypothesis that can be <u>tested</u> by carrying out <u>experiments</u>.

6) If the results from the experiments match the prediction, then the scientist can be <u>more confident</u> that the hypothesis is <u>correct</u>. This <u>doesn't</u> mean the hypothesis is <u>true</u> though — other predictions based on the hypothesis might turn out to be <u>wrong</u>.

Scientists <u>Work Together</u> to Test Hypotheses

1) Different scientists can look at the <u>same evidence</u> and interpret it in <u>different ways</u>. That's why scientists usually work in <u>teams</u> — they can share their <u>different ideas</u> on how to interpret the data they find.

2) Once a team has come up with (and tested) a hypothesis they all agree with, they'll present their work to the scientific community through <u>journals</u> and <u>scientific conferences</u> so it can be judged — this is called the <u>peer review</u> process.

Then we thought they looked like this.

3) Other scientists then <u>check</u> the team's results (by trying to <u>replicate</u> them) and carry out their own experiments to <u>collect more evidence</u>.

4) If all the experiments in the world back up the hypothesis, scientists start to have a lot of <u>confidence</u> in it. (A hypothesis that is <u>accepted</u> by pretty much every scientist is referred to as a <u>theory</u>.)

5) However, if another scientist does an experiment and the results <u>don't</u> fit with the hypothesis (and other scientists can <u>replicate</u> these results), then the hypothesis is in trouble. When this happens, scientists have to come up with a new hypothesis (maybe a <u>modification</u> of the old explanation, or maybe a completely <u>new</u> one).

Scientific Ideas <u>Change as New Evidence is Found</u>

Now we think it's more like this.

1) Scientific explanations are <u>provisional</u> because they only explain the evidence that's <u>currently available</u> — new evidence may come up that can't be explained.

2) This means that scientific explanations <u>never</u> become hard and fast, totally indisputable <u>fact</u>. As <u>new evidence</u> is found (or new ways of <u>interpreting</u> existing evidence are found), hypotheses can <u>change</u> or be <u>replaced</u>.

3) Sometimes, an <u>unexpected observation</u> or <u>result</u> will suddenly throw a hypothesis into doubt and further experiments will need to be carried out. This can lead to new developments that <u>increase</u> our <u>understanding</u> of science.

<u>You expect me to believe that — then show me the evidence...</u>

If scientists think something is true, they need to produce evidence to convince others — it's all part of <u>testing a hypothesis</u>. One hypothesis might survive these tests, while others won't — it's how things progress. And along the way some hypotheses will be disproved — i.e. shown not to be true.

Quality of Data

Evidence is the key to science — but not all evidence is equally good.
The way evidence is gathered can have a big effect on how trustworthy it is...

The Bigger the Sample Size the Better

1) Data based on small samples isn't as good as data based on large samples.
   A sample should be representative of the whole population (i.e. it should share as many of the various characteristics in the population as possible) — a small sample can't do that as well.

2) The bigger the sample size the better, but scientists have to be realistic when choosing how big.
   For example, if you were studying how lifestyle affects people's weight it'd be great to study everyone in the UK (a huge sample), but it'd take ages and cost a bomb. Studying a thousand people is more realistic.

Evidence Needs to be Reliable (Repeatable and Reproducible)

Evidence is only reliable if it can be repeated (during an experiment) AND other scientists can reproduce it too (in other experiments). If it's not reliable, you can't believe it.

> RELIABLE means that the data can be repeated, and reproduced by others.

EXAMPLE: In 1998, a scientist claimed that he'd found a link between the MMR (measles, mumps and rubella) vaccine and autism. However, no other scientist has been able to repeat the results since — they just weren't reliable. Because they couldn't be repeated, no-one has any reason to believe them.

Evidence Also Needs to Be Valid

> VALID means that the data is reliable AND answers the original question.

EXAMPLE: DO MOBILE PHONES CAUSE BRAIN TUMOURS?
Some studies have found that people who use mobile phones regularly are more likely to develop brain tumours. What they'd actually found was a correlation (relationship) between the variables "use of mobile phones" and "development of brain tumours" — they found that as one changed, so did the other. But this evidence is not enough to say that using a mobile phone causes brain tumours, as other explanations might be possible. For example, age, gender and family history can all increase the risk of developing a brain tumour. So these studies don't show a definite link and so don't answer the original question.

Don't Always Believe What You're Being Told Straight Away

1) People who want to make a point might present data in a biased way, e.g. by overemphasising a relationship in the data. (Sometimes without knowing they're doing it.)

2) And there are all sorts of reasons why people might want to do this — for example, companies might want to 'big up' their products. Or make impressive safety claims.

3) If an investigation is done by a team of highly-regarded scientists it's sometimes taken more seriously than evidence from less well known scientists.

4) But having experience, authority or a fancy qualification doesn't necessarily mean the evidence is good — the only way to tell is to look at the evidence scientifically (e.g. is it reliable, valid, etc.).

RRRR — Remember, Reliable means Repeatable and Reproducible...

By now you should have realised how important trustworthy evidence is (even more important than a good supply of spot cream). Without it (the evidence, not the spot cream), you just can't believe what you're being told.

Limits of Science and the Issues it Creates

Science can give us amazing things — cures for diseases, space travel, heated toilet seats...
But science has its limitations — there are questions that it just can't answer.

Some Questions Are Unanswered, Others are Unanswerable

1) Some questions are unanswered — we don't know everything and we never will. We'll find out more as new hypotheses are suggested and more experiments are done, but there'll always be stuff we don't know.

2) For example, we don't know what the exact impacts of global warming are going to be. At the moment scientists don't all agree on the answers because there isn't enough reliable and valid evidence.

3) Then there's the other type... questions that all the experiments in the world won't help us answer — the "Should we be doing this at all?" type questions. There are always two sides...

4) Take embryo screening (which allows you to choose an embryo with particular characteristics). It's possible to do it — but does that mean we should?

5) Different people have different opinions.

For example...

- Some people say it's good... couples whose existing child needs a bone marrow transplant, but who can't find a donor, will be able to have another child selected for its matching bone marrow. This would save the life of their first child — and if they want another child anyway... where's the harm?

- Other people say it's bad... they say it could have serious effects on the new child. In the above example, the new child might feel unwanted — thinking they were only brought into the world to help someone else. And would they have the right to refuse to donate their bone marrow (as anyone else would)?

THE GAZETTE
BONE MARROW BABY'S BROTHER SAVED

THE POST
BONE MARROW BABY BORN: WHAT RIGHTS DOES HE HAVE?

6) The question of whether something is morally or ethically right or wrong can't be answered by more experiments — there is no "right" or "wrong" answer.

7) The best we can do is get a consensus from society — a judgement that most people are more or less happy to live by. Science can provide more information to help people make this judgement, and the judgement might change over time. But in the end it's up to people and their conscience.

Scientific Developments are Great, but they can Raise Issues

Scientific knowledge is increased by doing experiments. And this knowledge leads to scientific developments, e.g. new technologies or new advice. These developments can create issues though. For example:

Economic issues: Society can't always afford to do things scientists recommend (e.g. investing heavily in alternative energy sources) without cutting back elsewhere.

Social issues: Decisions based on scientific evidence affect people — e.g. should fossil fuels be taxed more highly (to invest in alternative energy)? Should alcohol be banned (to prevent health problems)? Would the effect on people's lifestyles be acceptable...

Environmental issues: Genetically modified crops may help us produce more food — but some people think they could cause environmental problems.

Ethical issues: There are a lot of things that scientific developments have made possible, but should we do them? E.g. clone humans, develop better nuclear weapons.

Chips or rice? — totally unanswerable by science...

Science can't tell you whether you should or shouldn't do something. That is up to you and society to decide.

Planning Investigations

The next few pages show how <u>investigations</u> should be carried out — by both <u>professional scientists</u> and <u>you</u>.

To Make an Investigation a Fair Test You Have to Control the Variables

1) In a lab experiment you usually <u>change one variable</u> and <u>measure</u> how it affects the <u>other variable</u>.

> EXAMPLE: you might change only the temperature of an enzyme-controlled reaction and measure how it affects the rate of reaction.

2) To make it a fair test <u>everything else</u> that could affect the results should <u>stay the same</u> (otherwise you can't tell if the thing that's being changed is affecting the results or not — the data won't be reliable or valid).

> EXAMPLE continued: you need to keep the pH the same, otherwise you won't know if any change in the rate of reaction is caused by the change in temperature, or the change in pH.

3) The variable that you <u>change</u> is called the <u>independent</u> variable.

4) The variable that's <u>measured</u> is called the <u>dependent</u> variable.

5) The variables that you <u>keep the same</u> are called <u>control</u> variables.

> EXAMPLE continued:
> Independent = temperature
> Dependent = rate of reaction
> Control = pH

6) Because you can't always control all the variables, you often need to use a <u>control experiment</u> — an experiment that's kept under the <u>same conditions</u> as the rest of the investigation, but doesn't have anything done to it. This is so that you can see what happens when you don't change anything at all.

The Equipment Used has to be Right for the Job

1) The measuring equipment you use has to be <u>sensitive enough</u> to accurately measure the chemicals you're using, e.g. if you need to measure out 11 ml of a liquid, you'll need to use a measuring cylinder that can measure to 1 ml, not 5 or 10 ml.

> Accurate data is data that's close to the true value — see the next page.

2) The <u>smallest change</u> a measuring instrument can <u>detect</u> is called its RESOLUTION. E.g. some mass balances have a resolution of 1 g and some have a resolution of 0.1 g.

3) Also, equipment needs to be <u>calibrated</u> so that your data is <u>more accurate</u>. E.g. mass balances need to be set to zero before you start weighing things.

Experiments Must be Safe

1) Part of planning an investigation is making sure that it's <u>safe</u>.

2) A <u>hazard</u> is something that can <u>potentially cause harm</u>.

3) There are lots of <u>hazards</u> you could be faced with during an investigation, e.g. <u>radiation</u>, <u>electricity</u>, <u>gas</u>, <u>chemicals</u> and <u>fire</u>.

4) You should always make sure that you <u>identify</u> all the hazards that you might encounter.

5) You should also come up with ways of <u>reducing the risks</u> from the hazards you've identified.

6) One way of doing this is to carry out a <u>risk assessment</u>:

> For an experiment involving a <u>Bunsen burner</u>, the risk assessment might be something like this:

> <u>Hazard:</u> Bunsen burner is a fire risk.
> <u>Precautions:</u>
> • Keep flammable chemicals away from the Bunsen.
> • Never leave the Bunsen unattended when lit.
> • Always turn on the yellow safety flame when not in use.

Hazard: revision boredom. Precaution: use CGP books

Labs are dangerous places — you need to know the <u>hazards</u> of what you're doing <u>before you start</u>.

Collecting Data

There are a few things that can be done to make sure that you get the <u>best results</u> you possibly can.

Data Should be as Reliable, Accurate and Precise as Possible

1) When carrying out an investigation, you can <u>improve</u> the reliability of your results (see p.3) by <u>repeating</u> the readings and calculating the mean (average, see next page). You should repeat readings at least <u>twice</u> (so that you have at least <u>three</u> readings to calculate an average result).

2) To make sure your results are reliable you can cross check them by taking a <u>second set of readings</u> with <u>another instrument</u> (or a <u>different observer</u>).

3) Checking your results match with <u>secondary sources</u>, e.g. studies that other people have done, also increases the reliability of your data.

4) You should always make sure that your results are <u>accurate</u>. Really accurate results are those that are <u>really close</u> to the <u>true answer</u>.

5) You can get accurate results by doing things like making sure the <u>equipment</u> you're using is <u>sensitive enough</u> (see previous page), and by recording your data to a suitable <u>level of accuracy</u>. For example, if you're taking digital readings of something, the results will be more accurate if you include at least a couple of decimal places instead of rounding to whole numbers.

6) You should also always make sure your results are <u>precise</u>. Precise results are ones where the data is <u>all really close</u> to the <u>mean</u> (i.e. not spread out).

Trial Runs Help Figure out the Range and Interval of Variable Values

1) Before you carry out an experiment, it's a good idea to do a <u>trial run</u> first — a <u>quick version</u> of your experiment.

2) Trial runs help you work out whether your plan is <u>right or not</u> — you might decide to make some <u>changes</u> after trying out your method.

3) Trial runs are used to figure out the <u>range</u> of variable values used (the upper and lower limit).

4) And they're used to figure out the <u>interval</u> (gaps) between the values too.

> Enzyme-controlled reaction example from previous page continued:
>
> • You might do trial runs at 10, 20, 30, 40 and 50 °C. If there was no reaction at 10 or 50 °C, you might narrow the range to 20-40 °C.
>
> • If using 10 °C intervals gives you a big change in rate of reaction you might decide to use 5 °C intervals, e.g. 20, 25, 30, 35...

5) Trial runs can also help you figure out <u>how many times</u> the experiment has to be <u>repeated</u> to get reliable results. E.g. if you repeat it two times and the <u>results</u> are all <u>similar</u>, then two repeats is enough.

You Can Check For Mistakes Made When Collecting Data

1) When you've collected all the results for an experiment, you should have a look to see if there are any results that <u>don't seem to fit</u> in with the rest.

2) Most results vary a bit, but any that are totally different are called <u>anomalous results</u>.

3) They're <u>caused</u> by <u>human errors</u>, e.g. by a whoopsie when measuring.

4) The only way to stop them happening is by taking all your measurements as <u>carefully</u> as possible.

5) If you ever get any anomalous results, you should investigate them to try to <u>work out what happened</u>. If you can work out what happened (e.g. you measured something wrong) you can <u>ignore</u> them when processing your results.

Reliable data — it won't ever forget your birthday...

All this stuff is really important — without <u>good quality</u> data an investigation will be totally <u>meaningless</u>. So give this page a read through a couple of times and your data will be the envy of the whole scientific community.

Processing, Presenting and Interpreting Data

The fun doesn't stop once the data's been collected — it then needs to be <u>processed</u> and <u>presented</u>...

Data Needs to be Organised

1) Data that's been collected needs to be <u>organised</u> so it can be processed later on.
2) <u>Tables</u> are dead useful for <u>organising data</u>.
3) When drawing tables you should always make sure that <u>each column</u> has a <u>heading</u> and that you've included the <u>units</u>.
4) Annoyingly, tables are about as useful as a chocolate teapot for showing <u>patterns</u> or <u>relationships</u> in data. You need to use some kind of graph or mathematical technique for that...

Test tube	Result (ml)	Repeat 1 (ml)	Repeat 2 (ml)
A	28	37	32
B	47	51	60
C	68	72	70

Data Can be Processed Using a Bit of Maths

1) <u>Raw data</u> generally just ain't that useful. You usually have to <u>process</u> it in some way.
2) A couple of the most simple calculations you can perform are the <u>mean</u> (average) and the <u>range</u> (how spread out the data is):

- To calculate the <u>mean</u> <u>ADD TOGETHER</u> all the data values and <u>DIVIDE</u> by the total number of values. You usually do this to get a single value from several <u>repeats</u> of your experiment.
- To calculate the <u>range</u> find the <u>LARGEST</u> number and <u>SUBTRACT</u> the <u>SMALLEST</u> number. You usually do this to <u>check</u> the accuracy and reliability of the results — the <u>greater</u> the <u>spread</u> of the data, the <u>lower</u> the accuracy and reliability.

Test tube	Result (ml)	Repeat 1 (ml)	Repeat 2 (ml)	Mean (ml)	Range
A	28	37	32	(28 + 37 + 32) ÷ 3 = 32.3	37 − 28 = 9
B	47	51	60	(47 + 51 + 60) ÷ 3 = 52.7	60 − 47 = 13
C	68	72	70	(68 + 72 + 70) ÷ 3 = 70.0	72 − 68 = 4

Different Types of Data Should be Presented in Different Ways

1) Once you've carried out an investigation, you'll need to <u>present</u> your data so that it's easier to see <u>patterns</u> and <u>relationships</u> in the data.
2) Different types of investigations give you <u>different types</u> of data, so you'll always have to <u>choose</u> what the best way to present your data is.

Pie charts can be used to present the same sort of data as bar charts. They're mostly used when the data is in percentages or fractions though.

Bar Charts

If the independent variable is <u>categoric</u> (comes in distinct categories, e.g. blood types, metals) you should use a <u>bar chart</u> to display the data. You also use them if the independent variable is <u>discrete</u> (the data can be counted in chunks, where there's no in-between value, e.g. number of people is discrete because you can't have half a person).

There are some <u>golden rules</u> you need to follow for <u>drawing</u> bar charts:

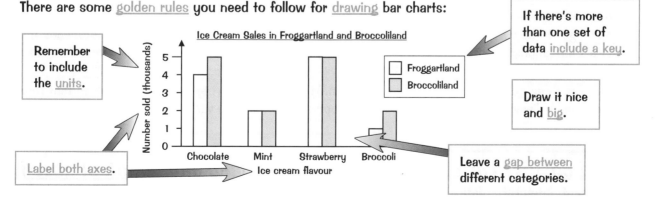

Remember to include the <u>units</u>.

Label both axes.

If there's more than one set of data <u>include a key</u>.

Draw it nice and <u>big</u>.

Leave a <u>gap between</u> different categories.

How Science Works

Processing, Presenting and Interpreting Data

Line Graphs

If the independent variable is <u>continuous</u> (numerical data that can have any value within a range, e.g. length, volume, temperature) you should use a <u>line graph</u> to display the data.

When plotting points, use a <u>sharp pencil</u> and make a <u>neat little cross</u> (don't do blobs).

nice clear mark

smudged unclear marks

Remember to include the <u>units</u>.

The <u>dependent</u> variable (the thing you measure) goes on the <u>y-axis</u> (the <u>vertical</u> one).

The <u>independent</u> variable (the thing you change) goes on the <u>x-axis</u> (the <u>horizontal</u> one).

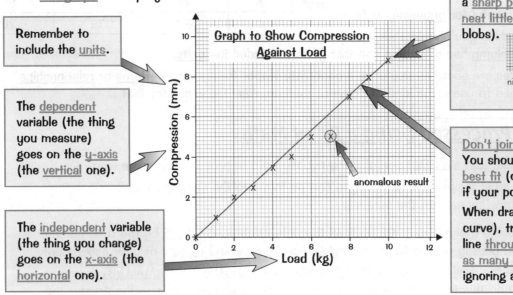

Graph to Show Compression Against Load

Compression (mm)

Load (kg)

anomalous result

<u>Don't join the dots up</u>. You should draw a <u>line of best fit</u> (or a <u>curve of best fit</u> if your points make a curve).

When drawing a line (or curve), try to draw the line <u>through</u> or as <u>near</u> to <u>as many points as possible</u>, ignoring anomalous results.

Line Graphs **Can Show** Relationships **in** Data

1) Line graphs are great for showing relationships <u>between two variables</u> (just like other graphs).

2) Here are some of the different types of <u>correlation</u> (relationship) shown on line graphs:

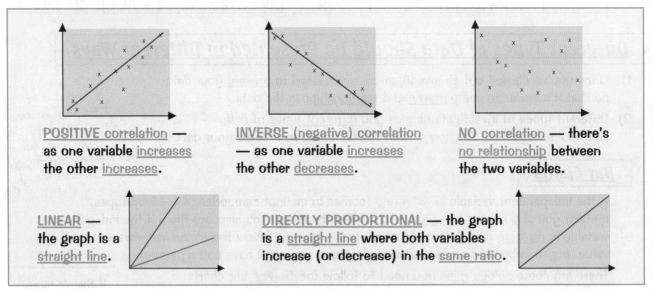

<u>POSITIVE</u> correlation — as one variable <u>increases</u> the other <u>increases</u>.

<u>INVERSE</u> (negative) correlation — as one variable <u>increases</u> the other <u>decreases</u>.

<u>NO</u> correlation — there's <u>no relationship</u> between the two variables.

<u>LINEAR</u> — the graph is a <u>straight line</u>.

<u>DIRECTLY PROPORTIONAL</u> — the graph is a <u>straight line</u> where both variables increase (or decrease) in the <u>same ratio</u>.

3) You've got to be careful not to <u>confuse correlation</u> with <u>cause</u> though. A <u>correlation</u> just means that there's a <u>relationship</u> between two variables. It <u>doesn't always mean</u> that the change in one variable is <u>causing</u> the change in the other.

4) There are <u>three possible reasons</u> for a correlation. It could be down to <u>chance</u>, it could be that there's a <u>third variable</u> linking the two things, or it might actually be that one variable is <u>causing</u> the other to change.

There's a positive correlation between age of man and length of nose hair...

<u>Process</u>, <u>present</u>, <u>interpret</u>... data's like a difficult child — it needs a lot of attention. Go on, make it happy.

Concluding and Evaluating

At the end of an investigation, the conclusion and evaluation are waiting. Don't worry, they won't bite.

A Conclusion is a Summary of What You've Learnt

1) Once all the data's been collected, presented and analysed, an investigation will always involve coming to a conclusion.

2) Drawing a conclusion can be quite straightforward — just look at your data and say what pattern you see.

EXAMPLE: The table on the right shows the heights of pea plant seedlings grown for three weeks with different fertilisers.

Fertiliser	Mean growth (mm)
A	13.5
B	19.5
No fertiliser	5.5

CONCLUSION: Fertiliser B makes pea plant seedlings grow taller over a three week period than fertiliser A.

3) However, you also need to use the data that's been collected to justify the conclusion (back it up).

EXAMPLE continued: Fertiliser B made the pea plants grow 6 mm more on average than fertiliser A.

4) There are some things to watch out for too — it's important that the conclusion matches the data it's based on and doesn't go any further.

5) Remember not to confuse correlation and cause (see previous page). You can only conclude that one variable is causing a change in another if you have controlled all the other variables (made it a fair test).

EXAMPLE continued: You can't conclude that fertiliser B makes any other type of plant grow taller than fertiliser A — the results could be totally different. Also, you can't make any conclusions beyond the three weeks — the plants could drop dead.

Evaluations — Describe How it Could be Improved

An evaluation is a critical analysis of the whole investigation.

I'd value this E somewhere in the region of 250-300k

1) You should comment on the method — was the equipment suitable? Was it a fair test?

2) Comment on the quality of the results — was there enough evidence to reach a valid conclusion? Were the results reliable, accurate and precise?

3) Were there any anomalies in the results — if there were none then say so.

4) If there were any anomalies, try to explain them — were they caused by errors in measurement? Were there any other variables that could have affected the results?

5) When you analyse your investigation like this, you'll be able to say how confident you are that your conclusion is right.

6) Then you can suggest any changes that would improve the quality of the results, so that you could have more confidence in your conclusion. For example, you might suggest changing the way you controlled a variable, or changing the interval of values you measured.

7) You could also make more predictions based on your conclusion, then further experiments could be carried out to test them.

8) When suggesting improvements to the investigation, always make sure that you say why you think this would make the results better.

Evaluation — in my next study I will make sure I don't burn the lab down...

I know it doesn't seem very nice, but writing about where you went wrong is an important skill — it shows you've got a really good understanding of what the investigation was about. It's difficult for me — I'm always right.

Cells

All living things are made of cells. When someone first peered down a microscope at a slice of cork and drew the boxes they saw, little did they know that they'd seen the building blocks of every organism on the planet.

Plant and Animal Cells Have Similarities and Differences

Most animal and plant cells have the following parts:

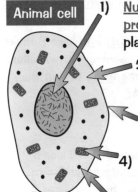
Animal cell

1) **Nucleus** — contains DNA (see page 25). DNA contains the instructions for making proteins, e.g. the enzymes used in the chemical reactions of respiration (in animal and plant cells, see page 18) and photosynthesis (in plant cells only, see page 43).

2) **Cytoplasm** — gel-like substance where proteins like enzymes (see page 13) are made. Some enzyme-controlled reactions take place in the cytoplasm, e.g. the reactions of anaerobic respiration (see page 19).

3) **Cell membrane** — holds the cell together and controls what goes in and out. It lets gases and water pass through freely while acting as a barrier to other chemicals.

4) **Mitochondria** — these are where the enzymes needed for the reactions of aerobic respiration are found, and where the reactions take place.

5) **Ribosomes** — these are where proteins are made in the cell.

Plant cells also have a few extra things that animal cells don't have:

1) Rigid **cell wall** — made of cellulose. It supports the cell and strengthens it.

2) **Vacuole** — contains cell sap, a weak solution of sugar and salts.

3) **Chloroplasts** — these are where the reactions for photosynthesis take place. They contain a green substance called chlorophyll and the enzymes needed for photosynthesis.

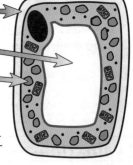
Plant cell

The cells of algae (e.g. seaweed) also have a rigid cell wall and chloroplasts.

Yeast is a Single-Celled Organism

Yeast is a microorganism. A yeast cell has a nucleus, cytoplasm, and a cell membrane surrounded by a cell wall.

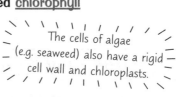
cell membrane | cytoplasm | cell wall | nucleus containing DNA

Bacteria Have a Simple Cell Structure

1) Bacterial cells are a bit different to plant, animal and yeast cells.

2) They don't have a nucleus. They have a circular molecule of DNA which floats around in the cytoplasm.

3) They don't have mitochondria either, but they can still respire aerobically.

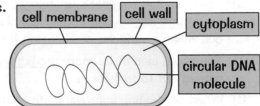
cell membrane | cell wall | cytoplasm | circular DNA molecule

At yeast it's an easy page...

It might look like there's lots on the page but don't let that put you off — it's not as mind boggling as it seems and there's a dead simple way of learning it all. Just draw a table showing the different parts of plant, animal, yeast and bacterial cells. Before you know it you'll be an expert on cells, just like me.

Specialised Cells

The previous page shows the structure of some typical cells. However, most cells are specialised for their specific function, so their structure can vary...

1) Palisade Leaf Cells Are Adapted for Photosynthesis

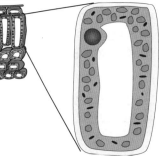

1) Packed with chloroplasts for photosynthesis. More of them are crammed at the top of the cell — so they're nearer the light.
2) Tall shape means a lot of surface area exposed down the side for absorbing CO_2 from the air in the leaf.
3) Thin shape means that you can pack loads of them in at the top of a leaf.

Palisade leaf cells are grouped together at the top of the leaf where most of the photosynthesis (see page 43) happens.

2) Guard Cells Are Adapted to Open and Close Pores

1) Special kidney shape which opens and closes the stomata (pores) in a leaf.
2) When the plant has lots of water the guard cells fill with it and go plump and turgid. This makes the stomata open so gases can be exchanged for photosynthesis.
3) When the plant is short of water, the guard cells lose water and become flaccid, making the stomata close. This helps stop too much water vapour escaping.
4) Thin outer walls and thickened inner walls make the opening and closing work.

5) They're also sensitive to light and close at night to save water without losing out on photosynthesis.

Guard cells are therefore adapted to their function of allowing gas exchange and controlling water loss within a leaf.

3) Red Blood Cells Are Adapted to Carry Oxygen

1) Concave shape gives a big surface area for absorbing oxygen. It also helps them pass smoothly through capillaries to reach body cells.
2) They're packed with haemoglobin — the pigment that absorbs the oxygen.
3) They have no nucleus, to leave even more room for haemoglobin.

Red blood cells are an important part of the blood.

4) Sperm and Egg Cells Are Specialised for Reproduction

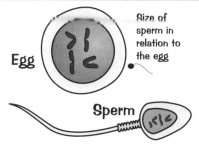

Egg

Size of sperm in relation to the egg

Sperm

1) The main functions of an egg cell are to carry the female DNA and to nourish the developing embryo in the early stages. The egg cell contains huge food reserves to feed the embryo.
2) When a sperm fuses with the egg, the egg's membrane instantly changes its structure to stop any more sperm getting in. This makes sure the offspring end up with the right amount of DNA.
3) The function of a sperm is basically to get the male DNA to the female DNA. It has a long tail and a streamlined head to help it swim to the egg. There are a lot of mitochondria in the cell to provide the energy needed.

4) Sperm also carry enzymes in their heads to digest through the egg cell membrane.
Sperm and eggs are very important cells in reproduction.

Beans, flying saucers, tadpoles — cells are masters of disguise...

These cells all have all the bits shown on the previous page, even though they look completely different and do totally different jobs. Apart from red blood cells that is, which are a bit special, e.g. they don't have a nucleus.

Cell Organisation

How, you might wonder, does having all these <u>specialised cells</u> mean you end up with a working <u>human</u> or <u>squirrel</u>... the answer's <u>organisation</u>. Otherwise you'd just have a meaty splodge.

Large Multicellular Organisms are Made Up of Organ Systems

1) As you know from the previous page, <u>specialised cells</u> carry out a <u>particular function</u>.
2) The <u>process</u> by which cells become specialised for a particular job is called <u>differentiation</u>.
3) Differentiation occurs during the <u>development</u> of a multicellular organism.
4) These <u>specialised cells</u> form <u>tissues</u>, which form <u>organs</u>, which form <u>organ systems</u> (see below).
5) <u>Large multicellular organisms</u> (e.g. squirrels) have different <u>systems</u> inside them for <u>exchanging</u> and <u>transporting</u> materials.

Similar Cells are Organised into Tissues

A <u>tissue</u> is a <u>group</u> of <u>similar cells</u> that work together to carry out a particular <u>function</u>. It can include <u>more than one type</u> of cell. In <u>mammals</u> (like humans), examples of tissues include:

1) <u>Muscular tissue</u>, which <u>contracts</u> (shortens) to <u>move</u> whatever it's attached to.
2) <u>Glandular tissue</u>, which <u>makes</u> and <u>secretes</u> chemicals like <u>enzymes</u> and <u>hormones</u>.
3) <u>Epithelial tissue</u>, which <u>covers</u> some parts of the body, e.g. the <u>inside</u> of the <u>gut</u>.

Epithelial cell

less than 0.1 mm

Epithelial tissue

Tissues are Organised into Organs

An <u>organ</u> is a group of <u>different tissues</u> that work together to perform a certain <u>function</u>. For example, the <u>stomach</u> is an organ made of these tissues:

1) <u>Muscular tissue</u>, which moves the stomach wall to <u>churn up the food</u>.
2) <u>Glandular tissue</u>, which makes <u>digestive juices</u> to digest food.
3) <u>Epithelial tissue</u>, which covers the <u>outside</u> and <u>inside</u> of the stomach.

Stomach

about 10 cm (over 1000 times longer than an epithelial cell)

Organs are Organised into Organ Systems

An <u>organ system</u> is a <u>group of organs</u> working together to perform a particular <u>function</u>. For example, the <u>digestive system</u> (found in humans and mammals) <u>breaks down food</u> and is made up of these organs:

1) <u>Glands</u> (e.g. the <u>pancreas</u> and <u>salivary glands</u>), which produce <u>digestive juices</u>.
2) The <u>stomach</u> and <u>small intestine</u>, which <u>digest</u> food.
3) The <u>liver</u>, which produces <u>bile</u>.
4) The <u>small intestine</u>, which <u>absorbs</u> soluble <u>food</u> molecules.
5) The <u>large intestine</u>, which <u>absorbs water</u> from undigested food, leaving <u>faeces</u>.

The digestive system <u>exchanges materials</u> with the <u>environment</u> by <u>taking in nutrients</u> and <u>releasing substances</u> such as bile.
There's more on the digestive system on pages 15-16.

Salivary glands

Liver

Digestive system
- Stomach
- Pancreas
- Small intestine
- Large intestine

See p.16 for a bigger diagram of the digestive system.

Soft and quilted — the best kind of tissues...

OK, <u>cells</u> are organised into <u>tissues</u>, the tissues into <u>organs</u>, and the organs into a whole <u>organism</u>. Or, to put it another way, an <u>organism</u> consists of <u>organs</u> which are made of <u>tissues</u> which are groups of <u>cells</u> working together.

Enzymes

Chemical reactions are what make you work. And enzymes are what make them work.

Enzymes Are Catalysts Produced by Living Things

1) Living things have thousands of different chemical reactions going on inside them all the time. These reactions need to be carefully controlled — to get the right amounts of substances.

2) You can usually make a reaction happen more quickly by raising the temperature. This would speed up the useful reactions but also the unwanted ones too... not good. There's also a limit to how far you can raise the temperature inside a living creature before its cells start getting damaged.

3) So... living things produce enzymes that act as biological catalysts. Enzymes reduce the need for high temperatures and we only have enzymes to speed up the useful chemical reactions in the body.

> A CATALYST is a substance which INCREASES the speed of a reaction,
> without being CHANGED or USED UP in the reaction.

4) Enzymes are all proteins and all proteins are made up of chains of amino acids. These chains are folded into unique shapes, which enzymes need to do their jobs (see below).

5) As well as catalysts, proteins act as structural components of tissues (e.g. muscles), hormones and antibodies.

Enzymes are Very Specific

1) Chemical reactions usually involve things either being split apart or joined together.

2) A substrate is a molecule that is changed in a reaction.

3) Every enzyme molecule has an active site — the part where a substrate joins on to the enzyme.

4) Enzymes are really picky — they usually only speed up one reaction. This is because, for an enzyme to work, a substrate has to be the correct shape to fit into the active site.

5) This is called the 'lock and key' model, because the substrate fits into the enzyme just like a key fits into a lock.

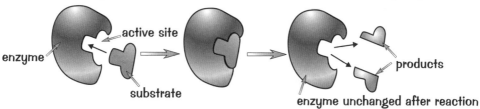

Enzymes Need the Right Temperature and pH

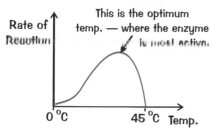

1) Changing the temperature changes the rate of an enzyme-catalysed reaction.

2) Like with any reaction, a higher temperature increases the rate at first. But if it gets too hot, some of the bonds holding the enzyme together break. This destroys the enzyme's special shape and so it won't work any more. It's said to be denatured.

3) Enzymes in the human body normally work best at around 37 °C.

4) The pH also affects enzymes. If it's too high or too low, the pH interferes with the bonds holding the enzyme together. This changes the shape and denatures the enzyme.

5) All enzymes have an optimum pH that they work best at. It's often neutral pH 7, but not always — e.g. pepsin is an enzyme used to break down proteins in the stomach. It works best at pH 2, which means it's well-suited to the acidic conditions there.

If the lock & key mechanism fails, you get in through a window...

Just like you've got to have the correct key for a lock, you've got to have the right substance for an enzyme. If the substance doesn't fit, the enzyme won't catalyse the reaction...

Enzymes and Reaction Rates

You can <u>measure</u> how a variable, e.g. temperature, affects the rate of an <u>enzyme-controlled reaction</u>. Goggles at the ready.

Measuring the Rate of an Enzyme-Controlled Reaction — Method

1) You can measure the rate of a reaction by using <u>amylase</u> as the <u>enzyme</u> and <u>starch</u> as the <u>substrate</u>.

2) <u>Amylase</u> catalyses the breakdown of <u>starch</u>, so you can <u>time</u> how long it takes for the <u>starch</u> to <u>disappear</u>.

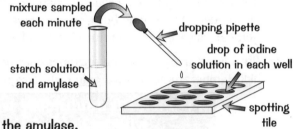

mixture sampled each minute

dropping pipette

drop of iodine solution in each well

starch solution and amylase

spotting tile

3) To do this, regularly take a <u>drop</u> of the amylase and starch mixture, and put it onto a drop of <u>iodine solution</u> on a spotting tile. Record the colour change — it'll turn <u>blue-black</u> if <u>starch</u> is present. Note the <u>time</u> when the iodine solution <u>no longer</u> turns blue-black — the starch has then been <u>broken down</u> by the amylase.

4) You can use the times to <u>compare reaction rates</u> under different <u>conditions</u> — see below.

Measuring the Rate of an Enzyme-Controlled Reaction — Variables

In the amylase/starch experiment above you need to choose which variable to change. For example:

- to investigate the effect of <u>temperature</u>, put the test tubes into <u>water baths</u> at a range of temperatures.

- to investigate the effect of <u>pH</u>, use a range of different <u>pH buffers</u>.

- to investigate the effect of <u>substrate concentration</u>, vary the initial <u>concentrations</u> of the <u>starch solutions</u>.

Remember to keep all the variables you're not investigating constant, e.g. use the same amylase concentration each time.

Q_{10} Values Show How Rate of Reaction Changes with Temperature

1) The Q_{10} <u>value</u> for a reaction shows how much the <u>rate changes</u> when the <u>temperature</u> is <u>raised</u> by <u>10 °C</u>.

2) You can <u>calculate it</u> using this <u>equation</u>:

$$Q_{10} = \frac{\text{rate at higher temperature}}{\text{rate at lower temperature}}$$

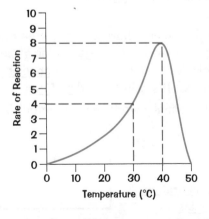

Rate of Reaction vs Temperature (°C)

3) The graph on the left shows the <u>rate of a reaction</u> between 0 °C and 50 °C. Here's how to calculate the Q_{10} value of the reaction using the rate at <u>30 °C</u> and at <u>40 °C</u>:

$$Q_{10} = \frac{\text{rate at 40 °C}}{\text{rate at 30 °C}} = \frac{8}{4} = 2$$

4) A Q_{10} value of <u>2</u> means that the <u>rate doubles</u> when the temperature is raised by 10 °C. A Q_{10} value of <u>3</u> would mean that the <u>rate trebles</u>.

If only enzymes could speed up revision...

A nice experimental <u>method</u> to start, an interlude on <u>variables</u> and the grand finale of an impressive looking <u>equation</u> and an interestingly-shaped <u>graph</u>. You can't say we don't spoil you rotten. No need to thank us.

Enzymes and Digestion

Not all enzymes work inside body cells — some work <u>outside</u> cells. For example, the enzymes used in <u>digestion</u> are produced by cells and then <u>released</u> into the <u>gut</u> to <u>mix</u> with <u>food</u>. Makes sense, really.

Digestive Enzymes *Break Down* Big Molecules *into* Smaller Ones

1) <u>Starch</u>, <u>proteins</u> and <u>fats</u> are BIG molecules.
   They're too big to pass through the walls of the digestive system.

2) <u>Sugars</u>, <u>amino acids</u>, <u>glycerol</u> and <u>fatty acids</u> are much smaller molecules.
   They can pass easily through the walls of the digestive system.

3) The <u>digestive enzymes</u> break down the BIG molecules into the smaller ones.

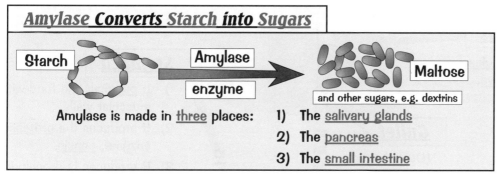

Amylase *Converts Starch into Sugars*

Starch → Amylase enzyme → Maltose
and other sugars, e.g. dextrins

Amylase is made in <u>three</u> places:
1) The <u>salivary glands</u>
2) The <u>pancreas</u>
3) The <u>small intestine</u>

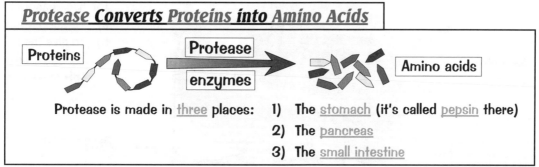

Protease *Converts Proteins into Amino Acids*

Proteins → Protease enzymes → Amino acids

Protease is made in <u>three</u> places:
1) The <u>stomach</u> (it's called <u>pepsin</u> there)
2) The <u>pancreas</u>
3) The <u>small intestine</u>

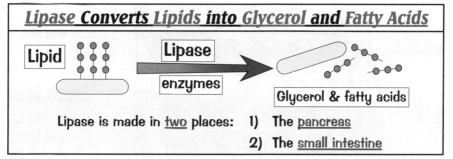

Lipase *Converts Lipids into Glycerol and Fatty Acids*

Lipid → Lipase enzymes → Glycerol & fatty acids

Lipase is made in <u>two</u> places:
1) The <u>pancreas</u>
2) The <u>small intestine</u>

Lipids are fats and oils.

Bile Neutralises *the Stomach Acid and* Emulsifies *Fats*

1) Bile is <u>produced</u> in the <u>liver</u>. It's <u>stored</u> in the <u>gall bladder</u> before it's released into the <u>small intestine</u>.

2) The <u>hydrochloric acid</u> in the stomach makes the pH <u>too acidic</u> for enzymes in the small intestine to work properly. Bile is <u>alkaline</u> — it <u>neutralises</u> the acid and makes conditions <u>alkaline</u>. The enzymes in the small intestine <u>work best</u> in these alkaline conditions.

3) It <u>emulsifies</u> fats. In other words it breaks the fat into <u>tiny droplets</u>. This gives a much <u>bigger surface area</u> of fat for the enzyme lipase to work on — which makes its digestion <u>faster</u>.

What do you call an acid that's eaten all the pies...

This all happens inside our digestive system, but there are some microorganisms that secrete their digestive enzymes <u>outside their body</u> onto the food. The food's digested, then the microorganism absorbs the nutrients. Nice. I wouldn't like to empty the contents of my stomach onto my plate before eating it.

More on Enzymes and Digestion

So now you know what the enzymes do, here's a nice big picture of the whole of the digestive system.

The Breakdown of Food is Catalysed by Enzymes

1) Enzymes used in the digestive system are produced by specialised cells in glands and in the gut lining.

2) Different enzymes catalyse the breakdown of different food molecules.

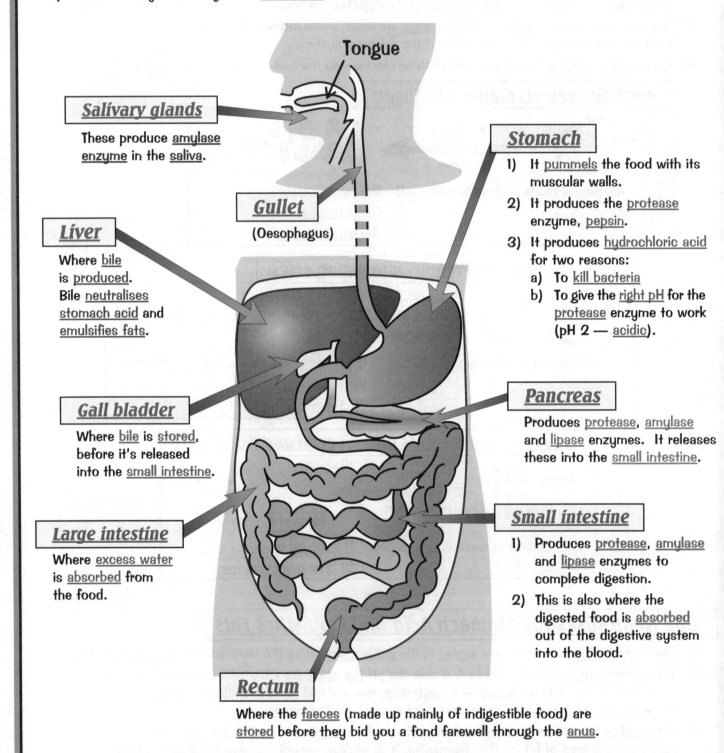

Tongue

Salivary glands

These produce amylase enzyme in the saliva.

Gullet
(Oesophagus)

Liver

Where bile is produced. Bile neutralises stomach acid and emulsifies fats.

Gall bladder

Where bile is stored, before it's released into the small intestine.

Large intestine

Where excess water is absorbed from the food.

Stomach

1) It pummels the food with its muscular walls.

2) It produces the protease enzyme, pepsin.

3) It produces hydrochloric acid for two reasons:
   a) To kill bacteria
   b) To give the right pH for the protease enzyme to work (pH 2 — acidic).

Pancreas

Produces protease, amylase and lipase enzymes. It releases these into the small intestine.

Small intestine

1) Produces protease, amylase and lipase enzymes to complete digestion.

2) This is also where the digested food is absorbed out of the digestive system into the blood.

Rectum

Where the faeces (made up mainly of indigestible food) are stored before they bid you a fond farewell through the anus.

Mmmm — so who's for a chocolate digestive...

Did you know that the whole of your digestive system is actually a hole that goes right through your body. Think about it. It just gets loads of food, digestive juices and enzymes piled into it. Most of it's then absorbed into the body and the rest is politely stored ready for removal.

Uses of Enzymes

Some microorganisms produce enzymes which pass out of their cells and catalyse reactions outside them (e.g. to digest the microorganism's food). These enzymes have many uses in the home and in industry.

Enzymes Are Used in Biological Detergents

1) Enzymes are the 'biological' ingredients in biological detergents and washing powders.
2) They're mainly protein-digesting enzymes (proteases) and fat-digesting enzymes (lipases).
3) Because the enzymes break down animal and plant matter, they're ideal for removing stains like food or blood.
4) Biological detergents are also more effective at working at low temperatures (e.g. 30 °C) than other types of detergents.

Enzymes Are Used to Change Foods

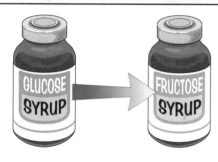

1) The proteins in some baby foods are 'pre-digested' using protein-digesting enzymes (proteases), so they're easier for the baby to digest.
2) Carbohydrate-digesting enzymes (carbohydrases) can be used to turn starch syrup (yuk) into sugar syrup (yum).
3) Glucose syrup can be turned into fructose syrup using an isomerase enzyme. Fructose is sweeter, so you can use less of it — good for slimming foods and drinks.

Using Enzymes in Industry Takes a Lot of Control

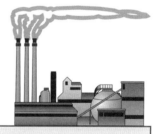

Enzymes are really useful in industry. They speed up reactions without the need for high temperatures and pressures. There are some advantages and disadvantages to using them, so here are a few to get you started:

ADVANTAGES

1) They're specific, so they only catalyse the reaction you want them to.
2) Using lower temperatures and pressures means a lower cost as it saves energy.
3) Enzymes work for a long time, so after the initial cost of buying them, you can continually use them.
4) They are biodegradable and therefore cause less environmental pollution.

DISADVANTAGES

1) Some people can develop allergies to the enzymes (e.g. in biological washing powders).
2) Enzymes can be denatured by even a small increase in temperature. They're also susceptible to poisons and changes in pH. This means the conditions in which they work must be tightly controlled.
3) Enzymes can be expensive to produce.
4) Contamination of the enzyme with other substances can affect the reaction.

There's a lot to learn — but don't be deterred gents...

Enzymes are so picky. Even tiny little changes in pH or temperature will stop them working at maximum efficiency. They only catalyse one reaction as well, so you need to use a different one for each reaction. Temperamental little things these enzymes...

Respiration

Many <u>chemical reactions</u> inside <u>cells</u> are controlled by <u>enzymes</u> — including the ones in <u>respiration</u>.

Respiration *is NOT "Breathing In and Out"*

<u>Respiration</u> involves many reactions, all of which are <u>catalysed</u> by <u>enzymes</u>.
These are really important reactions, as respiration releases the <u>energy</u>
that the cell needs to do just about everything.

1) <u>Respiration</u> is <u>not</u> breathing in and breathing out, as you might think.

2) <u>Respiration</u> is the process of <u>releasing energy</u> from the <u>breakdown of glucose</u>
   — and it goes on in <u>every cell</u> in your body.

3) It happens in <u>plants</u> too. <u>All</u> living things <u>respire</u>. It's how they release <u>energy</u> from their <u>food</u>.

> **RESPIRATION is the process of <u>RELEASING ENERGY FROM GLUCOSE</u>,
> which goes on <u>IN EVERY CELL</u>**

Aerobic Respiration *Needs Plenty of <u>Oxygen</u>*

1) <u>Aerobic respiration</u> is respiration using <u>oxygen</u>. It's the most <u>efficient</u> way to release energy from glucose.
   (You can also have <u>anaerobic</u> respiration, which happens <u>without</u> oxygen, but that doesn't release nearly
   as much energy — see next page.)

2) Aerobic respiration goes on <u>all the time</u> in <u>plants</u> and <u>animals</u>.

3) Most of the reactions in <u>aerobic respiration</u> happen inside <u>mitochondria</u> (see page 10).

4) Here are the overall <u>word and symbol equations</u> for respiration:

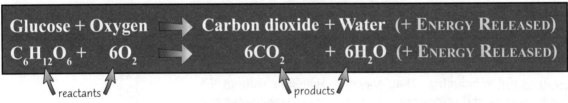

$$\text{Glucose} + \text{Oxygen} \Longrightarrow \text{Carbon dioxide} + \text{Water} \quad (+ \text{ENERGY RELEASED})$$
$$C_6H_{12}O_6 + 6O_2 \Longrightarrow 6CO_2 + 6H_2O \quad (+ \text{ENERGY RELEASED})$$

reactants / products

Reactants are turned into products during a reaction

Respiration Releases Energy *for All Kinds of Things*

Here are <u>four examples</u> of what the <u>energy</u> released by aerobic respiration is used for:

1) To build up <u>larger molecules</u> from <u>smaller</u> ones (like proteins from amino acids).

2) In animals, to allow the <u>muscles</u> to <u>contract</u> (which in turn allows them to <u>move</u> about).

3) In <u>mammals</u> and <u>birds</u> the energy is used to keep their <u>body temperature</u> steady
   (unlike other animals, mammals and birds keep their bodies constantly warm).

4) In <u>plants</u>, to build <u>sugars</u>, <u>nitrates</u> and other nutrients
   into <u>amino acids</u>, which are then built up into <u>proteins</u>.

Breathe, 2, 3, 4 — and release, 6, 7, 8...

So... respiration — that's a pretty important thing. <u>Cyanide</u> is a really nasty toxin that stops respiration by
<u>stopping enzymes</u> involved in the process from <u>working</u> — so it's pretty poisonous (it can kill you).
Your brain, heart and liver are affected first because they have the highest energy demands... nice.

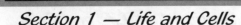

Exercise

When you exercise, your body quickly adapts so that your muscles get <u>more oxygen and glucose</u> to supply <u>energy</u>. If your body can't get enough oxygen or glucose to them, it has some back-up plans ready.

Exercise Increases the Heart Rate

1) Muscles are made of <u>muscle cells</u>. These use <u>oxygen</u> to <u>release energy</u> from <u>glucose</u> (<u>aerobic respiration</u> — see previous page), which is used to <u>contract</u> the muscles.

2) An <u>increase</u> in muscle activity requires <u>more glucose and oxygen</u> to be supplied to the muscle cells. Extra carbon dioxide needs to be <u>removed</u> from the muscle cells. For this to happen the blood has to flow at a <u>faster</u> rate.

3) This is why physical activity:
   - <u>increases</u> your <u>breathing rate</u> and makes you breathe <u>more deeply</u> to meet the demand for <u>extra oxygen</u>.
   - <u>increases</u> the speed at which the <u>heart pumps</u>.

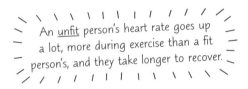
An <u>unfit</u> person's heart rate goes up a lot, more during exercise than a fit person's, and they take longer to recover.

Glycogen is Used During Exercise

1) Some <u>glucose</u> from food is <u>stored</u> as <u>glycogen</u>.

2) Glycogen's mainly stored in the liver, but each <u>muscle</u> also has its own store.

3) During vigorous exercise muscles use glucose <u>rapidly</u>, so some of the stored glycogen is converted back to <u>glucose</u> to provide more energy.

Anaerobic Respiration is Used if There's Not Enough Oxygen

1) When you do vigorous exercise and your body can't supply enough <u>oxygen</u> to your muscles, they start doing <u>anaerobic respiration</u> as well as aerobic respiration.

2) "<u>An</u>aerobic" just means "<u>without</u> oxygen". It's the <u>incomplete</u> breakdown of glucose, which produces <u>lactic acid</u>.

> glucose → energy + lactic acid

3) This is <u>NOT the best way to convert glucose into energy</u> because <u>lactic acid</u> builds up in the muscles, which gets <u>painful</u>. It also causes <u>muscle fatigue</u> — the muscles get <u>tired</u> and the <u>stop contracting efficiently</u>.

4) Another downside is that <u>anaerobic respiration</u> does <u>not release nearly as much energy</u> as aerobic respiration — but it's useful in emergencies.

5) The <u>advantage</u> is that at least you can keep on using your muscles for a while longer.

Anaerobic Respiration Leads to an Oxygen Debt

1) After resorting to anaerobic respiration, when you stop exercising you'll have an "<u>oxygen debt</u>".

2) In other words you have to "<u>repay</u>" the oxygen that you didn't get to your muscles in time, because your <u>lungs</u>, <u>heart</u> and <u>blood</u> couldn't keep up with the <u>demand</u> earlier on.

3) This means you have to keep breathing hard for a while <u>after you stop</u>, to get <u>more oxygen</u> into your blood. Blood flows through your muscles to <u>remove</u> the lactic acid by <u>oxidising</u> it to harmless CO_2 and water.

4) While <u>high levels</u> of $\underline{CO_2}$ and <u>lactic acid</u> are detected in the blood (by the brain), the <u>pulse</u> and <u>breathing rate</u> stay high to try and rectify the situation.

Oxygen debt — cheap to pay back...

Phew... bet you're exhausted after reading this. Still, best to read it through thoroughly before you have a pit stop. <u>Interpreting data</u> on the <u>effects of exercise</u> on the body is a handy skill to have.

Diffusion

Particles <u>move about randomly</u>, and after a bit they end up <u>evenly spaced</u>. And that's how most things move about in our bodies — by "diffusion".

Don't be Put Off by the Fancy Word

"<u>Diffusion</u>" is simple. It's just the <u>gradual movement</u> of particles from places where there are <u>lots</u> of them to places where there are <u>fewer</u> of them. That's all it is — just the <u>natural tendency</u> for stuff to <u>spread out</u>. There's a fancy way of saying the same thing, which is this:

DIFFUSION is the <u>spreading out</u> of particles from an area of <u>HIGH CONCENTRATION</u> to an area of <u>LOW CONCENTRATION</u>

Diffusion happens in both <u>liquids</u> and <u>gases</u> — that's because the <u>individual particles</u> in these substances are free to <u>move about randomly</u>. The <u>simplest type</u> is when different <u>gases</u> diffuse through each other. This is what's happening when the smell of perfume diffuses through the air in a room:

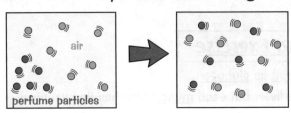

perfume particles diffused in the air

Cell Membranes are Kind of Clever...

They're clever because they <u>hold</u> the cell together <u>BUT</u> they let stuff <u>in and out</u> as well. Only very <u>small molecules</u> can <u>diffuse</u> through cell membranes though — things like <u>simple sugars</u>, <u>water</u> or <u>ions</u>. <u>Big</u> molecules like <u>starch</u> and <u>proteins</u> can't pass through the membrane.

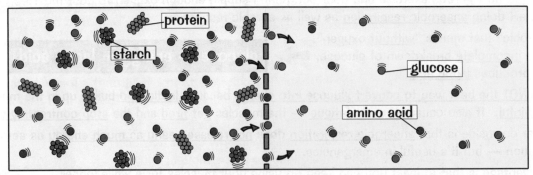

1)   Just like with diffusion in air, particles flow through the cell membrane from where there's a <u>higher concentration</u> (a lot of them) to where there's a <u>lower concentration</u> (not such a lot of them).

2)   They're only moving about <u>randomly</u> of course, so they go <u>both</u> ways — but if there are a lot <u>more</u> particles on one side of the membrane, there's obviously an <u>overall</u> movement <u>from</u> that side.

3)   The <u>rate</u> of diffusion depends on three main things:

   a)   <u>Distance</u> — substances diffuse <u>more quickly</u> when they haven't as <u>far</u> to move. Pretty obvious.

   b)   <u>Concentration difference</u> (<u>gradient</u>) — substances diffuse faster if there's a <u>big difference</u> in concentration. If there are <u>lots more</u> particles on one side, there are more there to move across.

   c)   <u>Surface area</u> — the <u>more surface</u> there is available for molecules to move across, the <u>faster</u> they can get from one side to the other.

Whoever smelt it dealt it... Whoever said the rhyme did the crime...

Because, of course, it's not just perfume that diffuses through a room. Anyway. All living cells have <u>membranes</u>, and their structure allows sugars, water and the rest to drift in and out as needed. Don't forget, the membrane doesn't <u>control</u> diffusion, it happens all by itself — but the membrane does stop <u>large molecules</u> passing through.

Osmosis

Trust me — osmosis really <u>isn't</u> as <u>scary</u> as it sounds.

Osmosis **is a Special Case** of Diffusion, That's All

> <u>Osmosis</u> is the net <u>movement of water molecules</u> across a <u>partially permeable</u> <u>membrane</u> from a region of <u>higher water concentration</u> (i.e. a dilute solution) to a region of <u>lower water concentration</u> (i.e. a concentrated solution).

1) A <u>partially permeable</u> membrane is just one with very small holes in it. So small, in fact, that only <u>tiny molecules</u> (like water) can pass through them, and bigger molecules (e.g. <u>sucrose</u>) can't.

2) The water molecules actually pass <u>both ways</u> through the membrane during osmosis. This happens because water molecules <u>move about randomly all the time</u>.

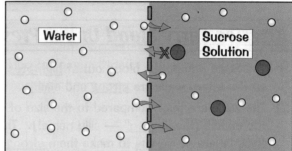

3) But because there are <u>more</u> water molecules on one side than on the other, there's a steady <u>net flow</u> of water into the region with <u>fewer</u> water molecules, i.e. into the <u>stronger sucrose</u> solution.

4) This means the <u>concentrated</u> sucrose solution gets more <u>dilute</u>. The water acts like it's trying to 'even up' the concentration either side of the membrane.

Net movement of water molecules

5) Osmosis is a type of <u>diffusion</u> — net movement of particles from an area of higher concentration to an area of lower concentration.

Turgor Pressure **Supports Plant Tissues**

1) When a plant is well watered, all its cells will draw water in by <u>osmosis</u> and become plump and swollen. When the cells are like this, they're said to be <u>turgid</u>.

2) The contents of the cell push against the <u>inelastic cell wall</u> — this is called <u>turgor pressure</u>. Turgor pressure helps <u>support</u> the plant tissues.

Normal Cell   Turgid Cell

3) If there's no water in the soil, a plant starts to <u>wilt</u> (droop). This is because the cells start to lose water and so <u>lose</u> their turgor pressure. They're then said to be <u>flaccid</u>.

4) If the plant's really short of water, the <u>cytoplasm</u> inside its cells starts to <u>shrink</u> and the membrane <u>pulls away</u> from the cell wall. The cell is now said to be <u>plasmolysed</u>. The plant doesn't totally lose its shape though, because the <u>inelastic cell wall</u> keeps things in position. It just droops a bit.

Flaccid Cell   Plasmolysed Cell

Animal Cells Don't **Have an Inelastic Cell Wall**

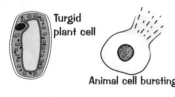

Turgid plant cell

Animal cell bursting

Plant cells aren't too bothered by changes in the amount of water because the <u>inelastic cell wall</u> keeps everything in place.

It's different in <u>animal cells</u> because they don't have a cell wall. If an animal cell <u>takes in</u> too much water, it <u>bursts</u> — this is known as <u>lysis</u>. If it <u>loses</u> too much water it gets all <u>shrivelled up</u> — this is known as <u>crenation</u>.

What all this means is that animals have to keep the amount of water in their cells pretty <u>constant</u> or they're in trouble, while plants are a bit more <u>tolerant</u> of periods of drought.

Revision by osmosis — you wish...

Wouldn't that be great — if all the ideas in this book would just gradually drift across into your mind, from an area of <u>higher concentration</u> (in the book) to an area of <u>lower concentration</u> (in your mind — no offence). Actually, that probably will happen if you <u>read it again</u>. Why don't you give it a go...

Blood Vessels

The blood in our bodies is constantly on the move, so it needs a good <u>transport system</u>.
Luckily, this is where <u>blood vessels</u> come in — they're a bit like the body's version of the M1...

Blood Vessels are Designed for Their Function

There are <u>three</u> different types of <u>blood vessel</u>:

> 1) <u>ARTERIES</u> — these carry the blood <u>away</u> from the heart.
> 2) <u>CAPILLARIES</u> — these are involved in the <u>exchange of materials</u> at the tissues.
> 3) <u>VEINS</u> — these carry the blood <u>to</u> the heart.

Arteries Carry Blood Under Pressure

1) The heart pumps the blood out at <u>high pressure</u> so the artery walls are <u>strong</u> and <u>elastic</u>.

2) The walls are <u>thick</u> compared to the size of the hole down the middle (the "<u>lumen</u>" — silly name!). They contain thick layers of <u>muscle</u> to make them <u>strong</u>.

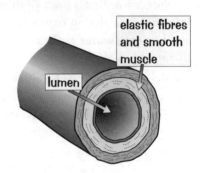

elastic fibres and smooth muscle

lumen

Capillaries are Really Small

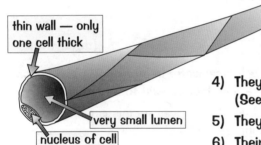

thin wall — only one cell thick

very small lumen

nucleus of cell

1) Arteries branch into <u>capillaries</u>.

2) Capillaries are really <u>tiny</u> — too small to see.

3) They carry the blood <u>really close</u> to <u>every cell</u> in the body to <u>exchange substances</u> with them.

4) They have <u>permeable</u> walls, so substances can <u>diffuse</u> in and out. (See page 20 for more on diffusion.)

5) They supply <u>food</u> and <u>oxygen</u>, and take away <u>wastes</u> like CO_2.

6) Their walls are usually <u>only one cell thick</u>. This <u>increases</u> the rate of diffusion by <u>decreasing</u> the <u>distance</u> over which it occurs.

Veins Take Blood Back to the Heart

1) Capillaries eventually <u>join up</u> to form <u>veins</u>.

2) The blood is at <u>lower pressure</u> in the veins so the walls don't need to be as <u>thick</u> as artery walls.

3) They have a <u>bigger lumen</u> than arteries to help the blood <u>flow</u> despite the lower pressure.

4) They also have <u>valves</u> to help keep the blood flowing in the <u>right direction</u>.

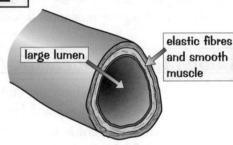

large lumen

elastic fibres and smooth muscle

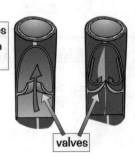

valves

Arteries don't need valves — the pressure in them is high enough to keep the blood flowing the right way.

Revise properly — don't struggle in vein...

Here's an interesting fact for you — your body contains about <u>60 000 miles</u> of blood vessels. That's about <u>six times</u> the distance from <u>London</u> to <u>Sydney</u> in Australia. Of course, capillaries are really tiny, which is how there can be such a big length — they can only be seen with a <u>microscope</u>.

The Heart

Blood doesn't just move around the body <u>on its own</u>, of course. It needs a <u>pump</u>.

Mammals *Have a Double Circulatory System*

1) The first system connects the <u>heart</u> to the <u>lungs</u>.
<u>Deoxygenated</u> blood is pumped to the <u>lungs</u> to take in <u>oxygen</u>.
The blood then <u>returns</u> to the heart.

2) The second system connects the <u>heart</u> to the <u>rest of the body</u>.
The <u>oxygenated</u> blood in the heart is pumped out to the <u>body</u>.
It <u>gives up</u> its oxygen, and then the <u>deoxygenated</u> blood
<u>returns</u> to the heart to be pumped out to the <u>lungs</u> again.

3) Not all animals have a double circulatory system
— <u>fish don't</u>, for example.

4) There are <u>advantages</u> to mammals having a double circulatory system though.
Returning the blood to the <u>heart</u> after it's picked up oxygen at the <u>lungs</u> means it can be pumped out
around the body at a much <u>higher pressure</u>. This <u>increases</u> the <u>rate of blood flow</u> to the tissues
(i.e. blood can be pumped around the body much <u>faster</u>), so <u>more oxygen</u> can be delivered to the cells.
This is important for mammals because they use up a lot of oxygen <u>maintaining their body temperature</u>.

Lungs

Rest of body

The Heart *has Four Chambers and Four Major Blood Vessels*

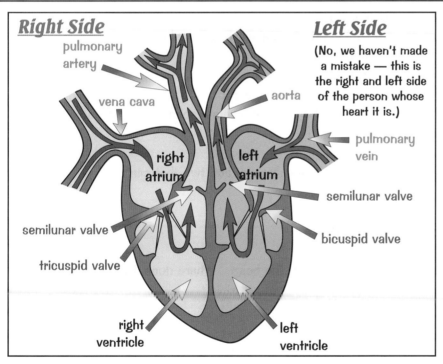

Right Side
pulmonary artery
vena cava
semilunar valve
tricuspid valve
right ventricle

Left Side
(No, we haven't made a mistake — this is the right and left side of the person whose heart it is.)
aorta
pulmonary vein
semilunar valve
bicuspid valve
left ventricle

right atrium
left atrium

1) The <u>right atrium</u> of the heart receives <u>deoxygenated</u> blood from the <u>body</u> (through the <u>vena cava</u>).
(The plural of atrium is atria.)

2) The deoxygenated blood moves through to the <u>right ventricle</u>, which pumps it to the <u>lungs</u> (via the <u>pulmonary artery</u>).

3) The <u>left atrium</u> receives <u>oxygenated</u> blood from the <u>lungs</u> (through the <u>pulmonary vein</u>).

4) The oxygenated blood then moves through to the <u>left ventricle</u>, which pumps it out round the <u>whole body</u> (via the <u>aorta</u>).

5) The <u>left</u> ventricle has a much <u>thicker wall</u> than the <u>right</u> ventricle. It needs more <u>muscle</u> because it has
to pump blood around the <u>whole body</u>, whereas the right ventricle only has to pump it to the <u>lungs</u>.

6) The <u>semilunar</u>, <u>tricuspid</u> and <u>bicuspid valves</u> prevent the <u>backflow</u> of blood.

Okay — let's get to the heart of the matter...

The human heart beats <u>100 000 times a day</u> on average — it's exhausting just thinking about it. You can feel a
pulse in your wrist or neck (where the vessels are close to the surface). This is the <u>blood</u> being pushed along by
another beat. Doctors use a <u>stethoscope</u> to listen to your heart — it's actually the <u>valves closing</u> that they hear.

Revision Summary for Section 1

And where do you think you're going? It's no use just reading through and thinking you've got it all — this stuff will only stick in your head if you've learnt it <u>properly</u>. And that's what these questions are for.
I won't pretend they'll be easy — they're not meant to be, but all the information's in the section somewhere.
Have a go at all the questions, then if there are any you can't answer, go back, look stuff up and try again.
Enjoy...

1) Name five parts of a cell that both plant and animal cells have.
   What three things do plant cells have that animal cells don't?
2) Where is the DNA found in:
   a) bacterial cells
   b) animal cells?
3) Give three ways that a palisade leaf cell is adapted for photosynthesis.
4) Give three ways that a sperm cell is adapted for swimming to an egg cell.
5) What is a tissue? What is an organ?
6) Give three examples of tissues in the human stomach, and say what job they do.
7) Name one organ system found in the human body.
8) What is an enzyme?
9) Describe the 'lock and key' model.
10) Name two things that affect how quickly an enzyme works.
11) What is a denatured enzyme?
12) What does a Q_{10} value show?
13) In which three places in the body is amylase produced?
14) Explain why the stomach produces hydrochloric acid.
15) Give two kinds of enzyme that would be useful in a biological washing powder.
16) Write the word equation for aerobic respiration.
17) Write the symbol equation for aerobic respiration.
18) Name three things that the energy released by respiration is used for.
19) What is anaerobic respiration? Give the word equation for anaerobic respiration in our bodies.
20) Explain how you repay an oxygen debt.
21) What is diffusion?
22) Name three substances that can diffuse through cell membranes, and two that can't.
23) Explain what osmosis is.
24) What is turgor pressure?
25) Why do arteries need very muscular, elastic walls?
26) Explain how capillaries are adapted to their function.
27) Name the blood vessel that joins to the right ventricle of the heart. Where does it take the blood?
28) Why does the left ventricle have a thicker wall than the right ventricle?

DNA

The first step in understanding genetics is getting to grips with DNA.

Chromosomes Are Really Long Molecules of DNA

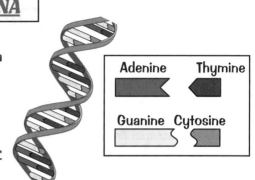

1) <u>DNA</u> stands for <u>d</u>eoxyribo<u>n</u>ucleic <u>a</u>cid.

2) A DNA molecule has <u>two strands</u> coiled together in the shape of a <u>double helix</u> (two spirals), as shown in the diagram opposite.

3) Each of the two DNA strands is made up of lots of small groups called "<u>nucleotides</u>". Each nucleotide contains a small molecule called a "<u>base</u>".

4) The two strands are held together by these <u>bases</u>. There are <u>four</u> different bases (shown in the diagram as different colours) — <u>adenine</u> (A), <u>cytosine</u> (C), <u>guanine</u> (G) and <u>thymine</u> (T).

5) The bases are <u>paired</u>, and they always pair up in the same way — it's always <u>A-T</u> and <u>C-G</u>. This is called <u>base-pairing</u> (or complimentary base-pairing).

6) The <u>base pairs</u> are joined together by <u>weak hydrogen bonds</u>.

Watson, Crick, Franklin and Wilkins Discovered The Structure of DNA

1) <u>Rosalind Franklin</u> and <u>Maurice Wilkins</u> worked out that DNA had a <u>helical structure</u> by directing beams of <u>x-rays</u> onto <u>crystallised DNA</u> and looking at the <u>patterns</u> the x-rays formed as they bounced off.

2) <u>James Watson</u> and <u>Francis Crick</u> used these ideas, along with the knowledge that the amount of <u>adenine + guanine</u> matched the amount of <u>thymine + cytosine</u>, to make a <u>model</u> of the DNA molecule where all the pieces <u>fitted together</u>.

You Can Do a Practical To Extract DNA From Cells

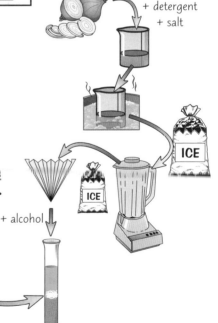

+ detergent
+ salt

ICE

ICE

+ alcohol

1) Chop up some <u>onion</u> and put it in a beaker containing a solution of <u>detergent</u> and <u>salt</u>. The detergent will <u>break down</u> the <u>cell membranes</u> and the salt will make the <u>DNA stick together</u>.

2) Put the beaker into a water bath at <u>60 °C</u> for <u>15 minutes</u> — this <u>denatures enzymes</u> (see p.13) that could digest the DNA and helps <u>soften</u> the onion cells.

3) Put the beaker in <u>ice</u> to <u>cool</u> the mixture down — this <u>stops</u> the DNA from <u>breaking down</u>.

4) Once the mixture is ice-cold, put it into a <u>blender</u> for a <u>few seconds</u> to <u>break open</u> the cell walls and <u>release</u> (but not break up) the DNA.

5) <u>Cool</u> the mixture down again, then <u>filter it</u> to get the froth and big bits of cell out.

6) <u>Gently</u> add some <u>ice-cold alcohol</u> to the filtered mixture. The <u>DNA</u> will start to <u>come out</u> of solution as it's <u>not soluble</u> in cold alcohol. It will appear as a <u>stringy white substance</u> that can be carefully fished out with a <u>glass rod</u>.

My band has a great rhythm section — it has paired basses...

Hope you enjoyed <u>extracting</u> all that DNA and learning about its <u>structure</u>. Sadly, though, you won't be getting a <u>Nobel prize</u> for your efforts — you're too late. Crick, Watson and Wilkins were awarded the Nobel prize for their work in <u>1962</u>. Unfortunately, by then Franklin had died and couldn't be nominated for the prize.

More on DNA

DNA has several really neat properties — not only can it replicate itself, but it's also unique to each and every person. Well... almost.

DNA Can Replicate Itself

1) DNA copies itself every time a cell divides, so that each new cell still has the full amount of DNA.

2) In order to copy itself, the DNA double helix first 'unzips' — to form two single strands.

3) New nucleotides (which float freely in the nucleus) then join on using base-pairing (A with T and C with G). This makes an exact copy of the DNA on the other strand.

4) The result is two double-stranded molecules of DNA that are identical to the original molecule of DNA.

Molecule
of DNA unzips.

Bases on free-floating nucleotides pair
up with matching bases on the DNA.

Cross links form between the bases and the
old DNA strands, and the nucleotides are
joined together to form double strands.

Everyone has Unique DNA...

...except identical twins and clones

Almost everyone's DNA is unique. The only exceptions are identical twins, where the two people have identical DNA, and clones.

DNA fingerprinting (or genetic fingerprinting) is a way of cutting up a person's DNA into small sections and then separating them. Every person's genetic fingerprint has a unique pattern (unless they're identical twins or clones of course). This means you can tell people apart by comparing samples of their DNA.

DNA fingerprinting is used in...

1) Forensic science — DNA (from hair, skin flakes, blood, semen etc.) taken from a crime scene is compared with a DNA sample taken from a suspect. In the diagram, suspect 1's DNA has the same pattern as the DNA from the crime scene — so suspect 1 was probably at the crime scene.

2) Paternity testing — to see if a man is the father of a particular child.

> Some people would like there to be a national genetic database of everyone in the country. That way, DNA from a crime scene could be checked against everyone in the country to see whose it was. But others think this is a big invasion of privacy, and they worry about how safe the data would be and what else it might be used for. There are also scientific problems — false positives can occur if errors are made in the procedure or if the data is misinterpreted.

So the trick is — frame your twin and they'll never get you...

Knowing about DNA comes in handy when interpreting data on DNA fingerprinting for identification. Say you're given the results of a paternity test — the DNA fingerprint of a child, their mother and some possible fathers. Half of the child's DNA fingerprint will match the mother's DNA fingerprint and half will match the actual father's.

Protein Synthesis

Your DNA is basically a long list of instructions on how to make <u>all the proteins</u> in your body.

A <u>Gene Codes</u> for a <u>Specific Protein</u>

1) A <u>gene</u> is a <u>section</u> of DNA. It contains the <u>instructions</u> to make a <u>specific protein</u>.

2) Cells make <u>proteins</u> by stringing <u>amino acids</u> together in a particular order.

3) Only <u>20</u> different amino acids are used to make up <u>thousands</u> of different <u>proteins</u>.

4) The <u>order of the bases</u> in a gene simply tells cells <u>in what order</u> to put the amino acids together:

> Each set of <u>three bases</u> (called a <u>triplet</u>) <u>codes</u> for a <u>particular amino acid</u>.
> Here's an <u>example</u> (don't worry — you don't have to remember the specific codes):
> TAT codes for tyrosine and GCA for alanine. If the order of the bases in the gene is
> TAT-GCA-TAT then the order of amino acids in the protein will be tyrosine-alanine-tyrosine.

5) DNA also determines which genes are <u>switched on or off</u> — and so which <u>proteins</u> the cell <u>produces</u>, e.g. haemoglobin or keratin. That in turn determines what <u>type of cell</u> it is, e.g. red blood cell, skin cell.

6) Some of the proteins <u>help to make</u> all the other things that <u>aren't made of protein</u> (like cell membranes) from substances that come from your diet (like fats and minerals).

Proteins <u>are Made by Ribosomes</u>

Proteins are made in the cell by <u>organelles</u> called <u>ribosomes</u>. DNA is found in the cell <u>nucleus</u> and can't move out of it because it's <u>really big</u>. The cell needs to get the information from the DNA to the <u>ribosome</u> in the cell cytoplasm. This is done using a molecule called <u>mRNA</u>, which is very similar to DNA, but it's shorter and only a <u>single strand</u>. mRNA is like a <u>messenger</u> between the DNA in the nucleus and the ribosome. Here's how it's done:

1) The two DNA strands <u>unzip</u>. The DNA is used as a <u>template</u> to make the <u>mRNA</u>. Base pairing ensures it's <u>complementary</u> (an exact match to the opposite strand). This step is called <u>TRANSCRIPTION</u>.

2) The mRNA molecule <u>moves out</u> of the nucleus and <u>joins</u> with a ribosome.

3) <u>Amino acids</u> that match the mRNA code are <u>brought</u> to the ribosome by molecules called <u>tRNA</u>.

4) The job of the ribosome is to <u>stick amino acids together</u> in a chain to make a <u>polypeptide</u> (protein). This follows the order of the triplet of bases (called a <u>codon</u>) in the mRNA. This step is called <u>TRANSLATION</u>.

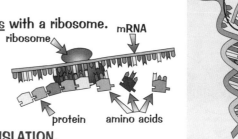

The result of all this molecular jiggery-pokery is that each type of <u>protein</u> gets made with its own specific <u>number</u> and <u>sequence</u> of <u>amino acids</u> — the ones described by its <u>DNA base sequence</u>. This is what makes it <u>fold up into the right shape</u> to do its specific <u>job</u>, e.g. as a particular <u>enzyme</u> (see page 13).

Mutations <u>can be</u> Harmful, Beneficial <u>or</u> Neutral

A <u>mutation</u> is a <u>change</u> to an organism's <u>DNA base sequence</u>. This could affect the sequence of <u>amino acids</u> in the protein, which could affect the <u>shape</u> of the protein and so its <u>function</u>. In turn, this could affect the <u>characteristics</u> of an organism. Mutations can be <u>harmful</u>, <u>beneficial</u> or <u>neutral</u>:

HARMFUL A mutation could cause a <u>genetic disorder</u>, for example <u>cystic fibrosis</u>.

BENEFICIAL A mutation could produce a <u>new characteristic</u> that is <u>beneficial</u> to an organism, e.g. mutations in genes on bacterial plasmids can make the bacteria <u>resistant</u> to <u>antibiotics</u>.

NEUTRAL Some mutations are <u>neither harmful nor beneficial</u>, e.g. they don't affect a protein's function.

4 bases, 20 amino acids, 1000s of proteins...

The <u>order of bases</u> says what amino acid is added and the <u>order of amino acids</u> determines the type of protein.

Cell Division — Mitosis

The cells of your body <u>divide</u> to <u>produce more cells</u>. This is so that your body can <u>grow</u> and <u>repair</u> damaged tissues. Of course, cell division doesn't just happen in humans — animals and plants do it too.

Mitosis Makes New Cells for Growth and Repair

1) <u>Human body cells</u> are <u>diploid</u>. This means they have <u>two versions</u> of each <u>chromosome</u> — one from the person's <u>mother</u>, and one from their <u>father</u>. This diagram shows the <u>23 pairs of chromosomes</u> in a human cell.

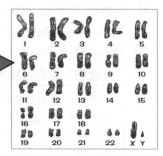

2) When a cell <u>divides</u> it makes <u>two</u> cells <u>identical</u> to the <u>original</u> cell — each with a <u>nucleus</u> containing the <u>same number</u> of chromosomes as the original cell.

3) This type of cell division is called <u>mitosis</u>. It's used when humans (and animals and plants) want to <u>grow</u> or to <u>replace</u> cells that have been <u>damaged</u>.

Mitosis Results in Two Identical Cells

In a cell that's not dividing, the DNA is all spread out in <u>long strings</u>.

If the cell gets a signal to <u>divide</u>, it needs to <u>duplicate</u> its DNA — so there's one copy for each new cell. The DNA is copied and forms <u>X-shaped</u> chromosomes. Each 'arm' of the chromosome is an <u>exact duplicate</u> of the other.

The left arm has the same DNA as the right arm of the chromosome.

The chromosomes then <u>line up</u> at the centre of the cell and <u>cell fibres</u> pull them apart. The <u>two arms</u> of each chromosome go to <u>opposite ends</u> of the cell.

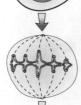

<u>Membranes</u> form around each of the sets of chromosomes. These become the <u>nuclei</u> of the two new cells.

Lastly, the <u>cytoplasm</u> divides.

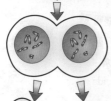

You now have <u>two new diploid cells</u> containing exactly the same DNA — they're <u>genetically identical</u>.

Asexual Reproduction Also Uses Mitosis

1) Some organisms also <u>reproduce</u> by mitosis, e.g. strawberry plants form runners in this way, which become new plants.

2) This is an example of <u>asexual reproduction</u>.

3) The offspring have exactly the <u>same genes</u> as the parent — so there's <u>no genetic variation</u>.

Now that I have your undivided attention...

The next page is about meiosis, which is quite similar to mitosis. It's easy to get them confused if you're not careful. A good plan is to make sure you understand mitosis <u>really thoroughly</u> before you move on. The best way to do this is to: 1) learn the diagram on this page, 2) cover it over, 3) sketch it out.

Cell Division — Meiosis

You thought mitosis was exciting. Hah. You ain't seen nothing yet.

Gametes Have Half the Usual Number of Chromosomes

1) Gametes are 'sex cells'. They're called ova (single, ovum) in females, and sperm in males. During sexual reproduction, two gametes combine to form a new cell which will grow to become a new organism.

2) Gametes are haploid — this means they only have one copy of each chromosome. This is so that when two gametes combine at fertilisation, the resulting cell (zygote) has the right number of chromosomes. Zygotes are diploid — they have two copies of each chromosome.

3) For example, human body cells have 46 chromosomes. The gametes have 23 chromosomes each, so that when an egg and sperm combine, you get 46 chromosomes again.

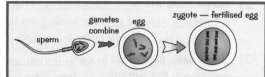

Meiosis Involves Two Divisions

1) To make new cells which only have half the original number of chromosomes, cells divide by meiosis.

2) Meiosis only happens in the reproductive organs (e.g. ovaries and testes).

3) Meiosis is when a cell divides to produce four haploid nuclei whose chromosomes are NOT identical.

chromosome pair

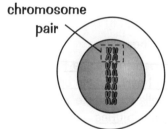

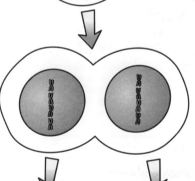

Meiosis — Division 1

1) As with mitosis, before the cell starts to divide, it duplicates its DNA — one arm of each chromosome is an exact copy of the other arm.

2) In the first division in meiosis (there are two divisions) the chromosome pairs (see previous page) line up in the centre of the cell.

3) They're then pulled apart, so each new cell only has one copy of each chromosome. Some of the father's chromosomes (shown in blue) and some of the mother's chromosomes (shown in red) go into each new cell.

4) Each new cell will have a mixture of the mother's and father's chromosomes. Mixing up the alleles in this way creates variation in the offspring. This is a huge advantage of sexual reproduction over asexual reproduction.

Meiosis — Division 2

5) In the second division the chromosomes line up again in the centre of the cell. It's a lot like mitosis. The arms of the chromosomes are pulled apart.

6) You get four haploid gametes, each with only a single set of chromosomes in it.

After two gametes join at fertilisation, the cell grows by repeatedly dividing by mitosis.

Relegation to the Second Division is inevitable...

Again, the best thing to do is to make sure you know the diagram. Cover it up and sketch it out.

Stem Cells

Stem cell research has exciting possibilities, but it's also pretty controversial.

Embryonic Stem Cells Can Turn into ANY Type of Cell

1) Differentiation is the process by which a cell changes to become specialised for its job (see page 11). In most animal cells, the ability to differentiate is lost at an early stage, but lots of plant cells don't ever lose this ability.

2) Some cells are undifferentiated. They can develop into different types of cell depending on what instructions they're given. These cells are called STEM CELLS.

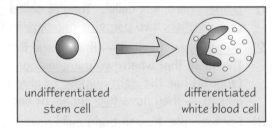

undifferentiated stem cell   differentiated white blood cell

3) Stem cells are found in early human embryos. They're exciting to doctors and medical researchers because they have the potential to turn into any kind of cell at all. This makes sense if you think about it — all the different types of cell found in a human being have to come from those few cells in the early embryo.

4) Adults also have stem cells, but they're only found in certain places, like bone marrow. These aren't as versatile as embryonic stem cells — they can't turn into any cell type at all, only certain ones.

Stem Cells May Be Able to Cure Many Diseases

1) Medicine already uses adult stem cells to cure disease. For example, people with some blood diseases (e.g. sickle cell anaemia) can be treated by bone marrow transplants. Bone marrow contains stem cells that can turn into new blood cells to replace the faulty old ones.

2) Scientists can also extract stem cells from very early human embryos and grow them.

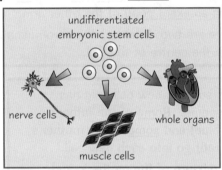

undifferentiated embryonic stem cells

nerve cells   whole organs

muscle cells

3) These embryonic stem cells could be used to replace faulty cells in sick people — you could make beating heart muscle cells for people with heart disease, insulin-producing cells for people with diabetes, nerve cells for people paralysed by spinal injuries, and so on.

4) To get cultures of one specific type of cell, researchers try to control the differentiation of the stem cells by changing the environment they're growing in. So far, it's still a bit hit and miss — lots more research is needed.

Some People Are Against Stem Cell Research

1) Some people are against stem cell research because they feel that human embryos shouldn't be used for experiments since each one is a potential human life.

2) Others think that curing patients who already exist and who are suffering is more important than the rights of embryos.

3) One fairly convincing argument in favour of this point of view is that the embryos used in the research are usually unwanted ones from fertility clinics which, if they weren't used for research, would probably just be destroyed. But of course, campaigners for the rights of embryos usually want this banned too.

4) These campaigners feel that scientists should concentrate more on finding and developing other sources of stem cells, so people could be helped without having to use embryos.

5) In some countries stem cell research is banned, but it's allowed in the UK as long as it follows strict guidelines.

But florists cell stems, and nobody complains about that...

The potential of stem cells is huge — but it's early days yet. Research has recently been done into getting stem cells from alternative sources. For example, some researchers think it might be possible to get cells from umbilical cords to behave like embryonic stem cells.

Growth and Development

Growth is an increase in size or mass. It can be measured in many different ways — read on...

Animals Stop Growing, Plants Can Grow Continuously

Plants and animals grow differently:

1) Animals tend to grow until they reach a finite size (full growth) and then stop growing. Plants often grow continuously — even really old trees will keep putting out new branches.

2) In animals, growth happens by cell division. In plants, growth in height is mainly due to cell enlargement (elongation). Growth by cell division usually just happens in areas of the plant called meristems (at the tips of the roots and shoots).

There are Different Methods for Measuring Growth

To work out if something's grown (i.e. increased in size), you need to take more than one measurement.

Growth of plants and animals can be quite tricky to measure — there are different methods, but they all have pros and cons.

Method	What it involves	Advantages	Disadvantages
LENGTH	Just measure the length (or height) of a plant or animal.	Easy to measure.	It doesn't tell you about changes in width, diameter, number of branches, etc.
WET MASS	Weigh the plant or animal and bingo — you have the wet mass.	Easy to measure.	Wet mass is very changeable. For example, a plant will be heavier if it's recently rained because it will have absorbed lots of water. Animals will be heavier if they've just eaten or if they've got a full bladder.
DRY MASS	Dry out the organism before weighing it.	It's not affected by the amount of water in a plant or animal or how much an organism has eaten.	You have to kill the organism to work it out. This might be okay for an area of grass, but it's not so good if you want to know the dry mass of a person.

Dry mass is actually the best measure of growth in plants and animals — it's not affected by changes in water content and it tells you the size of the whole organism.

Human Growth has Different Phases

1) Humans go through five main phases of growth:

PHASE	DESCRIPTION
Infancy	Roughly the first two years of life. Rapid growth.
Childhood	Period between infancy and puberty. Steady growth.
Adolescence	Begins with puberty and continues until body development and growth are complete. Rapid growth.
Maturity/adulthood	Period between adolescence and old age. Growth stops.
Old age	Usually considered to be between age 65 and death.

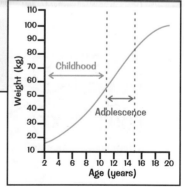

2) The two main phases of rapid growth take place just after birth and during adolescence. Growth stops when a person reaches adulthood.

3) The graph on the right is an example of a typical human growth curve. It shows how weight increases for boys between the ages of 2 and 20. When the line is steeper, growth is more rapid (e.g. during adolescence).

I'm growing rather sick of this topic...

Listen, you think you're sick of reading these lame jokes? Just think how I feel, having to make them up.

X and Y Chromosomes

Now for a couple of very important little chromosomes...

Your Chromosomes Control Whether You're Male or Female

There are <u>22 matched pairs</u> of <u>chromosomes</u> in every human body cell. The <u>23rd pair</u> are labelled <u>XX</u> or <u>XY</u>. They're the two chromosomes that decide whether you turn out <u>male</u> or <u>female</u>.

> <u>All men</u> have an <u>X</u> and a <u>Y</u> chromosome: **XY**
> The <u>Y chromosome</u> causes <u>male characteristics</u>.
>
> <u>All women</u> have <u>two X chromosomes</u>: **XX**
> The <u>XX combination</u> allows <u>female characteristics</u> to develop.

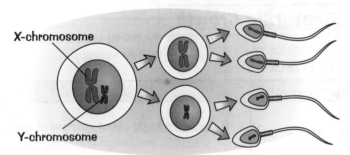

X-chromosome

Y-chromosome

When making sperm, the **X** and **Y** chromosomes are drawn apart in the first division in meiosis (page 29). There's a <u>50% chance</u> each sperm cell gets an <u>X-chromosome</u> and a <u>50% chance</u> it gets a <u>Y-chromosome</u>.

A similar thing happens when making eggs. But the original cell has two **X**-chromosomes, so all the eggs have one **X**-chromosome.

Genetic Diagrams Show the Possible Combinations of Gametes

1) To find the <u>probability</u> of getting a boy or a girl, you can draw a <u>genetic diagram</u>.

2) Put the <u>possible gametes</u> from <u>one</u> parent down the side, and those from the <u>other</u> parent along the top.

3) Then in each middle square you <u>fill in</u> the letters from the top and side that line up with that square. The <u>pairs of letters</u> in the middle show the possible combinations of the gametes.

4) There are <u>two XX results</u> and <u>two XY results</u>, so there's the same probability of getting a boy or a girl.

5) Don't forget that this <u>50:50 ratio</u> is only a <u>probability</u> at each pregnancy. If you had four kids they <u>could</u> all be <u>boys</u> — yes I know, terrifying isn't it?

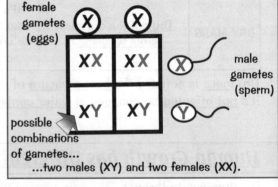

female gametes (eggs)

| XX | XX |
| XY | XY |

male gametes (sperm)

possible combinations of gametes...
...two males (XY) and two females (XX).

The other type of genetic diagram looks a bit more complicated, but it shows exactly the same thing.

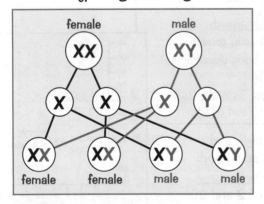

female   male

XX   XY

X   X   X   Y

XX   XX   XY   XY
female female male male

1) At the top are the <u>parents</u>.

2) The middle circles show the <u>possible gametes</u> that are formed. One gamete from the female combines with one gamete from the male (during fertilisation).

3) The criss-cross lines show <u>all</u> the <u>possible</u> ways the X and Y chromosomes <u>could</u> combine. The <u>possible combinations</u> of the offspring are shown in the bottom circles.

4) Remember, only <u>one</u> of these possibilities would <u>actually happen</u> for any one offspring.

Have you got the Y-factor...

Most genetic diagrams you'll come across concentrate on a <u>gene</u>, instead of a <u>chromosome</u>. But the principle's the same. Don't worry — there are loads of other examples on the following pages.

The Work of Mendel

Some people forget about Mendel but I reckon he's the <u>Granddaddy of Genetics</u>. Here's a whole page on him.

Mendel Did Genetic Experiments with Pea Plants

<u>Gregor Mendel</u> was an Austrian monk who trained in <u>mathematics</u> and <u>natural history</u> at the University of Vienna. On his garden plot at the monastery, Mendel noted how <u>characteristics</u> in <u>plants</u> were <u>passed on</u> from one generation to the next.

The results of his research were published in <u>1866</u> and eventually became the <u>foundation</u> of modern <u>genetics</u>.

The diagrams show two <u>crosses for height</u> in <u>pea plants</u> that Mendel carried out...

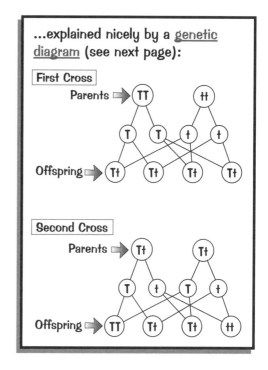

First Cross

A tall pea plant and a dwarf pea plant are crossed

Parents: Tall pea plant   Dwarf pea plant

All tall pea plants

Offspring:

Second Cross

Two pea plants from the 1st set of offspring are crossed

Parents: Tall pea plant   Tall pea plant

Three tall pea plants and one dwarf pea plant

Offspring:

...explained nicely by a <u>genetic diagram</u> (see next page):

First Cross

Parents ➡ TT   tt

T   T   t   t

Offspring ➡ Tt   Tt   Tt   Tt

Second Cross

Parents ➡ Tt   Tt

T   t   T   t

Offspring ➡ TT   Tt   Tt   tt

> Mendel had shown that the height characteristic in pea plants was determined by separately inherited "<u>hereditary units</u>" passed on from each parent. The ratios of tall and dwarf plants in the offspring showed that the unit for tall plants, <u>T</u>, was <u>dominant</u> over the unit for dwarf plants, <u>t</u>.

Mendel Reached Three Important Conclusions

Mendel reached these three important conclusions about <u>heredity in plants</u>:

1) Characteristics in plants are determined by "<u>hereditary units</u>".

2) Hereditary units are passed on from both parents, <u>one unit</u> from <u>each parent</u>.

3) Hereditary units can be <u>dominant</u> or <u>recessive</u> — if an individual has <u>both</u> the dominant and the recessive unit for a characteristic, the <u>dominant</u> characteristic will be expressed.

We now know that the "hereditary units" are of course <u>genes</u>. But in Mendel's time <u>nobody</u> knew anything about genes or DNA, and so the <u>significance</u> of his work was not to be realised until <u>after his death</u>.

Clearly, being a monk in the 1800s was a right laugh...

Well, there was no TV in those days, you see. Monks had to make their <u>own entertainment</u>. And in Mendel's case, that involved growing lots and lots of <u>peas</u>. He was a very clever lad, was Mendel, but unfortunately just a bit <u>ahead of his time</u>. Nobody had a clue what he was going on about.

Genetic Diagrams

Genetic diagrams can tell you about the inheritance of <u>any</u> kind of characteristic that's controlled by a <u>single gene</u>, as the principle's <u>always the same</u>. Here's a <u>bizarre</u> example, to show you the basics.

Genetic Diagrams Show the Possible Genes of Offspring

1) <u>Alleles</u> are <u>different versions</u> of the <u>same gene</u>.

2) In genetic diagrams <u>letters</u> are usually used to represent <u>alleles</u>.

3) If an organism has <u>two alleles</u> for a particular gene <u>the same</u>, then it's <u>homozygous</u>. If its two alleles for a particular gene are <u>different</u>, then it's <u>heterozygous</u>.

4) If the two alleles are <u>different</u>, only one can determine what <u>characteristic</u> is present. The allele for the <u>characteristic that's shown</u> is called the <u>dominant</u> allele (use a capital letter for dominant alleles — e.g. 'C'). The other one is called <u>recessive</u> (and you show these with small letters — e.g. 'c').

5) For an organism to display a <u>recessive</u> characteristic, <u>both</u> its alleles must be <u>recessive</u> (e.g. cc). But to display a <u>dominant</u> characteristic the organism can be <u>either</u> CC or Cc, because the dominant allele <u>overrules</u> the recessive one if the plant/animal/other organism is heterozygous.

> Remember, gametes only have one allele, but all the other cells in an organism have two.

Suppose You Find Yourself Cross-Breeding Crazy Hamsters...

Let's say that the gene which causes the <u>crazy</u> nature is <u>recessive</u>, so we use a <u>small</u> "b" for it, whilst <u>normal</u> (boring) behaviour is due to a <u>dominant</u> gene, so we represent it with a <u>capital</u> "B".

1) A <u>crazy</u> hamster <u>must</u> have the <u>genotype bb</u>. However, a normal hamster could have <u>two</u> possible genotypes — BB or Bb.

> <u>Genotype</u> means what alleles you have. <u>Phenotype</u> means the actual characteristic.

2) Here's what happens if you breed from two <u>homozygous</u> hamsters:

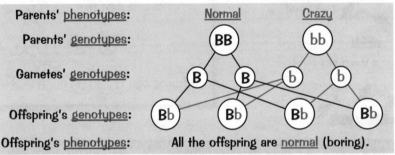

Parents' <u>phenotypes</u>: Normal   Crazy
Parents' <u>genotypes</u>: BB   bb
Gametes' <u>genotypes</u>: B B b b
Offspring's <u>genotypes</u>: Bb Bb Bb Bb
Offspring's <u>phenotypes</u>: **All the offspring are <u>normal</u> (boring).**

3) If two of these <u>offspring</u> now <u>breed</u>, you'll get the next generation:

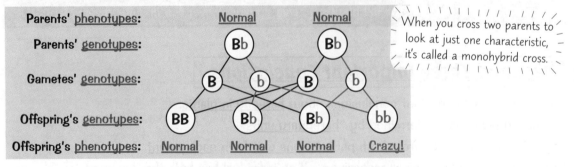

Parents' <u>phenotypes</u>: Normal   Normal
Parents' <u>genotypes</u>: Bb   Bb
Gametes' <u>genotypes</u>: B b B b
Offspring's <u>genotypes</u>: BB Bb Bb bb
Offspring's <u>phenotypes</u>: Normal Normal Normal Crazy!

> When you cross two parents to look at just one characteristic, it's called a monohybrid cross.

4) This gives a <u>3:1 ratio</u> of normal to crazy offspring in this generation. Remember that "results" like this are only <u>probabilities</u> — they don't say definitely what'll happen.

What do you get if you cross a kangaroo and a sheep...

...a ratio of 1:1 kangsheep to sheeparoos... bet you thought I was going to say a woolly jumper. If you want to work out whether a characteristic is <u>dominant</u> or <u>recessive</u> from the results of a <u>breeding experiment</u>, look at the <u>ratios</u> of the characteristic in <u>different generations</u> — just like in the diagrams. (If you have my luck, you'll end up trying to contain a mini-riot of nine lunatic baby hamsters.)

Genetic Disorders

It's not just characteristics that are passed on — some <u>disorders</u> are inherited.

Cystic Fibrosis is Caused by a Recessive Allele

<u>Cystic fibrosis</u> is a <u>genetic disorder</u> of the <u>cell membranes</u>. It <u>results</u> in the body producing a lot of thick sticky <u>mucus</u> in the <u>air passages</u> and in the <u>pancreas</u>.

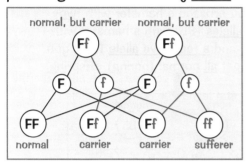

normal, but carrier   normal, but carrier

Ff   Ff

F   f   F   f

FF   Ff   Ff   ff

normal   carrier   carrier   sufferer

1) The allele which causes cystic fibrosis is a <u>recessive allele</u>, 'f', carried by about <u>1 person in 25</u>.

2) Because it's recessive, people with only <u>one copy</u> of the allele <u>won't</u> have the disorder — they're known as <u>carriers</u>.

3) For a child to have the disorder, <u>both parents</u> must be either <u>carriers</u> or <u>sufferers</u>.

4) As the diagram shows there's a <u>1 in 4 chance</u> of a child having the disorder if <u>both</u> parents are <u>carriers</u>.

Polydactyly is Caused by a Dominant Allele

<u>Polydactyly</u> is a <u>genetic disorder</u> where a baby's born with <u>extra fingers or toes</u>. It doesn't usually cause any other problems so <u>isn't life-threatening</u>.

1) The disorder is caused by a <u>dominant allele</u>, 'D', and so can be inherited if just <u>one parent</u> carries the defective allele.

2) The <u>parent</u> that <u>has</u> the defective allele will be a <u>sufferer</u> too since the allele is dominant.

3) As the genetic diagram shows, there's a <u>50% chance</u> of a child having the disorder if <u>one</u> parent has the D allele.

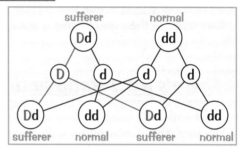

sufferer   normal

Dd   dd

D   d   d   d

Dd   dd   Dd   dd

sufferer   normal   sufferer   normal

Embryos Can Be Screened for Genetic Disorders

1) During <u>in vitro fertilisation</u> (IVF), embryos are fertilised in a <u>laboratory</u>, and then <u>implanted</u> into the mother's womb. <u>More</u> than one egg is fertilised, so there's a better chance of the IVF being <u>successful</u>.

2) Before being implanted, it's possible to <u>remove a cell</u> from each embryo and <u>analyse</u> its <u>genes</u>.

3) Many <u>genetic disorders</u> could be <u>detected</u> in this way, such as cystic fibrosis.

4) Embryos with '<u>good</u>' alleles would be <u>implanted</u> into the mother — the ones with '<u>bad</u>' alleles <u>destroyed</u>.

There is a <u>huge debate</u> raging about <u>embryonic screening</u>. Here are some arguments <u>for</u> and <u>against</u> it.

<u>Against Embryonic Screening</u>	<u>For Embryonic Screening</u>
1) There may come a point where everyone wants to screen their embryos so they can pick the most '<u>desirable</u>' one, e.g. they want a blue-eyed, blond-haired, intelligent boy.	1) It will help to stop people <u>suffering</u>.
	2) There are <u>laws</u> to stop it going too far. At the moment parents cannot even select the sex of their baby (unless it's for health reasons).
2) The rejected embryos are <u>destroyed</u> — they could have developed into humans.	3) During IVF, most of the embryos are <u>destroyed</u> anyway — screening just allows the selected one to be <u>healthy</u>.
3) It implies that <u>people</u> with <u>genetic problems</u> are 'undesirable' — this could increase <u>prejudice</u>.	4) Treating disorders costs the Government (and the taxpayers) a lot of <u>money</u>.
4) Screening is <u>expensive</u>.	

Many people think that embryonic screening <u>isn't justified</u> for genetic disorders that <u>don't</u> affect a person's health, such as <u>polydactyly</u>.

Embryonic screening — it's a tricky one...

There's a lot of debate surrounding embryonic screening, so make sure you've got your head around the <u>arguments</u>. There are no straightforward answers.

More Genetic Diagrams

Predicting and explaining the outcomes of crosses between individuals is much easier when you've got a genetic diagram. So here are a couple more examples for you.

All the Offspring are Normal

Let's take another look at the crazy hamster example from page 34:

In this cross, a hamster with two dominant alleles (BB) is crossed with a hamster with two recessive alleles (bb). All the offspring are normal (boring).

But, if you crossed a hamster with two dominant alleles (BB) with a hamster with a dominant and a recessive allele (Bb), you would also get all normal (boring) offspring.

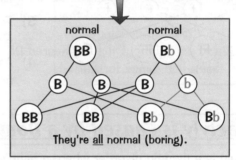

To find out which it was you'd have to breed the offspring together and see what kind of ratio you got that time — then you'd have a good idea. If it was 3:1, it's likely that you originally had BB and bb.

There's a 1:1 Ratio in the Offspring

A cat with long hair was bred with another cat with short hair. The long hair is caused by a dominant allele 'H', and the short hair by a recessive allele 'h'.

They had 8 kittens — 4 with long hair and 4 with short hair.

This is a 1:1 ratio — it's what you'd expect when a parent with only one dominant allele (Hh) is crossed with a parent with two recessive alleles (hh).

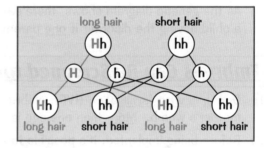

Family Trees Show How Genetic Disorders are Inherited

Knowing how inheritance works can help you to interpret a family tree — this is one for cystic fibrosis.

1) From the family tree, you can tell that the allele for cystic fibrosis isn't dominant because plenty of the family carry the allele but aren't sufferers.

2) There is a 25% chance that the new baby will be a sufferer and a 50% chance that it will be a carrier, as both of its parents are carriers but not sufferers. The case of the new baby is just the same as in the genetic diagram on page 35 — so the baby could be normal (FF), a carrier (Ff) or a sufferer (ff).

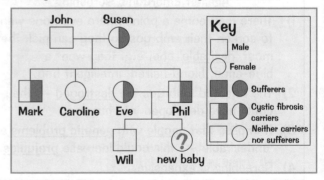

It's enough to make you go cross-eyed...

When you look at a family tree showing the inheritance of a dominant allele there won't be any carriers shown. Also, remember that a good way to work out a family tree is to write the genotype of each person onto it — you can practise by copying the family tree above and labelling the genotypes of everyone on it.

Genetic Engineering

Genetic engineering — playing around with genes. Cool.

Genetic Engineering is Great — Hopefully

The basic idea behind genetic engineering is to move genes (sections of DNA) from one organism to another so that it produces useful biological products. There are some advantages and risks involved in genetic engineering:

1) The main advantage is that you can produce organisms with new and useful features very quickly. There are some examples of this below.

2) The main risk is that the inserted gene might have unexpected harmful effects. For example, genes are often inserted into bacteria so they produce useful products. If these bacteria mutated and became pathogenic (disease-causing), the foreign genes might make them more harmful and unpredictable. People also worry about the engineered DNA 'escaping' — e.g. weeds could gain rogue genes from a crop that's had genes for herbicide resistance inserted into it. Then they'd be unstoppable. Eeek.

Genetic Engineering Involves These Important Stages:

1) First the gene that's responsible for producing the desirable characteristic is selected (say the gene for human insulin).

2) It's then 'cut' from the DNA using enzymes, and isolated.

3) The useful gene is inserted into the DNA of another organism (e.g. a bacterium).

4) The organism then replicates and soon there are loads of similar organisms all producing the same thing (e.g. loads of bacteria producing human insulin).

Here are Three Examples of Genetic Engineering:

1) In some parts of the world, the population relies heavily on rice for food. In these areas, vitamin A deficiency can be a problem, because rice doesn't contain much of this vitamin, and other sources are scarce. Genetic engineering has allowed scientists to take a gene that controls beta-carotene production from carrot plants, and put it into rice plants. Humans can then change the beta-carotene into vitamin A. Problem solved.

2) The gene for human insulin production has been put into bacteria. These are cultured in a fermenter, and the human insulin is simply extracted from the medium as they produce it. Great.

3) Some plants have resistance to things like herbicides, frost damage and disease. Unfortunately, it's not always the plants we want to grow that have these features. But now, thanks to genetic engineering, we can cut out the gene responsible and stick it into useful plants such as crops. Splendid.

There Are Moral and Ethical Issues Involved

All this is nice, but there are moral and ethical issues surrounding genetic modification:

1) Some people think it's wrong to genetically engineer other organisms purely for human benefit. This is a particular problem in the genetic engineering of animals, especially if the animal suffers as a result.

2) People worry that we won't stop at engineering plants and animals. In the future, those who can afford genetic engineering might be able to decide the characteristics they want their children to have — and those who can't afford it may become a 'genetic underclass'.

3) The evolutionary consequences of genetic engineering are unknown, so some people think it's irresponsible to carry on when we're not sure what the impact on future generations might be.

If only they could genetically engineer you to be better at exams...

You can do great things with genetic engineering. But some people worry that we don't know enough about it, or that some maniac is going to come along and combine David Cameron with a grapefruit. Possibly.

Cloning Mammals

If you've cloned a sheep before then you won't need to look at this page. If not, you'd better read on...

Cloned Mammals Can be Made by Adult Cell Cloning

Cloning is a type of asexual reproduction (see page 28). It produces cells that are genetically identical to an original cell. Here's how it's done:

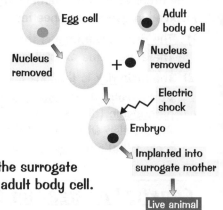

1) Adult cell cloning involves taking an unfertilised egg cell and removing its nucleus (the egg cell is enucleated).

2) A nucleus is taken from an adult body cell (e.g. skin cell). This is a diploid nucleus containing the full number of chromosomes.

3) The diploid nucleus is inserted into the 'empty' egg cell.

4) The egg cell is then stimulated by an electric shock — this makes it divide by mitosis, like a normal embryo.

5) When the embryo is a ball of cells, it's implanted into an adult female (the surrogate mother) to grow into a genetically identical copy (clone) of the original adult body cell.

6) This technique was used to create Dolly — the famous cloned sheep.

Cloning Has Many Uses

Cloning has several uses — here are just two examples:

1) Cloning mammals could help with the shortage of organs for transplants. For example, genetically-modified pigs are being bred that could provide suitable organs for humans. If this is successful, then cloning these pigs could help to meet the demand for organ transplants.

2) Human embryos could be produced by cloning adult body cells. The embryos could then be used to supply stem cells for stem cell therapy (see page 30). These cells would have exactly the same genetic information as the patient, reducing the risk of rejection (a common problem with transplants).

There are Many Issues Surrounding Cloning

1) Cloning mammals leads to a "reduced gene pool" — this means there are fewer different alleles in a population.

   • If a population are all closely related and a new disease appears, they could all be wiped out — because there may be no allele in the population giving resistance to the disease.

2) Cloned mammals mightn't live as long — Dolly the sheep only lived for 6 years (half as long as many sheep).

   • She was put down because she had lung disease, and she also had arthritis. These diseases are more usual in older sheep.

   • Dolly was cloned from an older sheep, so it's been suggested her 'true' age may have been older.

   • But it's possible she was just unlucky — and that her illnesses weren't linked to her being a clone.

3) There are other risks and problems associated with cloning:

   • The cloning process often fails. It took hundreds of attempts to clone Dolly.

   • Clones are often born with genetic defects.

   • Cloned mammals' immune systems are sometimes unhealthy — so they suffer from more diseases.

Thank goodness they didn't do that with my little brother...

Cloning can be a controversial topic — especially when it's to do with cloning mammals. More large-scale, long-term studies into cloned mammals are needed to find out what the dangers are.

Selective Breeding

'Selective breeding' sounds like it has the potential to be a tricky topic, but it's actually dead simple. You take the best plants or animals and breed them together to get the best possible offspring. That's it.

Selective Breeding is Very Simple

Selective breeding is when humans artificially select the plants or animals that are going to breed and have their genes remain in the population, according to what we want from them. Organisms are selectively bred to develop the best features, which are things like:

- Maximum yield of meat, milk, grain etc.
- Good health and disease resistance.
- Other qualities like temperament, speed, attractiveness, etc.

This is the basic process involved in selective breeding:

1) From your existing stock select the ones which have the best characteristics.
2) Breed them with each other.
3) Select the best of the offspring, and breed them together.
4) Continue this process over several generations, and the desirable trait gets stronger and stronger.

> **EXAMPLE:**
>
> In agriculture (farming), selective breeding can be used to improve yields. E.g. to improve meat yields, a farmer could breed together the cows and bulls with the best characteristics for producing meat, e.g. large size. After doing this for several generations the farmer would get cows with a very high meat yield.

The Main Drawback is a Reduction in the Gene Pool

1) The main problem with selective breeding is that it reduces the gene pool in a population — (see previous page). This is because the farmer keeps breeding from the "best" animals or plants — which are all closely related. This is known as inbreeding.

2) Inbreeding can cause health problems because there's more chance of the organisms developing harmful genetic disorders when the gene pool is limited. This is because lots of genetic conditions are recessive — you need two alleles to be the same for it to have an effect. Breeding from closely related organisms all the time means that recessive alleles are more likely to build up in the population (because the organisms are likely to share the same alleles).

3) There can also be serious problems if a new disease appears, because there's not much variation in the population (see previous page). All the stock are closely related to each other, so if one of them is going to be killed by a new disease, the others are also likely to succumb to it.

| Selective Breeding | → | Reduction in the number of different alleles | → | Less chance of any resistant alleles being present in the population |

I use the same genes all the time too — they flatter my hips...

Selective breeding's not a new thing. People have been doing it for absolutely yonks. That's how we ended up with something like a poodle from a wolf. Somebody thought 'I really like this small, woolly, yappy, wolf — I'll breed it with this other one'. And after thousands of generations, we got poodles. Hurrah.

Fossils

Fossils are great. If they're <u>well-preserved</u>, you can see what oldy-worldy creatures <u>looked</u> like. They also show how living things have <u>evolved</u>. Although we're not sure how life started in the first place...

Fossils are the Remains of Plants and Animals

Fossils are the <u>remains</u> of organisms from <u>many years ago</u>, which are found in <u>rocks</u>.
Fossils provide the <u>evidence</u> that organisms lived ages ago. Fossils form in rocks in one of <u>three</u> ways:

1) FROM <u>GRADUAL REPLACEMENT</u> BY MINERALS (Most fossils happen this way.)

1) Things like <u>teeth</u>, <u>shells</u>, <u>bones</u> etc., which <u>don't decay</u> easily, can last a long time when <u>buried</u>.

2) They're eventually <u>replaced by minerals</u> as they decay, forming a <u>rock-like substance</u> shaped like the original hard part.

3) The surrounding sediments also turn to rock, but the fossil stays <u>distinct</u> inside the rock and eventually someone <u>digs it up</u>.

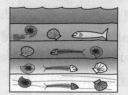

2) FROM <u>CASTS</u> AND <u>IMPRESSIONS</u>

1) Sometimes, fossils are formed when an organism is <u>buried</u> in a <u>soft</u> material like clay. The clay later <u>hardens</u> around it and the organism decays, leaving a <u>cast</u> of itself. An animal's <u>burrow</u> or a plant's <u>roots</u> can be preserved as casts.

2) Things like footprints can be <u>pressed</u> into these materials when soft, leaving an <u>impression</u> when it hardens.

3) FROM <u>PRESERVATION</u> IN PLACES WHERE NO DECAY HAPPENS

1) In <u>amber</u> (a clear yellow 'stone' made from fossilised resin) and <u>tar pits</u> there's no <u>oxygen</u> or <u>moisture</u> so <u>decay microbes</u> can't survive.

2) In <u>glaciers</u> it's too <u>cold</u> for the <u>decay microbes</u> to work.

3) <u>Peat bogs</u> are too <u>acidic</u> for <u>decay microbes</u>.
(A fully preserved man they named 'Pete Marsh' was found in a bog.)

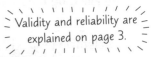

But No One Knows How Life Began

Fossils show how many of today's species have <u>evolved</u> (changed and developed) over millions of years. But where did the <u>first</u> living thing come from...

1) There are various <u>hypotheses</u> suggesting how life first came into being, but no one really <u>knows</u>.

2) Maybe the first life forms came into existence in a primordial <u>swamp</u> (or under the <u>sea</u>) here on <u>Earth</u>. Maybe simple organic molecules were brought to Earth on <u>comets</u> — these could have then become more <u>complex</u> organic molecules, and eventually very simple <u>life forms</u>.

3) These hypotheses can't be supported or disproved because there's a <u>lack</u> of <u>valid</u> and <u>reliable</u> evidence.

4) There's a lack of evidence because scientists believe many early organisms were <u>soft-bodied</u>, and soft tissue tends to decay away <u>completely</u>. So the fossil record is <u>incomplete</u>.

Validity and reliability are explained on page 3.

5) Plus, fossils that did form millions of years ago may have been <u>destroyed</u> by <u>geological activity</u>, e.g. the movement of tectonic plates may have crushed fossils already formed in the rock.

Don't get bogged down by all this information...

It's a bit mind-boggling really, how <u>fossils</u> of organisms can still exist even millions of years after they died. Right, testing time... scribble down the <u>three ways</u> that fossils form and why we can't be sure <u>how life began</u>.

Extinction and Speciation

Evolution leads to the development of lots of <u>different species</u>. But not every species is still around today... :(

Extinction *Happens if You Can't Evolve* Quickly Enough

The fossil record contains many species that <u>don't exist any more</u> — these species are said to be <u>extinct</u>. <u>Dinosaurs</u> and <u>mammoths</u> are extinct animals, with only <u>fossils</u> to tell us they existed at all.

Species become extinct for these reasons:
1) The <u>environment changes</u> too quickly (e.g. destruction of habitat).
2) A <u>new predator</u> kills them all (e.g. humans hunting them).
3) A <u>new disease</u> kills them all.
4) They can't <u>compete</u> with another (new) species for <u>food</u>.
5) A <u>catastrophic event</u> happens that kills them all (e.g. a volcanic eruption or a collision with an asteroid).
6) A <u>new species</u> develops (this is called speciation — see below).

Dodos are now extinct. Humans not only hunted them, but introduced other animals which ate all their eggs, and we destroyed the forest where they lived — they really didn't stand a chance...

Speciation *is the Development of a* New Species

1) A species is a group of <u>similar organisms</u> that can <u>reproduce</u> to give <u>fertile offspring</u>.
2) <u>Speciation</u> is the development of a <u>new species</u>.
3) Speciation occurs when <u>populations</u> of the <u>same species</u> become so <u>different</u> that they can <u>no longer breed</u> together to produce <u>fertile offspring</u>.

Isolation *and* Natural Selection *Lead to Speciation*

<u>Isolation</u> is where <u>populations</u> of a species are <u>separated</u>. This can happen due to a <u>physical barrier</u>. E.g. floods and earthquakes can cause barriers that <u>geographically isolate</u> some individuals from the main population. <u>Conditions</u> on either side of the barrier will be <u>slightly different</u>, e.g. they may have <u>different climates</u>. Because the environment is <u>different</u> on each side, <u>different characteristics</u> will become more common in each population due to <u>natural selection</u>:

1) Each population shows <u>variation</u> because they have a wide range of <u>alleles</u>.
2) In each population, individuals with characteristics that make them better adapted to their environment have a <u>better chance of survival</u> and so are more likely to <u>breed</u> successfully.
3) So the <u>alleles</u> that control the <u>beneficial characteristics</u> are more likely to be <u>passed on</u> to the <u>next generation</u>.

Eventually, individuals from the different populations will have <u>changed</u> so much that they <u>won't</u> be able to <u>breed</u> with one another to produce fertile offspring. The two groups will have become <u>separate species</u>.

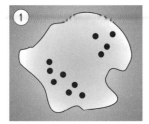 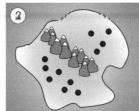 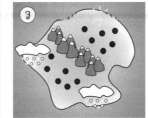 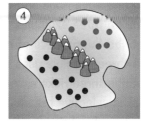

Two populations of ⇨ Physical barriers ⇨ Populations ⇨ Development of
the same species   separate populations.   adapt to new   a new species.
• = individual organism   environments.

Up for grabs — a top quality gag about speciation...*going once...going twice...*

So <u>speciation</u> happens if two or more populations of the same species change so much that they can <u>no longer breed together</u> to produce <u>fertile offspring</u>. It's caused by the populations becoming <u>separated</u> from each other. Right, I think it must be nearly time for a break before your brain cells become extinct...

Revision Summary for Section 2

Wow, that was quite a long section. First there was all the stuff on the basics of DNA, then came all the geneticsy bits and then even a bit on fossils and extinction. And just to finish off, some questions. Use these to find out what you know about it all — and what you don't. Then look back and learn the bits you don't know. Then try the questions again, and again...

1) What shape is a molecule of DNA?
2) Name the four different bases found in DNA. How do they pair up?
3) Name the four scientists who had major roles in discovering the structure of DNA.
4) Explain how DNA replicates itself.
5) Explain how DNA fingerprinting is used in forensic science.
6) What does a triplet of DNA bases code for?
7) Describe the stages of protein synthesis.
8) Are mutations always harmful? Explain your answer.
9) What is mitosis used for in the human body? Describe the four steps in mitosis.
10) Where does meiosis take place in the human body?
11) What is differentiation in a cell?
12) Give three ways that embryonic stem cells could be used to cure diseases.
13) Humans go through two main phases of rapid growth. When do these take place?
14) Which chromosome in the human body causes male characteristics?
15) Copy and complete the diagrams to show what happens to the X and Y chromosomes during reproduction.

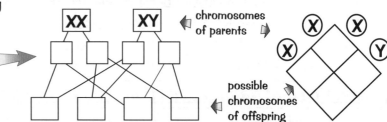

16) List three important conclusions that Mendel reached following his experiments with pea plants.
17) The significance of Mendel's work was not realised until 1900, 16 years after Mendel died. Suggest why the importance of the work wasn't understood at the time.
18) What is an allele?
19) What is meant by an organism being heterozygous? What about homozygous?
20) Describe the basic difference between a recessive allele and a dominant one.
21) If both parents carry recessive allele for cystic fibrosis, what is the probability of their child being a carrier?
22) What is polydactyly?
23)*Blue colour in a plant is carried on a recessive allele, b. The dominant allele, B, gives white flowers. In the first generation after a cross, all the flowers are white. These are bred together and the result is a ratio of 54 white : 19 blue. What were the alleles of the flowers used in the first cross?
24) Give one advantage and one risk of genetic engineering.
25) Describe three examples of genetic engineering.
26) Describe the process of cloning a mammal from an adult cell (e.g. cloning a sheep).
27) Give three possible uses of cloning mammals.
28) Describe three risks associated with trying to clone mammals.
29) What is selective breeding?
30) Give two disadvantages of selective breeding.
31) Describe the three ways that fossils can form. Give an example of each type.
32) Give three reasons why some species become extinct.
33) What is speciation? Explain how geographical isolation can lead to speciation.

* Answer on page 142.

Plant Structure and Photosynthesis

Plants carry out <u>photosynthesis</u> to produce food. You're about to find out all about it.

Plant Cells Are Organised Into Tissues And Organs

<u>Plants</u> are made of <u>organs</u> like <u>stems</u>, <u>roots</u> and <u>leaves</u>. These organs are made of <u>tissues</u>. For example, <u>leaves</u> are made of:

1) <u>Mesophyll tissue</u> — this is where most of the <u>photosynthesis</u> in a plant occurs.

2) <u>Xylem</u> and <u>phloem</u> — they <u>transport</u> things like <u>water</u>, <u>mineral ions</u> and <u>sucrose</u> around the plant.

3) <u>Epidermal tissue</u> — this <u>covers</u> the whole plant.

If you're wondering where these tissues are in a plant, check out the <u>leaf diagram</u> at the bottom of the page.

Photosynthesis Has An Equation:

$$\text{carbon dioxide} + \text{water} \xrightarrow{\text{LIGHT ENERGY}} \text{glucose} + \text{oxygen}$$
$$6CO_2 + 6H_2O \longrightarrow C_6H_{12}O_6 + 6O_2$$

reactants   products

Photosynthesis Produces Glucose Using Sunlight

1) <u>Photosynthesis</u> is the process that produces '<u>food</u>' in plants and algae. The 'food' it produces is <u>glucose</u>.

2) Photosynthesis happens inside the <u>chloroplasts</u>.

3) Chloroplasts contain a green substance called <u>chlorophyll</u>, which absorbs <u>sunlight</u> and uses its energy to convert <u>carbon dioxide</u> (from the air) and <u>water</u> (from the soil) into <u>glucose</u>. <u>Oxygen</u> is also produced as a by-product.

4) Photosynthesis happens in the <u>leaves</u> of all <u>green plants</u> — this is largely what the leaves are for.

   Below is a cross-section of a leaf showing the <u>four</u> raw materials needed for <u>photosynthesis</u>.

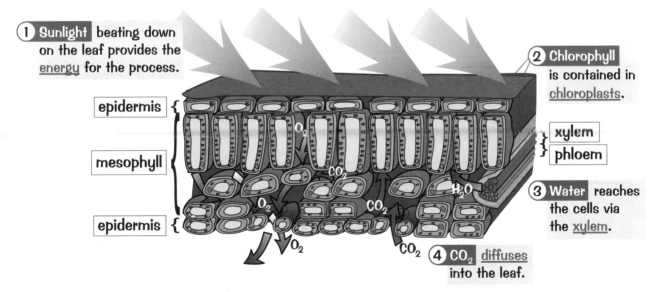

① <u>Sunlight</u> beating down on the leaf provides the <u>energy</u> for the process.

② <u>Chlorophyll</u> is contained in <u>chloroplasts</u>.

③ <u>Water</u> reaches the cells via the <u>xylem</u>.

④ CO_2 diffuses into the leaf.

epidermis

mesophyll

epidermis

xylem

phloem

Now you'll have something to bore the great-grandkids with...

You'll be able to tell them how in your day, all you needed was a bit of carbon dioxide and some water and you could make your own entertainment. See, when you're 109 you're allowed to get a bit confused, but in the middle of an exam you most certainly are not. So read it again my friend — you know you want to.

The Rate of Photosynthesis

The rate of photosynthesis is affected by the intensity of light, the volume of CO_2, and the temperature. Plants also need water for photosynthesis, but when a plant is so short of water that it becomes the limiting factor in photosynthesis, it's already in such trouble that this is the least of its worries.

The Limiting Factor Depends on the Conditions

1) Any of these three factors can become the limiting factor. This just means that it's stopping photosynthesis from happening any faster.

2) Which factor is limiting at a particular time depends on the environmental conditions:
   - at night it's pretty obvious that light is the limiting factor,
   - in winter it's often the temperature,
   - if it's warm enough and bright enough, the amount of CO_2 is usually limiting.

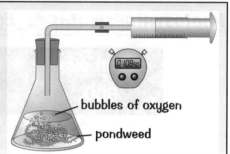

You can do experiments to work out the ideal conditions for photosynthesis in a particular plant. The easiest type to use is a water plant like Canadian pondweed — you can easily measure the amount of oxygen produced in a given time to show how fast photosynthesis is happening (remember, oxygen is made during photosynthesis).

bubbles of oxygen

pondweed

You could either count the bubbles given off, or if you want to be a bit more accurate you could collect the oxygen in a gas syringe.

Three Important Graphs for Rate of Photosynthesis

1) Not Enough Light Slows Down the Rate of Photosynthesis

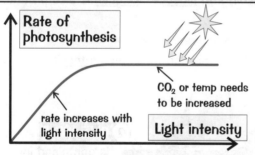

Rate of photosynthesis

CO_2 or temp needs to be increased

rate increases with light intensity

Light intensity

1) Light provides the energy needed for photosynthesis.

2) As the light level is raised, the rate of photosynthesis increases steadily — but only up to a certain point.

3) Beyond that, it won't make any difference because then it'll be either the temperature or the CO_2 level which is the limiting factor.

4) In the lab you can change the light intensity by moving a lamp closer to or further away from your plant.

5) But if you just plot the rate of photosynthesis against "distance of lamp from the beaker", you get a weird-shaped graph. To get a graph like the one above you either need to measure the light intensity at the beaker using a light meter or do a bit of nifty maths with your results.

2) Too Little Carbon Dioxide Also Slows it Down

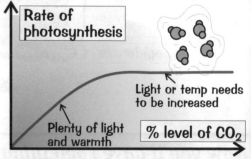

Rate of photosynthesis

Light or temp needs to be increased

Plenty of light and warmth

% level of CO_2

1) CO_2 is one of the raw materials needed for photosynthesis.

2) As with light intensity the amount of CO_2 will only increase the rate of photosynthesis up to a point. After this the graph flattens out showing that CO_2 is no longer the limiting factor.

3) As long as light and CO_2 are in plentiful supply then the factor limiting photosynthesis must be temperature.

4) There are loads of different ways to control the amount of CO_2. One way is to dissolve different amounts of sodium hydrogencarbonate in the water, which gives off CO_2.

The Rate of Photosynthesis

3) The Temperature has to be Just Right

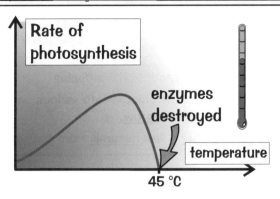

Rate of photosynthesis

enzymes destroyed

temperature

45 °C

1) Usually, if the temperature is the limiting factor it's because it's too low — the enzymes needed for photosynthesis work more slowly at low temperatures.

2) But if the plant gets too hot, the enzymes it needs for photosynthesis and its other reactions will be damaged.

3) This happens at about 45 °C (which is pretty hot for outdoors, although greenhouses can get that hot if you're not careful).

4) Experimentally, the best way to control the temperature of the flask is to put it in a water bath.

In all these experiments, you have to try and keep all the variables constant apart from the one you're investigating, so it's a fair test:

- use a bench lamp to control the intensity of the light (careful not to block the light with anything)
- keep the flask in a water bath to help keep the temperature constant
- you can't really do anything about the CO_2 levels — you just have to use a large flask, and do the experiments as quickly as you can, so that the plant doesn't use up too much of the CO_2 in the flask. If you're using sodium hydrogencarbonate make sure it's changed each time.

You can Artificially Create the Ideal Conditions for Farming

1) The most common way to artificially create the ideal environment for plants is to grow them in a greenhouse.

2) Greenhouses help to trap the sun's heat, and make sure that the temperature doesn't become limiting. In winter a farmer or gardener might use a heater as well to keep the temperature at the ideal level. In summer it could get too hot, so they might use shades and ventilation to cool things down.

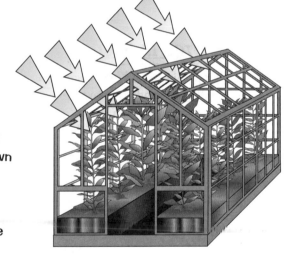

3) Light is always needed for photosynthesis, so commercial farmers often supply artificial light after the Sun goes down to give their plants more quality photosynthesis time.

4) Farmers and gardeners can also increase the level of carbon dioxide in the greenhouse. A fairly common way is to use a paraffin heater to heat the greenhouse. As the paraffin burns, it makes carbon dioxide as a by-product.

5) Keeping plants enclosed in a greenhouse also makes it easier to keep them free from pests and diseases. The farmer can add fertilisers to the soil as well, to provide all the minerals needed for healthy growth.

6) Sorting all this out costs money — but if the farmer can keep the conditions just right for photosynthesis, the plants will grow much faster and a decent crop can be harvested much more often, which can then be sold. It's important that a farmer supplies just the right amount of heat, light, etc. — enough to make the plants grow well, but not more than the plants need, as this would just be wasting money.

Don't blame it on the sunshine, don't blame it on the CO_2...

...don't blame it on the temperature, blame it on the plant. Right, and now you'll never forget the three limiting factors in photosynthesis. No... well, make sure you read these pages over and over again till you do. With your newly found knowledge of photosynthesis you could take over the world...

How Plants Use Glucose

Once plants have made glucose by photosynthesis (see p.43), there are a few ways they can use it.

① For Respiration

1) Plants manufacture glucose in their leaves.
2) They then use some of the glucose for respiration (see page 18).
3) This releases energy which enables them to convert the rest of the glucose into various other useful substances, which they can use to build new cells and grow.
4) To produce some of these substances they also need to gather a few minerals from the soil.

② Making Cell Walls

Glucose is converted into cellulose for making strong cell walls (see page 10), especially in a rapidly growing plant.

③ Making Proteins

Glucose is combined with nitrate ions (absorbed from the soil) to make amino acids, which are then made into proteins.

④ Stored in Seeds

Glucose is turned into lipids (fats and oils) for storing in seeds. Sunflower seeds, for example, contain a lot of oil — we get cooking oil and margarine from them. Seeds also store starch (see below).

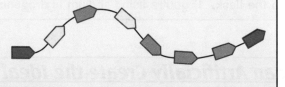

Algae also use glucose to make cellulose for cell walls, fats and oils for storage, and amino acids for proteins.

⑤ Stored as Starch

Glucose is turned into starch and stored in roots, stems and leaves, ready for use when photosynthesis isn't happening, like in the winter.
Starch is insoluble which makes it much better for storing than glucose — a cell with lots of glucose in would draw in loads of water and swell up.
Potato and parsnip plants store a lot of starch underground over the winter so a new plant can grow from it the following spring. We eat the swollen storage organs.

For making small ornamental birdcages...

Actually, I made that last one up. I was bored. So there are actually only five things that plants do with glucose. Right, shut the book right now. Or actually, finish reading this and then shut the book. Then write down all five uses of glucose from memory. Bet you forget one. Repeat until you don't.

Water Uptake and Loss in Plants

If you don't water a house plant for a few days it starts to go all droopy. Then it dies, and the people from the Society for the Protection of Plants come round and have you arrested. Plants need water.

Root Hairs Take in Water by Osmosis

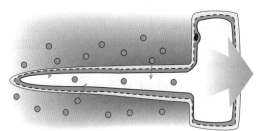

1) The cells on plant roots grow into long 'hairs' which stick out into the soil. Each branch of a root will be covered in millions of these microscopic hairs.

2) This gives the plant a big surface area for absorbing water from the soil.

3) There's usually a higher concentration of water in the soil than there is inside the plant, so the water enters the root hair cell by osmosis (see page 21).

Root Hairs Take In Minerals Using Active Transport

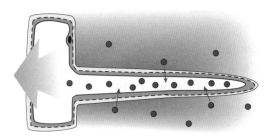

1) Root hairs also absorb minerals from the soil.

2) But the concentration of minerals in the soil is usually pretty low. It's normally higher in the root hair cell than in the soil around it.

3) So normal diffusion (page 20) doesn't explain how minerals are taken up into the root hair cell.

4) The answer is that a different process called 'active transport' is responsible.

5) Active transport uses energy from respiration to help the plant pull minerals into the root hair against the concentration gradient. This is essential for its growth.

Plants have tube networks to move substances to and from individual cells quickly:
- XYLEM tubes transport water and minerals from the root to the rest of the plant (e.g. the leaves).
- PHLOEM tubes transport sugars from the leaves (where they're made) to growing and storage tissues.

Transpiration is the Loss of Water from the Plant

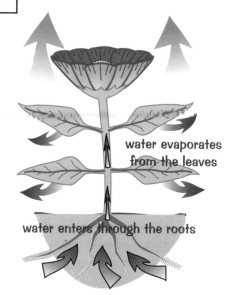

1) Transpiration is caused by the evaporation and diffusion of water from inside the leaves.

2) This creates a slight shortage of water in the leaf, and so more water is drawn up from the rest of the plant through the xylem vessels to replace it.

3) This in turn means more water is drawn up from the roots, and so there's a constant transpiration stream of water through the plant.

4) Transpiration is just a side-effect of the way leaves are adapted for photosynthesis. They have to have stomata in them so that gases can be exchanged easily. Because there's more water inside the plant than in the air outside, the water escapes from the leaves through the stomata.

water evaporates from the leaves

water enters through the roots

5) But, the transpiration stream does provide the plant with a constant supply of water for photosynthesis.

Transpiration — the plant version of perspiration...

A big tree loses about 1000 litres of water from its leaves every day. That's as much as an average person drinks in a year. The roots have to be very effective at drawing in water... which is why they have all those root hairs.

Plant Development

Plants, like animals, have stem cells. Page 30 will refresh your memory on stem cells. Then read on...

Meristems Contain Plant Stem Cells

1) In plants, the only cells that are mitotically active (i.e. divide by mitosis) are found in plant tissues called meristems.

2) Meristem tissue is found in the areas of a plant that are growing — such as the roots and shoots.

3) Meristems produce unspecialised cells that are able to divide and form any cell type in the plant — they act like embryonic stem cells (see page 30). But unlike human stem cells, these cells can divide to generate any type of cell for as long as the plant lives.

4) The unspecialised cells can become specialised and form tissues like xylem and phloem (the water and food transport tissues).

5) These tissues can group together to form organs like leaves, roots, stems and flowers.

Clones of Plants Can be Produced from Cuttings

1) A cutting is part of a plant that has been cut off it.

2) Cuttings taken from an area of the plant that's growing will contain unspecialised meristem cells which can differentiate to make any cell.

3) This means a whole new plant can grow from the cutting which will be a clone of the parent plant.

4) Gardeners often take cuttings from parent plants with desirable characteristics, and then plant them to produce identical copies of the parent plant.

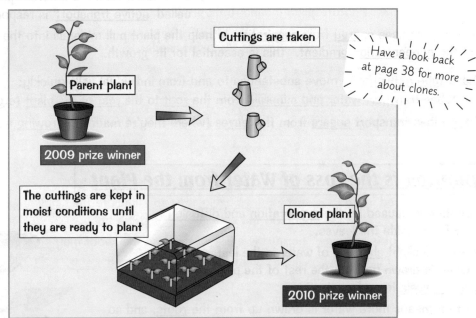

Parent plant

2009 prize winner

Cuttings are taken

The cuttings are kept in moist conditions until they are ready to plant

Cloned plant

2010 prize winner

Have a look back at page 38 for more about clones.

Rooting Powder Helps Cuttings to Grow into Complete Plants

1) If you stick cuttings in the soil they won't always grow.

2) If you add rooting powder, which contains plant hormones (auxins, see next page) they'll produce roots rapidly and start growing as new plants.

3) This helps growers to produce lots of clones of a really good plant very quickly.

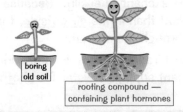

boring old soil

rooting compound — containing plant hormones

Cheery cells those Merry-stems...

So some plant cells can make any cell in the plant and for the whole time that the plant is alive. Nice.

Phototropism and Auxins

Unlike us humans, plants can't just get up and walk to something that they want. They can <u>grow</u> towards things though — <u>plant hormones</u> make sure they grow in a <u>useful direction</u> (e.g. toward light).

Phototropism **is** Growth Towards **or** Away **From** Light

1) Some parts of a plant, e.g. roots and shoots, can <u>respond</u> to <u>light</u> by <u>growing</u> in a certain <u>direction</u> — this is called <u>phototropism</u>.

2) Shoots are <u>positively phototropic</u> — they grow <u>towards</u> light.

3) Roots are <u>negatively phototropic</u> — they grow <u>away</u> from light.

4) Phototropism helps plants to <u>survive</u>:

Positive Phototropism

Plants need <u>sunlight</u> for <u>photosynthesis</u>. Without sunlight, plants can't photosynthesise and don't produce the food they need for <u>energy and growth</u>. Photosynthesis occurs <u>mainly</u> in the <u>leaves</u>, so it's important for plant shoots, which will grow leaves, to grow <u>towards light</u>.

Negative Phototropism

Plants need <u>nutrients and water</u> from the <u>soil</u> to grow. Phototropism means roots grow <u>away</u> from light, <u>down into the soil</u> where they can <u>absorb</u> the water and nutrients the plant needs for <u>healthy growth</u>.

Auxins **are Plant** Growth Hormones

1) <u>Auxins</u> are <u>chemicals</u> that control <u>growth</u> near the <u>tips</u> of <u>shoots</u> and <u>roots</u>.

2) Auxins are produced in the <u>tips</u> and <u>diffuses backwards</u> to stimulate the <u>cell elongation</u> (enlargement) process, which occurs in the cells <u>just behind</u> the tips.

3) If the tip of a shoot is <u>removed</u>, no auxins are available and the shoot may <u>stop growing</u>.

4) Auxins are involved in the responses of plants to <u>light</u>, <u>gravity</u> and <u>water</u>.

Auxins make shoots grow towards light

1) When a <u>shoot tip</u> is exposed to <u>light</u>, <u>more auxins</u> accumulate on the side that's in the <u>shade</u> than the side that's in the light.

2) This makes the cells grow (elongate) <u>faster</u> on the <u>shaded side</u>, so the shoot grows <u>towards</u> the light.

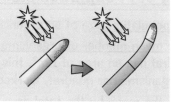

A plant auxin to a bar — 'ouch'...

<u>Phototropism</u> might not sound like the most exciting thing in the world, but it's pretty nifty stuff. If a plant grows towards <u>light</u> it can <u>photosynthesise</u> more — this means it can produce lots of <u>food</u> and <u>grow</u> quickly. A bigger plant is <u>better able</u> to <u>compete</u> with the other plants around it for resources, so it's more likely to <u>survive</u>.

Distribution of Organisms

This is where the <u>fun</u> starts. Studying <u>ecology</u> gives you the chance to <u>rummage around</u> in bushes, get your hands <u>dirty</u> and look at some <u>real organisms</u>, living in the <u>wild</u>. Hold on to your hats folks...

Organisms Live in Different Places Because The Environment Varies

1) A habitat is the place where an organism <u>lives</u>, e.g. a playing field.

2) The <u>distribution</u> of an organism is <u>where</u> an organism is <u>found</u>, e.g. in a part of the playing field.

3) Where an organism is found is affected by <u>environmental factors</u> such as:

- <u>Temperature</u>.
- Availability of <u>water</u>.
- Availability of <u>oxygen</u> and <u>carbon dioxide</u>.
- Availability of <u>nutrients</u>.
- Amount of <u>light</u>.

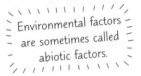
Environmental factors are sometimes called abiotic factors.

4) An organism might be <u>more common</u> in <u>one area</u> than another due to <u>differences</u> in <u>environmental factors</u> between the two areas. For example, in a field, you might find that daisies are <u>more common</u> in the open, than under trees, because there's <u>more light</u> available in the open.

5) There are a couple of ways to <u>study</u> the distribution of an organism. You can:
- <u>measure</u> how common an organism is in <u>two sample areas</u> (e.g. using <u>quadrats</u>) and compare them.
- study how the distribution <u>changes</u> across an area e.g. by placing quadrats along a <u>transect</u> (p.51).

Use Quadrats to Study The Distribution of Small Organisms

A <u>quadrat</u> is a <u>square</u> frame enclosing a <u>known area</u>, e.g. 1 m². To compare how common an organism is in <u>two sample areas</u>, just follow these simple steps:

A quadrat
1 m
1 m

1) Place a <u>1 m² quadrat</u> on the ground at a <u>random point</u> within the <u>first</u> sample area. E.g. divide the area into a grid and use a random number generator to pick coordinates.

2) <u>Count</u> all the organisms <u>within</u> the quadrat.

3) <u>Repeat</u> steps 1 and 2 as many times as you can.

4) <u>Work out</u> the <u>mean</u> number of organisms per quadrat within the first sample area.

- For example, Anna counted the number of daisies in 7 quadrats within her first sample area and recorded the following results: 18, 20, 22, 23, 23, 23, 25
- Here the MEAN is: $\dfrac{\text{TOTAL number of organisms}}{\text{NUMBER of quadrats}} = \dfrac{154}{7} = \underline{22}$ daisies per quadrat.
- The MODE is the MOST COMMON value. In this example it's <u>23</u>.
- And the MEDIAN is the MIDDLE value, when they're in order of size. In this example it's <u>23</u> also.

5) <u>Repeat</u> steps 1 to 4 in the <u>second</u> sample area.

6) Finally <u>compare</u> the two means. E.g. you might find 2 daisies per m² in the shade, and 22 daisies per m² (lots more) in the open field.

You Can Work Out Population Size Too

To work out the <u>population size</u> of an organism in one sample area:

1) Work out the <u>mean number of organisms per m²</u>. (If your quadrat has an area of 1 m², this is the <u>same</u> as the mean number of organisms per quadrat, worked out above.)

2) Then multiply the <u>mean</u> by the <u>total area</u> (in m²) of the habitat.

3) E.g. if the area of an open field is 800 m², and there are 22 daisies per m², then the size of the daisy population is 22 x 800 = 17 600.

Ben liked looking after his quad-rats.

Drat, drat, and double drat — my favourite use of quadrats...

You must put your quadrat down in a <u>random place</u> before you start counting. Anything, even chucking the quadrat over your shoulder*, is better than plonking it down right on the <u>first big patch</u> of organisms that you see.

*not an invitation to break equipment or maim fellow students, etc.

More on The Distribution of Organisms

So, now you think you know all about distribution. Well hold on — there's more ecology fun to be had.

Use Transects to Study The Distribution of Organisms Along a Line

You can use lines called transects to help find out how organisms (like plants) are distributed across an area — e.g. if an organism becomes more or less common as you move from a hedge towards the middle of a field. Here's what to do:

1) Mark out a line in the area you want to study using a tape measure.

2) Then collect data along the line.

3) You can do this by just counting all the organisms you're interested in that touch the line.

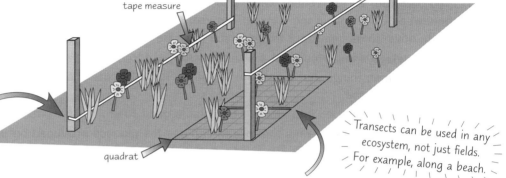

tape measure

quadrat

Transects can be used in any ecosystem, not just fields. For example, along a beach.

4) Or, you can collect data by using quadrats. These can be placed next to each other along the line or at intervals, for example, every 2 m.

When Collecting Environmental Data You Need to Think About...

❶ Reliability

1) Quadrats and transects are pretty good tools for finding out how an organism is distributed.

2) But, you have to work hard to make sure your results are reliable — which means making sure they are repeatable and reproducible (see page 3).

3) To make your results more reliable you need to:
   - Take a large sample size, e.g. use as many quadrats and transects as possible in your sample area. Bigger samples are more representative of the whole population.
   - Use random samples, e.g. randomly put down or mark out your quadrat or transect. If all your samples are in one spot, and everywhere else is different, the results you get won't be reproducible.

❷ Validity

1) For your results to be valid they must be reliable (see above) and answer the original question.

2) To answer the original question, you need to control all the variables.

3) The question you want to answer is whether a difference in distribution between two sample areas is due to a difference in one environmental factor.

4) If you've controlled all the other variables that could be affecting the distribution, you'll know whether a difference in distribution is caused by the environmental factor or not.

5) If you don't control the other variables you won't know whether any correlation you've found is because of chance, because of the environmental factor you're looking at or because of a different variable — the study won't give you valid data.

A slug that's been run over — definitely a widely-spread organism...

Isn't it exciting — after reading these pages, you can go out and count bugs. You can use quadrats and transects to study the distribution of organisms, and you can even do a nifty calculation to work out population size. If that's not enough, you can also ponder whether your data is reliable and valid.

Revision Summary for Section 3

Believe it or not, it's already time for another round of questions. Do as many as you can and if there are some that you're finding really fiddly, don't panic. Have a quick flick over the relevant topics and give the questions another go once you've had another chance to read the pages. Good luck — not that you need it.

1) Write down the word equation for photosynthesis.
2) What is the green substance in leaves that absorbs sunlight?
3) Name the three factors that can limit the rate of photosynthesis.
4) You carry out an experiment where you change the light intensity experienced by a piece of Canadian pondweed by changing the distance between the pondweed and a lamp supplying it with light.
Write down three important things which must be kept constant for this experiment to be a fair test.
5) Explain why it's important that a plant doesn't get too hot.
6) Describe three things that a gardener could do to make sure she grows a good crop of tomatoes in her greenhouse.
7) Why is glucose turned into starch when plants need to store it for later?
8) Write down four other ways that plants can use the glucose produced by photosynthesis.
9) What is the advantage to a plant of having root hairs?
10) What is transpiration?
11) What name is given to the parts of plants where mitotically active cells are found?
12) Name two types of tissue that the unspecialised cells in plants can turn into.
13) What is a cutting?
14) What do cuttings grow into?
15) Why are cuttings useful?
16) What can be added to soil to encourage cuttings to grow roots?
17) What is phototropism?
18) Are shoots negatively or positively phototropic?
19) Explain how auxins cause plant shoots to grow towards light.
20) What is a habitat?
21) Give five environmental factors that can affect the distribution of organisms.
22) Briefly describe how you could find out how common an organism is in two sample areas using quadrats.
23) Describe one way of using a transect to find out how an organism is distributed across an area.

Atoms, Compounds and Isotopes

Atoms are really <u>small</u> but very important. They contain <u>three</u> even smaller types of particle —
<u>protons</u>, <u>neutrons</u> and <u>electrons</u>.

Atomic Number **and Mass Number Describe an Atom**

These two numbers tell you how many of each kind of particle an atom has.

The Mass Number ➡ **²³Na**
— Total number of
protons and neutrons

The Atomic Number ➡ **₁₁Na**
— Number of protons

1) The <u>atomic number</u> tells you
how many <u>protons</u> there are.

2) Atoms of the <u>same</u> element all have the <u>same</u>
number of <u>protons</u> — so atoms of <u>different</u>
elements will have <u>different</u> numbers of <u>protons</u>.

3) To get the number of <u>neutrons</u>, just <u>subtract</u>
the <u>atomic number</u> from the <u>mass number</u>.
Electrons aren't counted in the mass number
because their <u>relative mass</u> is very small.

- <u>Protons</u> are <u>heavy</u> and <u>positively charged</u>
- <u>Neutrons</u> are <u>heavy</u> and <u>neutral</u>
- <u>Electrons</u> are <u>tiny</u> and <u>negatively charged</u>

PARTICLE	MASS	CHARGE
Proton	1	+1
Neutron	1	0
Electron	0.0005	−1

(<u>Electron mass</u> is often
taken as <u>zero</u>.)

Compounds Are *Chemically Bonded*

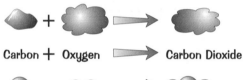

Carbon + Oxygen ⟶ Carbon Dioxide

1) Compounds are formed when <u>atoms</u> of <u>two or more</u>
elements are <u>chemically combined</u> together.
For example, carbon dioxide is a <u>compound</u> formed from a
<u>chemical reaction</u> between carbon and oxygen.

2) It's difficult to <u>separate</u> the two original elements out again.

Isotopes **Are the Same Except for an Extra** Neutron **or Two**

Isotopes are: <u>different atomic forms</u> of the <u>same element</u>, which have
the <u>SAME</u> number of <u>PROTONS</u> but a <u>DIFFERENT</u> number of <u>NEUTRONS</u>.

1) The upshot is: isotopes must have the <u>same</u> atomic number but <u>different</u> mass numbers.
2) <u>If</u> they had <u>different</u> atomic numbers, they'd be <u>different</u> elements altogether.
3) <u>Carbon-12</u> and <u>carbon-14</u> are a very popular pair of isotopes.

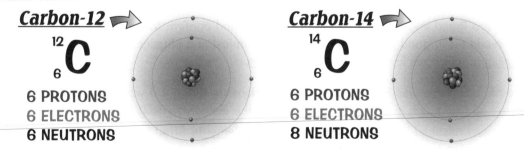

Carbon-12 ➡ **¹²C₆**

6 PROTONS
6 ELECTRONS
6 NEUTRONS

Carbon-14 ➡ **¹⁴C₆**

6 PROTONS
6 ELECTRONS
8 NEUTRONS

Isotope you get learning this stuff...

Read this page until you know this stuff as well as you know not to eat yellow snow. Ahem.
Remember that an isotope is just a slight variation on the <u>same element</u>.

History of The Periodic Table

We haven't always known as much about Chemistry as we do now. No sirree. Early chemists looked to try and understand <u>patterns</u> in the elements' properties to get a bit of understanding.

Döbereiner Tried to Organise Elements into Triads

Back in the 1800's the only thing they could measure was <u>relative atomic mass</u> (page 67), and so the <u>known</u> elements were arranged <u>in order of atomic mass</u>.

In 1828 a guy called <u>Döbereiner</u> started to put this list of elements into groups based on their <u>chemical properties</u>. He put the elements into groups of <u>three</u>, which he called <u>triads</u>. E.g. Cl, Br and I were one triad, and Li, Na and K were another.

The <u>middle element</u> of each triad had a relative atomic mass that was the <u>average</u> of the other two.

Element	Relative atomic mass
Lithium	7
Sodium	23
Potassium	39

$(7 + 39) \div 2 = 23$

Newlands' Law of Octaves Was the First Good Effort

A chap called <u>Newlands</u> noticed that when you arranged the elements in order of relative atomic mass, every <u>eighth</u> element had similar properties, and so he listed some of the known elements in rows of seven:

H	Li	Be	B	C	N	O
F	Na	Mg	Al	Si	P	S
Cl	K	Ca	Cr	Ti	Mn	Fe

These sets of eight were called <u>Newlands' Octaves</u>. Unfortunately the pattern <u>broke down</u> on the <u>third row</u>, with <u>transition metals</u> like titanium (Ti) and iron (Fe) messing it up.

It was because he left <u>no gaps</u> that his work was <u>ignored</u>. But he was getting <u>pretty close</u>.

Newlands presented his ideas to the Chemical Society in 1865. But his work was criticised because:

1) His groups contained elements that didn't have <u>similar properties</u>, e.g. <u>carbon</u> and <u>titanium</u>.
2) He <u>mixed up metals and non-metals</u> e.g. <u>oxygen</u> and <u>iron</u>.
3) He <u>didn't leave any gaps</u> for elements that hadn't been discovered yet.

Dmitri Mendeleev Left Gaps and Predicted New Elements

1) In <u>1869</u>, <u>Dmitri Mendeleev</u> in Russia, armed with about 50 known elements, arranged them into his Table of Elements — with various <u>gaps</u> as shown.

2) Mendeleev put the elements in order of <u>atomic mass</u> (like Newlands did). But Mendeleev found he had to leave <u>gaps</u> in order to keep elements with <u>similar properties</u> in the same <u>vertical groups</u> — and he was prepared to leave some <u>very big gaps</u> in the first two rows before the transition metals come in on the <u>third</u> row.

```
                 Mendeleev's Table of the Elements
H
Li Be                                           B  C  N  O  F
Na Mg                                           Al Si P  S  Cl
K  Ca *  Ti V  Cr Mn Fe Co Ni Cu Zn *  *  As Se Br
Rb Sr Y  Zr Nb Mo *  Ru Rh Pd Ag Cd In Sn Sb Te I
Cs Ba *  *  Ta W  *  Os Ir Pt Au Hg Tl Pb Bi
```

3) The <u>gaps</u> were the really clever bit because they <u>predicted</u> the properties of so far <u>undiscovered elements</u>. When they were found and they <u>fitted the pattern</u> it helped confirm Mendeleev's ideas. For example, Mendeleev made really good predictions about the chemical and physical properties of an element he called <u>ekasilicon</u>, which we know today as <u>germanium</u>.

- When the periodic table was first released, many scientists thought it was just a bit of <u>fun</u>. At that time, there wasn't all that much <u>evidence</u> to suggest that the elements really did fit together in that way.
- After Mendeleev released his work, <u>newly discovered elements</u> fitted into the <u>gaps</u> he left. This was convincing evidence in favour of the periodic table.

Julie Andrews' octaves — do-re-mi-fa-so-la-ti-do...

This is a good example of how science often works. A scientist has a <u>basically good</u> (though incomplete) idea. Other scientists disagree with it. Eventually, it gets modified a bit and voilà — into the textbooks it goes.

The Modern Periodic Table

There are about <u>100 known elements</u>. The modern <u>periodic table</u> is a refined version of Mendeleev's Table of Elements (see previous page) but the difference is that it shows the elements in order of <u>atomic number</u> (see page 53). Carry on reading to see it in all its glory...

Metals and Non-metals are on Opposite Sides of the Periodic Table

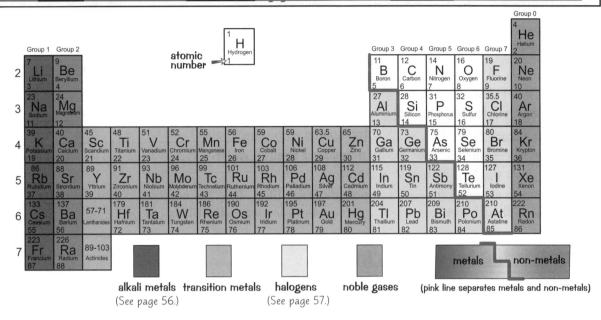

alkali metals transition metals halogens noble gases (pink line separates metals and non-metals)
(See page 56.) (See page 57.)

The Periodic Table is Arranged in Periods and Groups

Periods

1) The <u>rows</u> of the periodic table are called <u>periods</u>.

2) The elements are arranged in order of <u>increasing atomic number</u> along each row. E.g. the atomic numbers of the Period 2 elements <u>increase</u> from 3 for Li to 10 for Ne.

3) The period number is the <u>same</u> as the number of <u>electron shells</u>. E.g. the Period <u>3</u> elements have <u>3</u> electron shells.

4) The <u>properties</u> of elements <u>change</u> as you go along a period (sometimes quite dramatically).

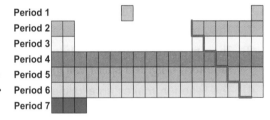

Groups

1) The <u>columns</u> of the periodic table are called <u>groups</u>.

2) Elements in the same group have <u>similar properties</u>. This is because they have the <u>same number of electrons in their outer shell</u>.

3) The <u>group number</u> is always <u>equal</u> to the number of <u>electrons</u> in the outer shell. E.g. the <u>Group 2</u> elements all have <u>two electrons in their outer shell</u>.

4) The <u>properties</u> of <u>elements</u> (such as reactivity) often <u>gradually change</u> as you go down a group (as the atomic number increases).

I've got a periodic table — Queen Anne legs and everything...

The periodic table is jam-packed with useful information. I like to think of it as a library and a crystal ball all rolled into one. For example, you can find out at a glance whether an element is a metal or a non-metal, and you can <u>predict</u> some of its properties too. Just don't forget the difference between <u>groups</u> and <u>periods</u>.

Group 1 — The Alkali Metals

Welcome to the wonderful world of the alkali metals. May I introduce Li, Na, K, Rb, Cs and Fr...

Group 1 Metals are Known as the 'Alkali Metals'

Group 1 metals include lithium, sodium and potassium... know those names real well.

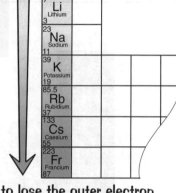

As you go DOWN Group 1, the alkali metals become more reactive — the outer electron is more easily lost, because it's further from the nucleus (the atomic radius is larger) so less energy is needed to remove it.

1) The alkali metals all have ONE outer electron.
   This makes them very reactive and gives them all similar properties.

2) They all have the following physical properties:
   - Low melting point and boiling point (compared with other metals).
   - Low density — lithium, sodium and potassium float on water.
   - Very soft — they can be cut with a knife.

3) The alkali metals always form ionic compounds (page 58). They are so keen to lose the outer electron there's no way they'd consider sharing, so covalent bonding (page 61) is out of the question.

Oxidation is the Loss of Electrons

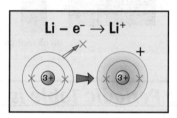

1) Group 1 metals are keen to lose an electron to form a 1^+ ion with a stable electronic structure.

2) The more reactive the metal the happier it is to lose an electron.

3) Loss of electrons is called OXIDATION.

Reaction with Cold Water Produces Hydrogen Gas

1) When lithium, sodium or potassium are put in water, they react very vigorously.

2) They move around the surface, fizzing furiously.

3) They produce hydrogen. Potassium gets hot enough to ignite it. If it hasn't already been ignited by the reaction, a lighted splint will indicate hydrogen by producing the notorious "squeaky pop" as it ignites.

4) The reaction makes an alkaline solution — this is why Group 1 is known as the alkali metals.

5) A hydroxide of the metal forms, e.g. sodium hydroxide (NaOH), potassium hydroxide (KOH) or lithium hydroxide (LiOH).

$$2Na_{(s)} + 2H_2O_{(l)} \rightarrow 2NaOH_{(aq)} + H_2{(g)}$$
$$2K_{(s)} + 2H_2O_{(l)} \rightarrow 2KOH_{(aq)} + H_2{(g)}$$

6) This experiment shows the relative reactivities of the alkali metals. The more violent the reaction, the more reactive the alkali metal is.

Reaction with Chlorine Produces Salts

1) Alkali metals react vigorously with chlorine.

2) The reaction produces colourless crystalline salts, e.g. lithium chloride (LiCl), sodium chloride (NaCl) and potassium chloride (KCl).

$$2Na_{(s)} + Cl_2{(g)} \rightarrow 2NaCl_{(s)}$$
$$2K_{(s)} + Cl_2{(g)} \rightarrow 2KCl_{(s)}$$

Notorious Squeaky Pop — a.k.a. the Justin Timberlake test...

Alkali metals are ace. They're so reactive you have to store them in oil — because otherwise they'd react with the water vapour in the air. AND they fizz in water and explode and everything. Cool.

Group 7 — The Halogens

The 'trend thing' happens in Group 7 as well — no surprise there.

Group 7 Elements are Known as the 'Halogens'

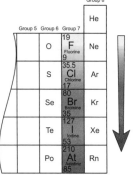

1) Group 7 is made up of fluorine, chlorine, bromine, iodine and astatine.
2) All Group 7 elements have 7 electrons in their outer shell — so they all react by gaining one electron to form a negative ion.
3) This means they've all got similar properties.

> As you go DOWN Group 7, the halogens become less reactive — there's less inclination to gain the extra electron to fill the outer shell when it's further out from the nucleus (there's a larger atomic radius).

4) As you go down group 7 the melting points and boiling points of the halogens increase.
5) This means that at room temperature:

- Chlorine (Cl_2) is a fairly reactive, poisonous, dense green gas (low boiling point).
- Bromine (Br_2) is a dense, poisonous, orange liquid.
- Iodine (I_2) is a dark grey crystalline solid (high boiling point).

Reduction is the Gain of Electrons

1) Halogens are keen to gain an electron to form a 1^- ion with a stable electronic structure.
2) The more reactive the halogen the happier it is to gain an electron.
3) Gain of electrons is called REDUCTION.

$$Cl_2 + 2e^- \rightarrow 2Cl^-$$

Halogen molecule   Halide ion

Halogens become Less Reactive Down the Group

Chlorine is more reactive than bromine, which is more reactive than iodine.

The trend in reactivity of the halogens can be shown by looking at different reactions.

REACTIONS WITH ALKALI METALS

The halogens react with alkali metals like lithium, sodium and potassium to form salts called metal halides e.g. sodium chloride (NaCl), potassium bromide (KBr) and lithium iodide (LiI). The reactions become less vigorous as you go down the group.

$$2Na_{(s)} + Cl_{2(g)} \rightarrow 2NaCl_{(s)}$$
$$2K_{(s)} + Br_{2(g)} \rightarrow 2KBr_{(s)}$$

REACTIONS WITH IRON

They react with iron to form coloured solids called iron halides.
Again, the reactions become less vigorous as you go down the group.

$$2Fe_{(s)} + 3Cl_{2(g)} \rightarrow 2FeCl_{3(s)}$$
$$2Fe_{(s)} + 3Br_{2(g)} \rightarrow 2FeBr_{3(s)}$$

DISPLACEMENT REACTIONS

A displacement reaction is where a more reactive element 'pushes out' (displaces) a less reactive element from a compound.

These displacement reactions can be used to determine the relative reactivity of the halogens.

Chlorine is more reactive than iodine. So chlorine reacts with potassium iodide solution to form potassium chloride, and the iodine is left in solution.
Chlorine can also displace bromine from solutions of bromides.
Bromine will displace iodine because of the trend in reactivity.

$$Cl_{2(g)} + 2KI_{(aq)} \rightarrow I_{2(aq)} + 2KCl_{(aq)}$$
$$Cl_{2(g)} + 2KBr_{(aq)} \rightarrow Br_{2(aq)} + 2KCl_{(aq)}$$

They're great, the halogens — you have to hand it to them...

The halogens are another group from the periodic table, and just like the alkali metals (see page 56) they follow certain trends. This can be shown in various reactions — exciting stuff...

Ionic Bonding

Ionic Bonding — Transferring Electrons

In ionic bonding, atoms lose or gain electrons to form charged particles (called ions) which are then strongly attracted to one another (because of the attraction of opposite charges, + and −).

A Shell with Just One Electron is Well Keen to Get Rid...

All the atoms over at the left-hand side of the periodic table, e.g. sodium, potassium, calcium etc. have just one or two electrons in their outer shell (highest energy level). And they're pretty keen to get shot of them, because then they'll only have full shells left, which is how they like it. (They try to have the same electronic structure as a noble gas.) So given half a chance they do get rid, and that leaves the atom as an ion instead. Now ions aren't the kind of things that sit around quietly watching the world go by. They tend to leap at the first passing ion with an opposite charge and stick to it like glue.

A Nearly Full Shell is Well Keen to Get That Extra Electron...

On the other side of the periodic table, the elements in Group 6 and Group 7, such as oxygen and chlorine, have outer shells which are nearly full. They're obviously pretty keen to gain that extra one or two electrons to fill the shell up. When they do of course they become ions (you know, not the kind of things to sit around) and before you know it, pop, they've latched onto the atom (ion) that gave up the electron a moment earlier. The reaction of sodium and chlorine is a classic case:

The sodium atom gives up its outer electron and becomes an Na⁺ ion.

The chlorine atom has picked up the spare electron and becomes a Cl⁻ ion.

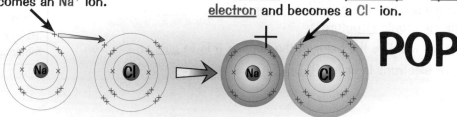

POP!

Ionic Compounds Have A Regular Lattice Structure

1) Ionic compounds always have giant ionic lattices.
2) The ions form a closely packed regular lattice arrangement.
3) There are very strong electrostatic forces of attraction between oppositely charged ions, in all directions.
4) A single crystal of sodium chloride (salt) is one giant ionic lattice, which is why salt crystals tend to be cuboid in shape. The Na⁺ and Cl⁻ ions are held together in a regular lattice.

● = Cl⁻
● = Na⁺

Ionic Compounds All Have Similar Properties

1) They all have high melting points and high boiling points due to the strong attraction between the ions. It takes a large amount of energy to overcome this attraction. When ionic compounds melt, the ions are free to move and they'll carry electric current.

2) They do dissolve easily in water though. The ions separate and are all free to move in the solution, so they'll carry electric current.

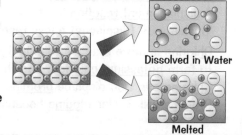

Dissolved in Water

Melted

Giant ionic lattices — all over your chips...

These guys are tough nuts to crack, but if you do crack 'em, they get all excited and start conducting electricity.

Ions and Formulas

Make sure you've really got your head around the idea of ionic bonding before you start on this page.

Groups 1 & 2 and 6 & 7 are the Most Likely to Form Ions

1) Remember, atoms that have <u>lost</u> or <u>gained</u> an electron (or electrons) are <u>ions</u>.

2) Ions have the <u>electronic structure</u> of a <u>noble gas</u>.

3) The elements that most readily form ions are those in <u>Groups 1, 2, 6 and 7</u>.

4) <u>Group 1 and 2 elements</u> are <u>metals</u> and they <u>lose</u> electrons to form <u>positive ions</u>.

5) For example, <u>Group 1</u> elements (the <u>alkali metals</u>) form ionic compounds with <u>non-metals</u> where the metal ion has a 1^+ charge. E.g. K^+Cl^-.

6) <u>Group 6 and 7 elements</u> are <u>non-metals</u>. They <u>gain</u> electrons to form <u>negative ions</u>.

7) For example, <u>Group 7</u> elements (the <u>halogens</u>) form ionic compounds with the <u>alkali metals</u> where the halide ion has a 1^- charge. E.g. Na^+Cl^-.

8) The <u>charge</u> on the <u>positive ions</u> is the <u>same</u> as the <u>group number</u> of the element:

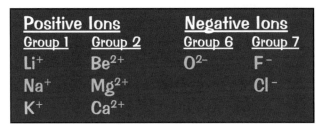

Positive Ions		Negative Ions	
Group 1	Group 2	Group 6	Group 7
Li^+	Be^{2+}	O^{2-}	F^-
Na^+	Mg^{2+}		Cl^-
K^+	Ca^{2+}		

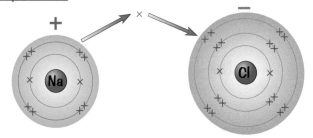

9) Any of the positive ions above can <u>combine</u> with any of the negative ions to form an <u>ionic compound</u>.

10) Only elements at <u>opposite sides</u> of the periodic table will form ionic compounds, e.g. Na and Cl, where one of them becomes a <u>positive ion</u> and one becomes a <u>negative ion</u>.

> Remember, the $+$ and $-$ charges we talk about, e.g. Na^+ for sodium, just tell you <u>what type of ion the atom WILL FORM</u> in a chemical reaction. In sodium <u>metal</u> there are <u>only neutral sodium atoms, Na</u>. The Na^+ ions <u>will only appear</u> if the sodium metal <u>reacts</u> with something like water or chlorine.

Look at Charges to Work Out the Formula of an Ionic Compound

1) Ionic compounds are made up of a <u>positively charged</u> part and a <u>negatively charged</u> part.

2) The <u>overall charge</u> of <u>any compound</u> is <u>zero</u>.

3) So all the <u>negative charges</u> in the compound must <u>balance</u> all the <u>positive charges</u>.

4) You can use the charges on the <u>individual ions</u> present to work out the formula for the ionic compound:

> Sodium chloride contains Na^+ $(+1)$ and Cl^- (-1) ions.
> $(+1) + (-1) = 0$. The charges are balanced with one of each ion, so the formula for sodium chloride = NaCl

> Magnesium chloride contains Mg^{2+} $(+2)$ and Cl^- (-1) ions.
> Because a chloride ion only has a 1^- charge we will need <u>two</u> of them to balance out the 2^+ charge of a magnesium ion. This gives us the formula $MgCl_2$.

The formula for exam success = revision...

Remember, the $+$ and $-$ charges only appear when an element <u>reacts</u> with something. So, don't be fooling yourself, sodium isn't always a flashy Na^+ ion — when he's being sodium metal he's just made up of boring old <u>neutral sodium atoms, Na</u>. But wave some chlorine at him and he gets positively charged.

Electronic Structure of Ions

I heard the examiner fancies himself as a bit of an artist. This page is full of lovely drawings of <u>electronic structures</u> that should put a smile on his face.

Show the Electronic Structure of Simple Ions With Diagrams

A useful way of representing ions is by <u>drawing</u> out their electronic structure. Just use a big <u>square bracket</u> and a + or − to show the charge. A few <u>ions</u> and the <u>ionic compounds</u> they form are shown below.

Sodium Chloride

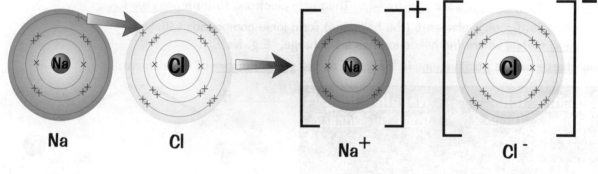

Na   Cl   Na$^+$ Cl$^-$

NaCl (Sodium Chloride)

Magnesium Oxide

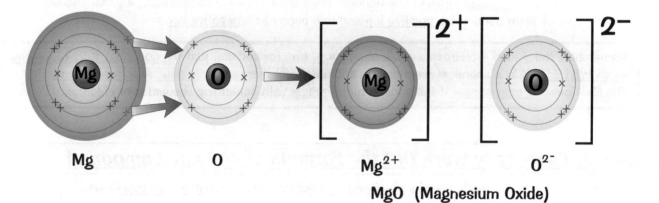

Mg   O   Mg^{2+} O^{2-}

MgO (Magnesium Oxide)

Calcium Chloride

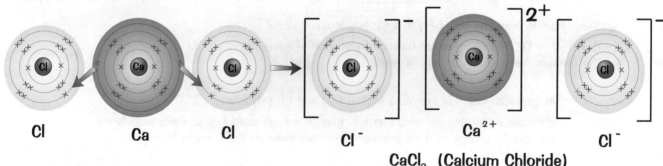

Cl   Ca   Cl   Cl$^-$ Ca^{2+} Cl$^-$

CaCl$_2$ (Calcium Chloride)

Any old ion, any old ion — any, any, any old ion...

3 ionic compounds, 3 drawings, 1 exam hall. It's like the start of a bad Game Show. Whether or not you're able to produce some lovely drawings of these bad boys all comes down to how well you've understood <u>ionic bonding</u>. (So if you're struggling, try reading the last few pages again — I know I had to).

Covalent Bonding

Some elements bond ionically (see page 58) but others form strong <u>covalent bonds</u>.
This is where atoms <u>share electrons</u> with each other so that they've got <u>full outer shells</u>.

Covalent **Bonds** — **Sharing Electrons**

1) Sometimes atoms prefer to make <u>covalent bonds</u> by <u>sharing</u> electrons with other atoms.

2) They only share electrons in their <u>outer shells</u> (highest energy levels).

3) This way <u>both</u> atoms feel that they have a <u>full outer shell</u>, and that makes them happy. Having a full outer shell gives them the electronic structure of a <u>noble gas</u>.

4) Each <u>covalent bond</u> provides one <u>extra</u> shared electron for each atom.

5) So, a covalent bond is a <u>shared pair</u> of electrons.

6) Each atom involved has to make <u>enough</u> covalent bonds to <u>fill up</u> its outer shell.

> Fancy sharing spare electrons?

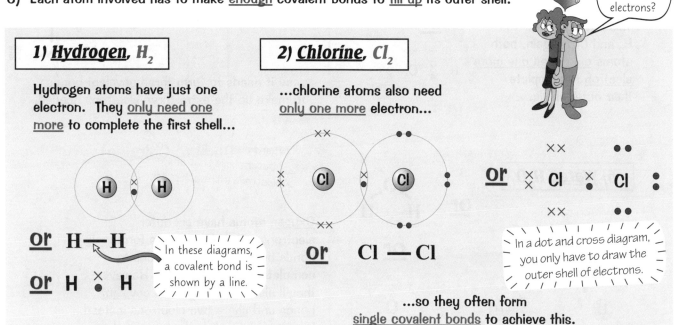

1) **Hydrogen**, H_2

Hydrogen atoms have just one electron. They <u>only need one</u> <u>more</u> to complete the first shell...

Or H — H

In these diagrams, a covalent bond is shown by a line.

Or H × • H

2) **Chlorine**, Cl_2

...chlorine atoms also need <u>only one more</u> electron...

Or Cl — Cl

In a dot and cross diagram, you only have to draw the outer shell of electrons.

...so they often form <u>single covalent bonds</u> to achieve this.

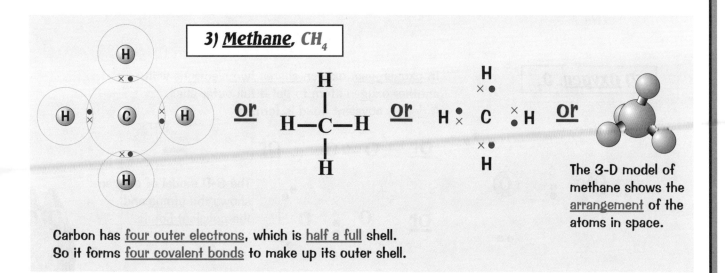

3) **Methane**, CH_4

Or H—C—H (with H above and H below)

Or (dot and cross diagram of methane)

The 3-D model of methane shows the <u>arrangement</u> of the atoms in space.

Carbon has <u>four outer electrons</u>, which is <u>half a full</u> shell.
So it forms <u>four covalent bonds</u> to make up its outer shell.

Covalent bonding — it's good to share...

There's another page of covalent bonding diagrams yet to come, but make sure you understand the ones on this page first. When you've drawn a dot and cross diagram, it's a really good idea to count up the number of electrons, just to <u>double check</u> you've definitely got a full outer shell.

More Covalent Bonding

You lucky thing. There are four more examples of covalent bonding on this page — and for each compound there are three possible <u>diagrams</u>. I make that twelve diagrams in total... and just a smattering of words. So, this page is a breeze compared to others out there.

4) <u>Hydrogen Chloride</u>, HCl

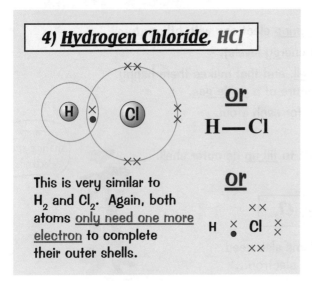

or

H—Cl

This is very similar to H_2 and Cl_2. Again, both atoms <u>only need one more electron</u> to complete their outer shells.

or

5) <u>Ammonia</u>, NH_3

Nitrogen has <u>five</u> outer electrons...

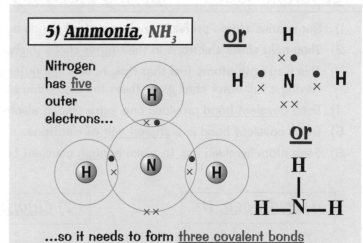

or

or

...so it needs to form <u>three covalent bonds</u> to make up the extra <u>three</u> electrons needed.

Remember — it's only the outer shells that share electrons with each other.

6) <u>Water</u>, H_2O

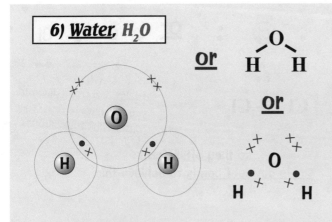

or

or

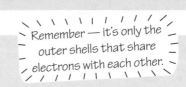

<u>Oxygen</u> atoms have <u>six</u> outer electrons. They sometimes form <u>ionic</u> bonds by <u>taking</u> two electrons to complete their outer shell. However they'll also cheerfully form <u>covalent bonds</u> and <u>share</u> two electrons instead. In <u>water molecules</u>, the oxygen <u>shares</u> electrons with the two H atoms.

7) <u>Oxygen</u>, O_2

In <u>oxygen gas</u>, oxygen <u>shares two electrons</u> with another oxygen atom to get a full outer shell. A <u>double</u> covalent bond is formed.

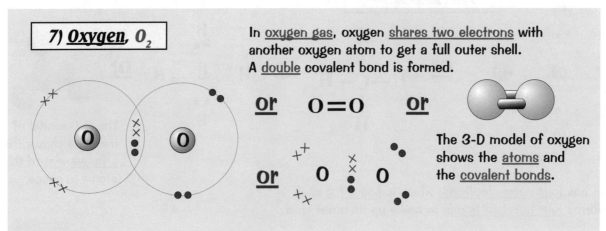

or   O=O   **or**

or

The 3-D model of oxygen shows the <u>atoms</u> and the <u>covalent bonds</u>.

<u>The name's Bond, Covalent Bond...</u>

These pages give you some basic examples and tell you <u>why they work</u>. Every atom wants a full outer shell, and they can get that either by becoming an <u>ion</u> (see page 58) or by <u>sharing electrons</u>. Once you understand that, you should be able to apply it if it comes up in your exam. Now go get 'em...

Covalent Substances: Two Kinds

Substances with covalent bonds (electron sharing) can either be simple molecules or giant structures.

Simple Molecular Substances

1) The atoms form very strong covalent bonds to form small molecules of several atoms.

2) By contrast, the forces of attraction between these molecules are very weak.

3) The result of these feeble intermolecular forces is that the melting and boiling points are very low, because the molecules are easily parted from each other. It's the intermolecular forces that get broken when simple molecular substances melt or boil — not the much stronger covalent bonds.

4) Most molecular substances are gases or liquids at room temperature, but they can be solids.

5) Molecular substances don't conduct electricity — there are no ions so there's no electrical charge.

Very weak intermolecular forces

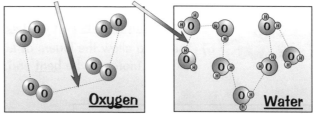

Giant Covalent Structures Are Macromolecules

1) These are similar to giant ionic structures (lattices) except that there are no charged ions.

2) All the atoms are bonded to each other by strong covalent bonds.

3) This means that they have very high melting and boiling points.

4) They don't conduct electricity — not even when molten (except for graphite).

5) The main examples are diamond and graphite, which are both made only from carbon atoms, and silicon dioxide (silica).

Diamond

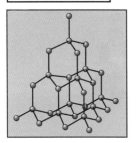

Each carbon atom forms four covalent bonds in a very rigid giant covalent structure.
This structure makes diamond the hardest natural substance, so it's used for drill tips.
And it's pretty and sparkly too.

Silicon Dioxide (Silica)

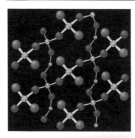

Sometimes called silica, this is what sand is made of.
Each grain of sand is one giant structure of silicon and oxygen.

Graphite

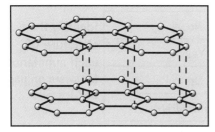

Each carbon atom only forms three covalent bonds. This creates layers which are free to slide over each other, like a pack of cards — so graphite is soft and slippery. The layers are held together so loosely that they can be rubbed off onto paper — that's how a pencil works. This is because there are weak intermolecular forces between the layers.

Graphite is the only non-metal which is a good conductor of heat and electricity. Each carbon atom has one delocalised (free) electron and it's these free electrons that conduct heat and electricity.

Carbon is a girl's best friend...

The two different types of covalent substance are very different — simple and weak, or giant and strong. Easy.

Metallic Structures

Ever wondered what makes <u>metals</u> tick? Well, either way, this is the page for you.

Metal Properties <u>Are All Due to the</u> Sea of Free Electrons

1) <u>Metals</u> also consist of a <u>giant structure</u>.

2) <u>Metallic bonds</u> involve the all-important '<u>free electrons</u>' which produce <u>all</u> the properties of metals. These delocalised (free) electrons come from the <u>outer shell</u> of <u>every</u> metal atom in the structure.

3) These electrons are <u>free to move</u> through the whole structure and so metals are good conductors of <u>heat and electricity</u>.

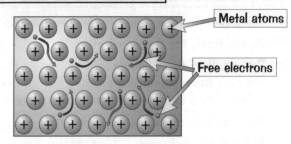

Metal atoms

Free electrons

4) These electrons also <u>hold</u> the <u>atoms</u> together in a <u>regular</u> structure. There are strong forces of <u>electrostatic attraction</u> between the <u>positive metal ions</u> and the <u>negative electrons</u>.

5) They also allow the layers of atoms to <u>slide</u> over each other, allowing metals to be <u>bent</u> and <u>shaped</u>.

Alloys <u>are Harder</u> <u>Than</u> Pure Metals

1) <u>Pure metals</u> often aren't quite right for certain jobs. So scientists <u>mix two or more metals together</u> — creating an <u>alloy</u> with the properties they want.

2) Different elements have <u>different sized atoms</u>. So when another metal is mixed with a pure metal, the new metal atoms will <u>distort</u> the layers of metal atoms, making it more difficult for them to slide over each other. So alloys are <u>harder</u>.

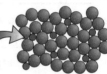

Identifying <u>the Structure of a Substance</u> by Its Properties

You should be able to easily <u>identify</u> most substances just by the way they <u>behave</u> as either:

- <u>giant ionic</u>,
- <u>simple molecular</u>,
- <u>giant covalent</u>,
- or <u>giant metallic</u>.

That's the guy.

You can tell what <u>type</u> of <u>structure</u> a substance has from its <u>physical properties</u>.

<u>Example:</u> Four substances were tested for various properties with the following results:

Substance	Melting point (°C)	Boiling point (°C)	Good electrical conductor?
A	−218.4	−182.96	No
B	1535	2750	Yes
C	1410	2355	No
D	801	1413	When molten

Identify the structure of each substance. (Answers on page 142.)

A few free electrons and my knees have gone all bendy...

If you know the <u>properties</u> of a substance then you can work out its <u>structure</u>. Now ain't that useful.

New Materials

New materials are continually being developed, with new properties. Two of these are smart materials and nanoparticles — and guess what, they're coming up on this page...

Smart Materials Have Some Really Weird Properties

1) Smart materials behave differently depending on the conditions, e.g. temperature.

2) A good example is nitinol — a "shape memory alloy".
It's a metal alloy (about half nickel, half titanium) but when it's cool you can bend it and twist it like rubber. Bend it too far, though, and it stays bent. But here's the really clever bit — if you heat it above a certain temperature, it goes back to a "remembered" shape.

3) It's really handy for glasses frames. If you accidentally bend them, you can just pop them into a bowl of hot water and they'll jump back into shape.

4) Nitinol is also used for dental braces. In the mouth it warms and tries to return to a 'remembered' shape, and so it gently pulls the teeth with it.

Nanoparticles Are Really Really Really Really Tiny

...smaller than that.

1) Really tiny particles, 1–100 nanometres across, are called 'nanoparticles' (1 nm = 0.000 000 001 m).

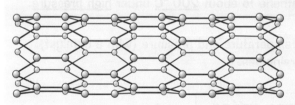

2) Nanoparticles contain roughly a few hundred atoms.

3) Nanoparticles include fullerenes. These are molecules of carbon, shaped like hollow balls or closed tubes. The carbon atoms are arranged in hexagonal rings. Different fullerenes contain different numbers of carbon atoms.

4) A nanoparticle has very different properties from the 'bulk' chemical that it's made from — e.g. fullerenes have different properties from big lumps of carbon.

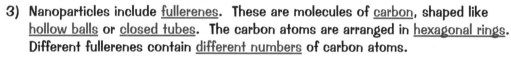

1) Fullerenes can be joined together to form nanotubes — teeny tiny hollow carbon tubes, a few nanometres across.

2) All those covalent bonds make carbon nanotubes very strong. They can be used to reinforce graphite in tennis rackets.

5) Using nanoparticles is known as nanoscience. Many new uses of nanoparticles are being developed:

- They have a huge surface area to volume ratio, so they could help make new industrial catalysts (see page 84).

- You can use nanoparticles to make sensors to detect one type of molecule and nothing else. These highly specific sensors are already being used to test water purity.

- Nanotubes can be used to make stronger, lighter building materials.

- New cosmetics, e.g. sun tan cream and deodorant, have been made using nanoparticles. The small particles do their job but don't leave white marks on the skin.

- Nanomedicine is a hot topic. The idea is that tiny fullerenes are absorbed more easily by the body than most particles. This means they could deliver drugs right into the cells where they're needed.

- New lubricant coatings are being developed using fullerenes. These coatings reduce friction a bit like ball bearings and could be used in all sorts of places from artificial joints to gears.

- Nanotubes conduct electricity, so they can be used in tiny electric circuits for computer chips.

Bendy specs, tennis rackets and computer chips — cool...

Some nanoparticles have really unexpected properties. Silver's normally very unreactive, but silver nanoparticles can kill bacteria. Cool. On the flipside, we also need to watch out for any unexpected harmful properties.

Polymers

There's plastic and there's... well, plastic. You wouldn't want to make a chair with the same plastic that gets used for flimsy old carrier bags. But whatever the plastic, it's always a polymer.

Forces Between Molecules Determine the Properties of Plastics

Strong covalent bonds hold the atoms together in long chains. But it's the bonds between the different molecule chains that determine the properties of the plastic.

Weak Forces:

Individual tangled chains of polymers, held together by weak intermolecular forces, are free to slide over each other.

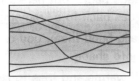

THERMOSOFTENING POLYMERS don't have cross-linking between chains. The forces between the chains are really easy to overcome, so it's dead easy to melt the plastic. When it cools, the polymer hardens into a new shape. You can melt these plastics and remould them as many times as you like.

Strong Forces:

Some plastics have stronger intermolecular forces between the polymer chains, called crosslinks, that hold the chains firmly together.

THERMOSETTING POLYMERS have crosslinks. These hold the chains together in a solid structure. The polymer doesn't soften when it's heated. Thermosetting polymers are the tough guys of the plastic world. They're strong, hard and rigid.

How You Make a Polymer Affects Its Properties

1) The starting materials and reaction conditions will both affect the properties of a polymer.

2) Two types of polythene can be made using different conditions:

- Low density (LD) polythene is made by heating ethene to about 200 °C under high pressure. It's flexible and is used for bags and bottles.

- High density (HD) polythene is made at a lower temperature and pressure (with a catalyst). It's more rigid and is used for water tanks and drainpipes.

The Use of a Plastic Depends on Its Properties

Because plastics have different properties, you use different ones for different things. For example:

Choose from the table the plastic that would be best suited for making:

a) a disposable cup for hot drinks,

b) clothing,

c) a measuring cylinder.

Give reasons for each choice.

Plastic	Cost	Resistance to chemicals	Melting point	Transparency	Rigidity	Can be made into fibres
W	High	High	High	Low	High	No
X	Low	Low	Low	Low	Low	Yes
Y	High	High	High	High	High	No
Z	Low	Low	High	High	High	No

Answers

a) Z — low cost (disposable) and high melting point (for hot drinks),

b) X — flexible (essential for clothing) and able to be made into fibres (clothing is usually woven),

c) Y — transparent and resistant to chemicals (you need to be able to see the liquid inside and the liquid and measuring cylinder mustn't react with each other).

Platinum cards — my favourite sort of plastic...

The properties of thermosoftening and thermosetting polymers are really different — it's all to do with the intermolecular forces between the chains. Different properties make different plastics suited for certain jobs.

Relative Formula Mass

The biggest trouble with <u>relative atomic mass</u> and <u>relative formula mass</u> is that they <u>sound</u> so blood-curdling. Take a few deep breaths, and just enjoy, as the mists slowly clear...

Relative Atomic Mass, A_r — Easy Peasy

1) This is just a way of saying how <u>heavy</u> different atoms are <u>compared</u> with the mass of an atom of carbon-12. So carbon-12 has A_r of <u>exactly 12</u>.

2) It turns out that the <u>relative atomic mass</u> A_r is usually just the same as the <u>mass number</u> of the element.

3) In the periodic table, the elements all have <u>two</u> numbers. The smaller one is the atomic number (how many protons it has). But the <u>bigger one</u> is the <u>mass number</u> or <u>relative atomic mass</u>.

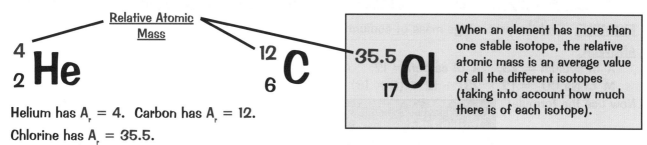

Helium has A_r = 4. Carbon has A_r = 12.
Chlorine has A_r = 35.5.

When an element has more than one stable isotope, the relative atomic mass is an average value of all the different isotopes (taking into account how much there is of each isotope).

Relative Formula Mass, M_r — Also Easy Peasy

If you have a compound like $MgCl_2$ then it has a <u>relative formula mass</u>, M_r, which is just all the relative atomic masses <u>added together</u>.
For $MgCl_2$ it would be:

The relative atomic mass of chlorine is multiplied by 2 because there are two chlorine atoms.

$$24 + (35.5 \times 2) = 95$$

So M_r for $MgCl_2$ is simply <u>95</u>.

You can easily get A_r for any element from the periodic table (see inside front cover), but in a lot of questions they give you them anyway. And that's all it is. A big fancy name like <u>relative formula mass</u> and all it means is "<u>add up all the relative atomic masses</u>". What a swizz, eh?

"ONE MOLE" of a Substance is Equal to its M_r in Grams

The <u>relative formula mass</u> (A_r or M_r) of a substance <u>in grams</u> is known as <u>one mole</u> of that substance.

<u>Examples</u>:
Iron has an A_r of 56.
Nitrogen gas, N_2, has an M_r of 28 (2×14).

So one mole of iron weighs exactly 56 g
So one mole of N_2 weighs exactly 28 g

You can convert between moles and grams using this formula:

$$\text{NUMBER OF MOLES} = \frac{\text{Mass in g (of element or compound)}}{M_r \text{ (of element or compound)}}$$

<u>Example:</u> How many moles are there in 42 g of carbon?
<u>Answer:</u> No. of moles = Mass (g) / M_r = 42/12 = <u>3.5 moles</u>   Easy Peasy

Numbers? — and you thought you were doing chemistry...

Use the definitions of <u>relative atomic mass</u> and <u>relative formula mass</u> to have a go at these:
1) Use the periodic table to find the relative atomic mass of these elements: Cu, K, Kr, Cl
2) Find the relative formula mass of: NaOH, Fe_2O_3, C_6H_{14}, $Mg(NO_3)_2$ Answers on page 142.

Two Formula Mass Calculations

Although relative atomic mass and relative formula mass are <u>easy enough</u>, it can get just a tad <u>trickier</u> when you start getting into other calculations which use them. It depends on how good your maths is basically, because it's all to do with ratios and percentages.

Calculating % Mass of an Element in a Compound

This is actually dead easy — so long as you've learnt this formula:

$$\text{Percentage mass OF AN ELEMENT IN A COMPOUND} = \frac{A_r \times \text{No. of atoms (of that element)}}{M_r \text{ (of whole compound)}} \times 100$$

<u>EXAMPLE:</u> Find the percentage mass of sodium in sodium carbonate, Na_2CO_3.
<u>ANSWER:</u>

A_r of sodium = 23, A_r of carbon = 12, A_r of oxygen = 16
M_r of Na_2CO_3 = $(2 \times 23) + 12 + (3 \times 16) = 106$

Now use the formula:

$$\underline{\text{Percentage mass}} = \frac{A_r \times n}{M_r} \times 100 = \frac{23 \times 2}{106} \times 100 = 43.4\%$$

And there you have it. Sodium makes up <u>43.4%</u> of the mass of sodium carbonate.

Finding the Empirical Formula (from Masses or Percentages)

This also sounds a lot worse than it really is. Try this for an easy peasy <u>stepwise method</u>:

1) <u>List all the elements</u> in the compound (there are usually only two or three!)

2) <u>Underneath them</u>, write their <u>experimental masses or percentages</u>.

3) <u>Divide</u> each mass or percentage <u>by the A_r</u> for that particular element.

4) Turn the numbers you get into <u>a nice simple ratio</u> by multiplying and/or dividing them by well-chosen numbers.

5) Get the ratio in its <u>simplest form</u>, and that tells you the <u>empirical formula</u> of the compound.

<u>Example:</u> Find the empirical formula of the iron oxide produced when 44.8 g of iron react with 19.2 g of oxygen. (A_r for iron = 56, A_r for oxygen = 16)

<u>Method:</u>

1) <u>List the two elements:</u>	Fe	O
2) Write in the <u>experimental masses:</u>	44.8	19.2
3) <u>Divide by the A_r</u> for each element:	$\frac{44.8}{56} = 0.8$	$\frac{19.2}{16} = 1.2$
4) Multiply by 10...	8	12
...then divide by 4:	2	3

5) So the <u>simplest formula</u> is 2 atoms of Fe to 3 atoms of O, i.e. <u>Fe_2O_3</u>. And that's it done.

> You need to realise that this <u>empirical method</u> (i.e. based on <u>experiment</u>) is the <u>only way</u> of finding out the formula of a compound. Rust is iron oxide, sure, but is it FeO, or Fe_2O_3? Only an experiment to determine the empirical formula will tell you for certain.

With this empirical formula I can rule the world! — mwa ha ha ha...

Make sure you read the formula and the five steps in the red box thoroughly. Then try these: Answers on page 142.

1) Find the percentage mass of oxygen in each of these: a) Fe_2O_3 b) H_2O c) $CaCO_3$ d) H_2SO_4.
2) Find the empirical formula of the compound formed from 2.4 g of carbon and 0.8 g of hydrogen.

Calculating Masses in Reactions

These can be kinda scary too, but chill out, little trembling one — just relax and enjoy.

The Three Important Steps — Not to Be Missed...

(Miss one out and it'll all go horribly wrong, believe me.)

> 1) <u>Write out</u> the balanced <u>equation</u>
> 2) <u>Work out M_r</u> — just for the <u>two bits you want</u>
> 3) Apply the rule: <u>Divide to get one, then multiply to get all</u>
>   (But you have to apply this first to the substance they
>   give you information about, and then the other one!)

Don't worry — these steps should all make sense when you look at the example below.

<u>Example</u>: What mass of magnesium oxide is produced when 60 g of magnesium is burned in air?

<u>Answer</u>:

1) Write out the <u>balanced equation</u>: $\qquad$ $2Mg + O_2 \rightarrow 2MgO$

2) Work out the <u>relative formula masses</u>:
   (don't do the oxygen — we don't need it) $\qquad$ $2 \times 24 \quad \rightarrow \quad 2 \times (24+16)$
   $\qquad\qquad\qquad\qquad\qquad\qquad\qquad\qquad\qquad 48 \qquad \rightarrow \qquad 80$

3) Apply the rule: <u>Divide to get one, then multiply to get all</u>:
   The two numbers, 48 and 80, tell us that <u>48 g of Mg react to give 80 g of MgO</u>.
   Here's the tricky bit. You've now got to be able to write this down:

> 48 g of Mg ......reacts to give.....80 g of MgO
>
> 1 g of Mg ......reacts to give.....
>
> 60 g of Mg .....reacts to give......

<u>The big clue</u> is that in the question they've said we want to burn "<u>60 g of magnesium</u>",
i.e. they've told us how much <u>magnesium</u> to have, and that's how you know to write down the
<u>left-hand side</u> of it first, because:

> We'll first need to ÷ by 48 to get 1 g of Mg
> and then need to × by 60 to get 60 g of Mg.

<u>Then</u> you can work out the numbers on the other side (shown in purple below) by realising that you must
<u>divide both sides by 48</u> and then <u>multiply both sides by 60</u>. It's tricky.

$÷48$ { 48 g of Mg .... 80 g of MgO } $+48$
$\qquad$ 1 g of Mg .... 1.67 g of MgO
$×60$ { 60 g of Mg .... 100 g of MgO } $×60$

The mass of product is called the <u>yield</u> of a reaction. You should realise that <u>in practice</u> you never get 100% of the yield, so the amount of product will be <u>slightly less than calculated</u> (see p.71).

This finally tells us that <u>60 g of magnesium will produce 100 g of magnesium oxide</u>.
If the question had said "Find how much magnesium gives 500 g of magnesium oxide", you'd fill in the
MgO side first, <u>because that's the one you'd have the information about</u>. Got it? Good-O!

Reaction mass calculations — no worries, matey...

The only way to get good at these is to practise. So have a go at these: $\qquad$ Answers on page 142.

1) Find the mass of calcium which gives 30 g of calcium oxide (CaO) when burnt in air.
2) What mass of fluorine fully reacts with potassium to make 116 g of potassium fluoride (KF)?

Atom Economy

It's important in industrial reactions that as much of the reactants as possible get turned into useful products. This depends on the atom economy and the percentage yield (see next page) of the reaction.

"Atom Economy" — % of Reactants Changed to Useful Products

1) A lot of reactions make more than one product. Some of them will be useful, but others will just be waste, e.g. when you make quicklime from limestone, you also get CO_2 as a waste product.

2) The atom economy of a reaction tells you how much of the mass of the reactants is wasted when manufacturing a chemical. It's calculated using this:

$$\text{atom economy} = \frac{\text{total } M_r \text{ of desired products}}{\text{total } M_r \text{ of all products}} \times 100$$

3) 100% atom economy means that all the atoms in the reactants have been turned into useful (desired) products. The higher the atom economy the 'greener' the process.

Example: Hydrogen gas is made on a large scale by reacting natural gas (methane) with steam.

$$CH_4(g) + H_2O(g) \rightarrow CO(g) + 3H_2(g)$$

Calculate the atom economy of this reaction.

Method: 1) Identify the useful product — that's the hydrogen gas.

2) Work out the M_r of all the products and the useful product:

CO	$3H_2$	$3H_2$
12 + 16	3 × (2 × 1)	3 × (2 × 1)
34		6

3) Use the formula to calculate the atom economy: $\text{atom economy} = \frac{6}{34} \times 100 = \underline{17.6\%}$

So in this reaction, over 80% of the starting materials are wasted.

High Atom Economy is Better for Profits and the Environment

1) Pretty obviously, if you're making lots of waste, that's a problem.

2) Reactions with low atom economy use up resources very quickly. At the same time, they make lots of waste materials that have to be disposed of somehow. That tends to make these reactions unsustainable — the raw materials will run out and the waste has to go somewhere.

3) For the same reasons, low atom economy reactions aren't usually profitable. Raw materials are expensive to buy, and waste products can be expensive to remove and dispose of responsibly.

4) The best way around the problem is to find a use for the waste products rather than just throwing them away. There's often more than one way to make the product you want, so the trick is to come up with a reaction that gives useful "by-products" rather than useless ones.

5) The reactions with the highest atom economy are the ones that only have one product. Those reactions have an atom economy of 100%.

Atom economy — important but not the whole story...

The same stuff about atom economy applies to any industrial reaction. In the real world, high atom economy isn't enough, though. You need to think about the percentage yield of the reaction (next page) and the energy cost as well. And then you're flying. Well... not literally.

Section 4 — The Periodic Table, Bonding and Calculations

Percentage Yield and Reversible Reactions

Percentage yield tells you about the <u>overall success</u> of an experiment. It compares what you calculate you should get (<u>predicted yield</u>) with what you get in practice (<u>actual yield</u>).

Percentage Yield Compares Actual and Predicted Yield

The amount of product you get is known as the <u>yield</u>. The more reactants you start with, the higher the <u>actual yield</u> will be — that's pretty obvious. But the <u>percentage yield doesn't</u> depend on the amount of reactants you started with — it's a <u>percentage</u>.

1) The <u>predicted yield</u> of a reaction can be calculated from the <u>balanced reaction equation</u>.

2) Percentage yield is given by the formula:

$$\text{percentage yield} = \frac{\text{actual yield (grams)}}{\text{predicted yield (grams)}} \times 100$$

(The predicted yield is sometimes called the theoretical yield.)

3) Percentage yield is <u>always</u> somewhere between 0 and 100%.

4) A 100% percentage yield means that you got <u>all</u> the product you expected to get.

5) A 0% yield means that <u>no</u> reactants were converted into product, i.e. no product at all was <u>made</u>.

Yields Are Always Less Than 100%

Even though <u>no atoms are gained or lost</u> in reactions, in real life, you <u>never</u> get a 100% percentage yield. Some product or reactant <u>always</u> gets lost along the way — and that goes for big <u>industrial processes</u> as well as school lab experiments. There are several reasons for this:

1) The reaction is <u>reversible</u>:

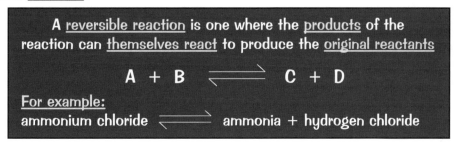

A <u>reversible reaction</u> is one where the <u>products</u> of the reaction can <u>themselves react</u> to produce the <u>original reactants</u>

A + B $\rightleftharpoons$ C + D

<u>For example:</u>
ammonium chloride $\rightleftharpoons$ ammonia + hydrogen chloride

This means that the reactants will never be completely converted to products because the reaction goes both ways. Some of the <u>products</u> are always <u>reacting together</u> to change back to the original reactants. This will mean a <u>lower yield</u>.

2) When you <u>filter a liquid</u> to remove <u>solid particles</u>, you nearly always <u>lose</u> a bit of liquid or a bit of solid. So, some of the product may be lost when it's <u>separated</u> from the reaction mixture.

3) Things don't always go exactly to plan. Sometimes there can be other <u>unexpected reactions</u> happening which <u>use up the reactants</u>. This means there's not as much reactant to make the <u>product</u> you want.

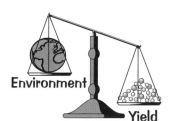

Environment

Yield

Thinking about product yield is important for <u>sustainable development</u>. Sustainable development is about making sure that we don't use <u>resources</u> faster than they can be <u>replaced</u> — there needs to be enough for <u>future generations</u> too. So, for example, using as <u>little energy</u> as possible to create the <u>highest product yield possible</u> means that resources are <u>saved</u>. A low yield means wasted chemicals — not very sustainable.

You can't always get what you want...

A high percentage yield means there's <u>not much waste</u> — which is good for <u>preserving resources</u>, and keeping production <u>costs down</u>. If a reaction's going to be worth doing commercially, it generally has to have a high percentage yield or recyclable reactants. The <u>formula</u> lets you work out the all-important percentage yield.

Revision Summary for Section 4

Some people skip these pages. But what's the point in reading that great big section if you're not going to check if you really know it or not? Look, just read the first ten questions, and I guarantee there'll be an answer you'll have to look up. And when it comes up in the exam, you'll be so glad you did.

1) What do the mass number and atomic number represent?
2) Draw a table showing the relative masses of the three types of particle in an atom.
3) What is a compound?
4) Define the term isotope.
5) What size groups did Döbereiner organise the elements into? What were these groups called?
6) Give two reasons why Newlands' Octaves were criticised.
7) Why did Mendeleev leave gaps in his Table of Elements?
8) What feature of atoms determines the order of the periodic table?
9) What are groups in the periodic table? Explain their significance in terms of electrons.
10) Which group contains the alkali metals? How many electrons do they each have in their outer shell?
11) Give details of the reactions of the alkali metals with water.
12)* Write a balanced equation for the reaction between lithium and chlorine.
13) Describe the trend in reactivity of the halogens as you go down the group.
14) Name a type of experiment that could be used to determine the relative reactivity of the halogens.
15) Describe the process of ionic bonding.
16) Describe the structure of a crystal of sodium chloride.
17) List the main properties of ionic compounds.
18)* Use information from the periodic table to help you work out the formulas of these ionic compounds:
      a) potassium chloride   b) calcium chloride
19)*Draw a diagram to show the electronic structure of an Mg^{2+} ion (magnesium's atomic number is 12).
20) What is covalent bonding?
21) Sketch dot and cross diagrams showing the bonding in molecules of:
      a) hydrogen,   b) hydrogen chloride,   c) water,   d) ammonia

22) What are the two types of covalent substance? Give three examples of each.
23) List three properties of metals and explain how metallic bonding causes these properties.
24) Explain why alloys are harder than pure metals.
25) Give an example of a "smart" material and describe how it behaves.
26) What are nanoparticles? Give two different applications of nanoparticles.
27) Explain the difference between thermosoftening and thermosetting polymers.
28) Define relative atomic mass and relative formula mass.
29)*Find A_r or M_r for these (use the periodic table at the front of the book):
      a) Ca   b) Ag   c) CO_2 d) $MgCO_3$ e) Na_2CO_3 f) ZnO   g) KOH   h) NH_3
30) What is the link between moles and relative formula mass?
31)*a) Calculate the percentage mass of carbon in: i) $CaCO_3$ ii) CO_2 iii) CH_4
      b) Calculate the percentage mass of metal in: i) Na_2O ii) Fe_2O_3 iii) Al_2O_3
32)*What is an empirical formula? Find the empirical formula of the compound formed when
      21.9 g of magnesium, 29.2 g of sulfur and 58.4 g of oxygen react.
33)*What mass of sodium is needed to produce 108.2 g of sodium oxide (Na_2O)?
34) Write the equation for calculating the atom economy of a reaction.
35) Explain why it is important to use industrial reactions with a high atom economy.
36) Describe three factors that can reduce the percentage yield of a reaction.

* Answers on page 142.

Section 4 — The Periodic Table, Bonding and Calculations

Identifying Positive Ions

Say you've got a compound, but you <u>don't know</u> what it is. Well, you'd want to <u>identify</u> it...
that's only natural. And that's what the next couple of pages are all about. Tests for <u>positive ions</u> first...

Flame Tests — *Spot the* <u>Colour</u>

Compounds of some <u>metals</u> give a characteristic <u>colour</u> when heated.
This is the idea behind <u>flame tests</u>.

*   <u>Sodium</u>, Na^+, gives an orange/yellow flame.
*   <u>Potassium</u>, K^+, gives a lilac flame.
*   <u>Calcium</u>, Ca^{2+}, gives a brick-red flame.
*   <u>Copper</u>, Cu^{2+}, gives a blue-green flame.

You can use these <u>colours</u> to <u>detect</u> and <u>identify</u> different ions.

Add <u>Sodium Hydroxide</u> *and Look for a* <u>Coloured Precipitate</u>

A precipitation reaction is where two solutions react to form an <u>insoluble solid compound</u> called a <u>precipitate</u>.

1) Many <u>metal hydroxides</u> are <u>insoluble</u> and precipitate out of solution when you add an alkali.
2) Some of these hydroxides have a <u>characteristic colour</u>.
3) So in this test you add a few drops of <u>sodium hydroxide</u> solution to a solution
    of your mystery compound — in the hope of forming an insoluble hydroxide.
4) If you get a <u>coloured insoluble hydroxide</u> you can then identify the metal ion that was in the compound.

"Metal"	Colour of precipitate	Ionic Reaction
Calcium, Ca^{2+}	White	$Ca^{2+}(aq) + 2OH^-(aq) \rightarrow Ca(OH)_2 (s)$
Copper(II), Cu^{2+}	Blue	$Cu^{2+}(aq) + 2OH^-(aq) \rightarrow Cu(OH)_2 (s)$
Iron(II), Fe^{2+}	Sludgy green	$Fe^{2+}(aq) + 2OH^-(aq) \rightarrow Fe(OH)_2 (s)$
Iron(III), Fe^{3+}	Reddish brown	$Fe^{3+}(aq) + 3OH^-(aq) \rightarrow Fe(OH)_3 (s)$
Zinc, Zn^{2+}	White at first. But then redissolves in excess NaOH to form a colourless solution.	$Zn^{2+}(aq) + 2OH^-(aq) \rightarrow ZN(OH)_2 (s)$ then $Zn(OH)_2 (s) + 2OH^-(aq) \rightarrow Zn(OH)_4^{2-}(aq)$

NaOH isn't the only solution that can be used for precipitation reactions — you can use other solutions of ionic compounds too.

Ionic Equations *Show Just the* <u>Useful Bits</u> *of Reactions*

1) The reactions in the above table are <u>ionic equations</u>. Ionic equations are 'half' a full equation, if you like.
2) They just show the bit of the equation you're <u>interested</u> in — nothing else. For example:

$$Ca^{2+}(aq) + 2OH^-(aq) \longrightarrow Ca(OH)_2(s)$$

3) This shows the formation of (solid) <u>calcium hydroxide</u> from the <u>calcium ions</u> and the
    <u>hydroxide ions</u> in solution. And it's the formation of this that helps identify the compound.
4) The <u>full</u> equation in the above reaction would be (if you started off with <u>calcium chloride</u>, say):

$$CaCl_2(aq) + 2NaOH(aq) \longrightarrow Ca(OH)_2(s) + 2NaCl(aq)$$

5) But the formation of <u>sodium chloride</u> is of no great interest here
    — it's not helping to <u>identify</u> the compound, after all.
6) So the ionic equation just concentrates on the <u>good bits</u>.

It isn't any old ion — get a positive identification...

Pay <u>full attention</u> to the bits on <u>ionic equations</u> for each test with NaOH <u>as well as</u> all the <u>test results</u>.
Just think of an ionic equation as a bit like Match of the Day — an <u>edited highlights package</u>.

Identifying Negative Ions

It's not just positive ions you can identify. Yep, you can also identify <u>negative ions</u>.
They're often tested for by adding a <u>reagent</u> and looking for an <u>insoluble solid</u> — so the fun goes on...

Hydrochloric Acid Can Help Detect Carbonates

With dilute <u>hydrochloric acid</u>, <u>carbonates</u> (CO_3^{2-}) will fizz because they give off <u>carbon dioxide</u>.

$$CO_3^{2-}(s) + 2H^+(aq) \longrightarrow CO_2(g) + H_2O(l)$$

You can test for carbon dioxide using <u>limewater</u>.

Carbon dioxide <u>turns limewater cloudy</u> — just bubble the gas
through a test tube of limewater and watch what happens.
If the water goes cloudy you've identified a <u>carbonate ion</u>.

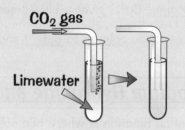

CO_2 gas

Limewater

Test for Sulfates with HCl and Barium Chloride

To identify a <u>sulfate</u> ion (SO_4^{2-}), add dilute HCl, followed by <u>barium chloride solution</u>, $BaCl_2(aq)$.

$$Ba^{2+}(aq) + SO_4^{2-}(aq) \longrightarrow BaSO_4(s)$$

A <u>white precipitate</u> of <u>barium sulfate</u> means the original compound was a sulfate.

(The <u>hydrochloric acid</u> is added to get rid of any traces of <u>carbonate</u> ions before you do the test.
These would also produce a precipitate, so they'd <u>confuse</u> the results.)

Test for Halides (Cl⁻, Br⁻, I⁻) with Nitric Acid and Silver Nitrate

To identify a <u>halide</u> ion, add dilute <u>nitric acid</u> (HNO_3), followed by <u>silver nitrate solution</u>, $AgNO_3(aq)$.

$$Ag^+(aq) + Cl^-(aq) \longrightarrow AgCl(s)$$ A <u>chloride</u> gives a **white** precipitate of <u>silver chloride</u>.

$$Ag^+(aq) + Br^-(aq) \longrightarrow AgBr(s)$$ A <u>bromide</u> gives a **cream** precipitate of <u>silver bromide</u>.

$$Ag^+(aq) + I^-(aq) \longrightarrow AgI(s)$$ An <u>iodide</u> gives a **yellow** precipitate of <u>silver iodide</u>.

(Again, the <u>acid</u> is added to get rid of <u>carbonate</u> ions before the test.
You use <u>nitric acid</u> in this test, though, <u>not HCl</u>.)

These tests just detect negative ions — not happy cheery ones...

How to learn this page — don't stare at the whole thing till your eyes swim and you don't want to see the word
"precipitate" ever again. It's been handily divided into <u>three subsections</u>, so tackle them one by one.

Chemical Analysis and Instrumental Methods

Nowadays there are some pretty clever ways of identifying substances, from using filter paper to machines...

Artificial Colours Can Be Separated Using Paper Chromatography

A food colouring might contain one dye or it might be a mixture of dyes. Here's how you can tell:

1) Extract the colour from a food sample by placing it in a small cup with a few drops of solvent (can be water, ethanol, salt water, etc).

2) Put spots of the coloured solution on a pencil baseline on filter paper. (Don't use pen because it might dissolve in the solvent and confuse everything.)

3) Roll up the sheet and put it in a beaker with some solvent — but keep the baseline above the level of the solvent.

4) The solvent seeps up the paper, taking the dyes with it. Different dyes form spots in different places.

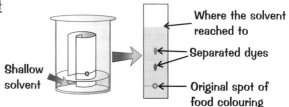

Shallow solvent

Where the solvent reached to

Separated dyes

Original spot of food colouring

5) Watch out though — a chromatogram with four spots means at least four dyes, not exactly four dyes. There could be five dyes, with two of them making a spot in the same place. It can't be three dyes though, because one dye can't split into two spots.

Machines Can Also Analyse Unknown Substances

You can identify elements and compounds using instrumental methods — this just means using machines.

Advantages of Using Machines

- Very sensitive — can detect even the tiniest amounts of substances.
- Very fast and tests can be automated.
- Very accurate

Gas Chromatography Can be Used to Identify Substances

Gas chromatography can separate out a mixture of compounds and help you identify the substances present.

1) A gas is used to carry substances through a column packed with a solid material.

2) The substances travel through the tube at different speeds, so they're separated.

3) The time they take to reach the detector is called the retention time. It can be used to help identify the substances.

4) The recorder draws a gas chromatograph. The number of peaks shows the number of different compounds in the sample.

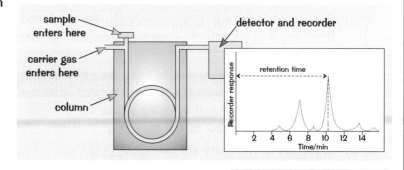

sample enters here

detector and recorder

carrier gas enters here

column

retention time

Time/min

5) The position of the peaks shows the retention time of each substance.

6) The gas chromatography column can also be linked to a mass spectrometer. This process is known as GC-MS and can identify the substances leaving the column very accurately.

7) You can work out the relative molecular mass of each of the substances from the graph it draws. You just read off from the molecular ion peak.

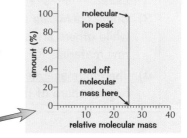

molecular ion peak

read off molecular mass here

relative molecular mass

Unfortunately, machines can't do the exam for you...

Make sure you don't get the two types of chromatography muddled up... there's paper and then there's gas.

Industrial Chemical Synthesis

Chemical synthesis sounds a bit scary, but it's just the term used by those in the know to describe the process of making complex chemical compounds from simpler ones. The chemical industry does this every day...

The Chemical Industry Makes Useful Products

Chemicals aren't just found in the laboratory. Most of the products you come across in your day-to-day life will have been carefully researched, formulated and tested by chemists. Here are a few examples...

1) Food additives — the chemical industry produces additives like preservatives, colourings and flavourings for food producers.

2) Cleaning and decorating products — things like paints contain loads of different pigments and dyes, all of which have been developed by chemists. Cleaning products like bleach, oven cleaner and washing-up liquid will all have been developed by chemists.

3) Drugs — the pharmaceutical industry is huge (see below). Whenever you have a headache or an upset tummy the drugs you take will have gone through loads of development and testing before you get to use them.

4) Fertilisers — we use about a million tonnes of fertiliser every year. Amongst other things fertilisers contain loads of ammonia, all of which has to be produced by the chemical industry.

As well as figuring out how to make chemicals, chemists must also figure out how to make them in the way that produces the highest yield (p.71) — they do this by controlling the rate of the reaction (p.78). They must also think about the environment, choosing processes with a low impact.

The Chemical Industry is Huge

It's absolutely massive, in terms of both the amount of chemicals it produces and the money it generates.

Scale — chemicals can be produced on a large or small scale.

1) Some chemicals are produced on a massive scale — for example, over 150 million tonnes of sulfuric acid are produced around the world every year.

2) Sulfuric acid has loads of different uses, for example in car batteries and fertiliser production.

3) Other chemicals, e.g. pharmaceuticals, are produced on a smaller scale, but this doesn't make them any less important — we just need less of them.

Sectors — there are loads of different sectors within the chemical industry.

1) In the UK, the chemical industry makes up a significant chunk of the economy.

2) In the UK alone, there are over 200 000 people employed in the chemical industry.

3) Some chemicals are sold directly to consumers, while others are sold to other industries as raw materials for other products.

4) The pharmaceutical industry has the largest share of the industry.

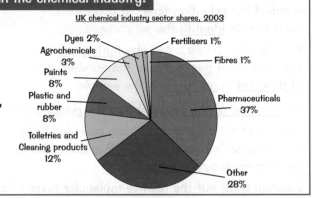

UK chemical industry sector shares, 2003

Dyes 2%
Agrochemicals 3%
Paints 8%
Plastic and rubber 8%
Toiletries and Cleaning products 12%
Fertilisers 1%
Fibres 1%
Pharmaceuticals 37%
Other 28%

You'd need a big fish to make all those chemicals on a scale...

The chemical industry has certainly got its fingers in lots of different pies. It's pretty exhausting to think about. But don't fall asleep just yet, there's still more on chemical synthesis on the next page...

More on Industrial Chemical Synthesis

When you're manufacturing drugs there are lots of things you have to think about...

The Type of Manufacturing Process Depends on the Product

Batch Production Only Operates at Certain Times

Pharmaceutical drugs are complicated to make and there's fairly low demand for them. Batch production is often the most cost-effective way to produce small quantities of different drugs to order, because:

1) It's flexible — several different products can be made using the same equipment.

2) Start-up costs are relatively low — small-scale, multi-purpose equipment can be bought off the shelf.

But batch production does have disadvantages:

1) It's labour-intensive — the equipment needs to be set up and manually controlled for each batch and then cleaned out at the end.

2) It can be tricky to keep the same quality from batch to batch.

Continuous Production Runs All the Time

Large-scale industrial manufacture of popular chemicals, e.g. the Haber process for making ammonia uses continuous production because:

1) Production never stops, so you don't waste time emptying the reactor and setting it up again.

2) It runs automatically — you only need to interfere if something goes wrong.

3) The quality of the product is very consistent.

But, start-up costs to build the plant are huge, and it isn't cost-effective to run at less than full capacity.

Pharmaceutical Drugs Often Cost A Lot — For Several Reasons

1) Research and Development — finding a suitable compound, testing it, modifying it, testing again, until it's ready. This involves the work of lots of highly paid scientists.

2) Trialling — no drug can be sold until it's gone through loads of time-consuming tests including animal trials and human trials. The manufacturer has to prove that the drug meets legal requirements so it works and it's safe.

3) Manufacture — multi-step batch production is labour-intensive and can't be automated. Other costs include energy and raw materials. The raw materials for pharmaceuticals are often rare and sometimes need to be extracted from plants (an expensive process).

> It takes about 12 years and £900 million to develop a new drug and get it onto the market. Ouch.

To extract a substance from a plant, it has to be crushed then boiled and dissolved in a suitable solvent. Then, you can extract the substance you want by chromatography.

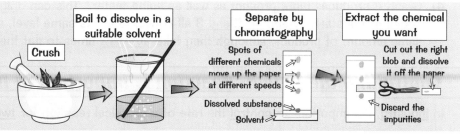

Test For Purity Using Chromatography And Boiling and Melting Points

You can carry out tests which will tell you how pure a substance is. For example:

1) Pure substances won't be separated by chromatography — it'll all move as one blob.

2) Pure substances have a specific melting point and boiling point (e.g. pure ice melts at 0 °C, and pure water boils at 100 °C). If a substance is impure, the melting point will be too low and the boiling point will be too high (so if some ice melts at −2 °C, it's probably got an impurity in it e.g. salt).

I wish they'd find a drug to cure exams...

£900 million. You could buy yourself an island. And one for your mum. And a couple for your mates...

Rate of Reaction

Reactions can be <u>fast</u> or <u>slow</u> — you've probably already realised that. This page covers the things that affect the <u>rate of a reaction</u>, as well as what you can do to <u>measure it</u>. You'll be on the edge of your seat. Honest.

Reactions Can Go at All Sorts of Different Rates

1) One of the <u>slowest</u> is the <u>rusting</u> of iron.
2) A <u>moderate speed</u> reaction is a <u>metal</u> (like magnesium) reacting with <u>acid</u> to produce a gentle stream of <u>bubbles</u>.
3) A <u>really fast</u> reaction is an <u>explosion</u>, where it's all over in a <u>fraction</u> of a second.

The Rate of a Reaction Depends on Four Things:

1) <u>Temperature</u>   2) <u>Concentration</u> (or <u>pressure</u> for gases)   3) <u>Catalyst</u>   4) <u>Surface area of solids</u> (or <u>size</u> of solid pieces)

Typical Graphs for Rate of Reaction

The plot below shows how the rate of a particular reaction varies under <u>different conditions</u>. The <u>quickest reaction</u> is shown by the line with the <u>steepest slope</u>. Also, the faster a reaction goes, the sooner it finishes, which means that the line becomes <u>flat</u> earlier.

1) <u>Graph 1</u> represents the original <u>fairly slow</u> reaction. The graph is not too steep.
2) <u>Graphs 2 and 3</u> represent the reaction taking place <u>quicker</u> but with the <u>same initial amounts</u>. The slope of the graphs gets steeper.
3) The <u>increased rate</u> could be due to <u>any</u> of these:

   a) increase in <u>temperature</u>
   b) increase in <u>concentration</u> (or pressure)
   c) <u>catalyst</u> added
   d) solid reactant crushed up into <u>smaller bits</u>.

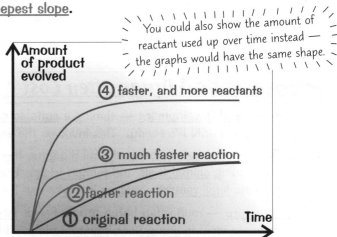

You could also show the amount of reactant used up over time instead — the graphs would have the same shape.

4) <u>Graph 4</u> produces <u>more product</u> as well as going <u>faster</u>. This can <u>only</u> happen if <u>more reactant(s)</u> are added at the start. <u>Graphs 1, 2 and 3</u> all converge at the same level, showing that they all produce the same amount of product, although they take <u>different</u> times to get there.

Controlling the Rate of Reaction is Important in Industry

In <u>industry</u>, it's important to <u>control</u> the rate of a chemical reaction for <u>two</u> main reasons:

1) <u>Safety</u> — if the reaction is <u>too fast</u> it could cause an <u>explosion</u>, which can be a bit <u>dangerous</u>.
2) <u>Economic reasons</u> — changing the conditions can be <u>costly</u>. For example, using very high <u>temperatures</u> means there'll be bigger <u>fuel bills</u>, so the cost of production is pushed up. But, a <u>faster rate</u> means that <u>more product</u> will be produced in <u>less time</u>. Companies often have to choose optimum conditions that give <u>low production costs</u>, but this may mean compromising on the <u>rate of production</u>, or the <u>yield</u>.

How to get a fast, furious reaction — crack a wee joke...

<u>Industrial</u> reactions generally use a <u>catalyst</u> and are done at <u>high temperature and pressure</u>. Time is money, so the faster an industrial reaction goes the better... but only <u>up to a point</u>. Chemical plants are quite expensive to rebuild if they get blown into lots and lots of teeny tiny pieces.

Measuring Rates of Reaction

Ways to Measure the Rate of a Reaction

The rate of a reaction can be observed either by measuring how quickly the reactants are used up or how quickly the products are formed. It's usually a lot easier to measure products forming.

The rate of reaction can be calculated using the following formula:

$$\text{Rate of Reaction} = \frac{\text{Amount of reactant used or amount of product formed}}{\text{Time}}$$

There are different ways that the rate of a reaction can be measured. Take a look at these three:

1) Precipitation

1) This is when the product of the reaction is a precipitate which clouds the solution.

2) Observe a mark through the solution and measure how long it takes for it to disappear.

3) The quicker the mark disappears, the quicker the reaction.

4) This only works for reactions where the initial solution is rather see-through.

5) The result is very subjective — different people might not agree over the exact point when the mark 'disappears'.

2) Change in Mass (Usually Gas Given Off)

1) Measuring the speed of a reaction that produces a gas can be carried out on a mass balance.

2) As the gas is released the mass disappearing is easily measured on the balance.

3) The quicker the reading on the balance drops, the faster the reaction.

4) Rate of reaction graphs are particularly easy to plot using the results from this method.

5) This is the most accurate of the three methods described on this page because the mass balance is very accurate. But it has the disadvantage of releasing the gas straight into the room.

3) The Volume of Gas Given Off

1) This involves the use of a gas syringe to measure the volume of gas given off.

2) The more gas given off during a given time interval, the faster the reaction.

3) A graph of gas volume against time elapsed could be plotted to give a rate of reaction graph.

4) Gas syringes usually give volumes accurate to the nearest millilitre, so they're quite accurate. You have to be quite careful though — if the reaction is too vigorous, you can easily blow the plunger out of the end of the syringe!

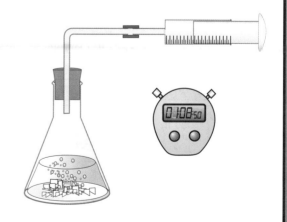

OK have you got your stopwatch ready *BANG!* — oh...

Each method has its pros and cons. The mass balance method is only accurate as long as the flask isn't too hot, otherwise you lose mass by evaporation as well as by the reaction. The first method isn't very accurate, but if you're not producing a gas you can't use either of the other two. Ah well.

Rate of Reaction Experiments

Remember: Any reaction can be used to investigate any of the four factors that affect the rate. These pages illustrate four important reactions, but only one factor has been considered for each. But we could just as easily use, say, the marble chips/acid reaction to test the effect of temperature instead.

1) Reaction of Hydrochloric Acid and Marble Chips

This experiment is often used to demonstrate the effect of breaking the solid up into small bits.

1) Measure the volume of gas evolved with a gas syringe and take readings at regular intervals.

2) Make a table of readings and plot them as a graph. You choose regular time intervals, and time goes on the x-axis and volume goes on the y-axis.

3) Repeat the experiment with exactly the same volume of acid, and exactly the same mass of marble chips, but with the marble more crunched up.

4) Then repeat with the same mass of powdered chalk instead of marble chips.

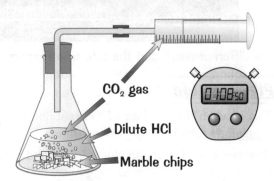

CO₂ gas

Dilute HCl

Marble chips

This graph shows the effect of using finer particles of solid

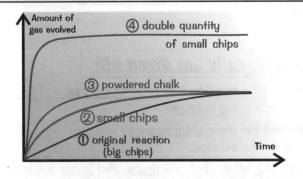

1) Using finer particles means that the marble has a larger surface area.

2) A larger surface area causes more frequent collisions (see page 83) so the rate of reaction is faster.

3) Line 4 shows the reaction if a greater mass of small marble chips is added. The extra surface area gives a quicker reaction and there is also more gas evolved overall.

2) Reaction of Magnesium Metal with Dilute HCl

1) This reaction is good for measuring the effects of increased concentration (as is the marble/acid reaction).

2) This reaction gives off hydrogen gas, which we can measure with a mass balance, as shown.

3) In this experiment, time also goes on the x-axis and volume goes on the y-axis.

   (The other method is to use a gas syringe, as above.)

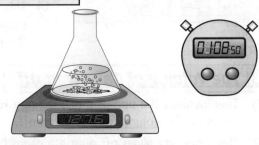

This graph shows the effect of using more concentrated acid solutions

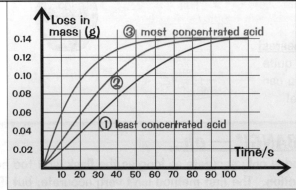

1) Take readings of mass at regular time intervals.

2) Put the results in a table and work out the loss in mass for each reading. Plot a graph.

3) Repeat with more concentrated acid solutions, but always with the same amount of magnesium.

4) The volume of acid must always be kept the same too — only the concentration is increased.

5) The three graphs show the same old pattern — a higher concentration giving a steeper graph, with the reaction finishing much quicker.

More Rate of Reaction Experiments

3) Sodium Thiosulfate and HCl Produce a Cloudy Precipitate

1) These two chemicals are both clear solutions.

2) They react together to form a yellow precipitate of sulfur.

3) The experiment involves watching a black mark disappear through the cloudy sulfur and timing how long it takes to go.

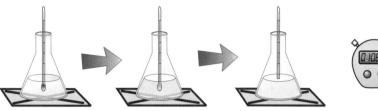

4) The reaction can be repeated for solutions at different temperatures. In practice, that's quite hard to do accurately and safely (it's not a good idea to heat an acid directly). The best way to do it is to use a water bath to heat both solutions to the right temperature before you mix them.

5) The depth of liquid must be kept the same each time, of course.

6) The results will of course show that the higher the temperature the quicker the reaction and therefore the less time it takes for the mark to disappear. These are typical results:

Temperature (°C)	20	25	30	35	40
Time taken for mark to disappear (s)	193	151	112	87	52

This reaction can also be used to test the effects of concentration. One sad thing about this reaction is it doesn't give a set of graphs. Well I think it's sad. All you get is a set of readings of how long it took till the mark disappeared for each temperature. Boring.

4) The Decomposition of Hydrogen Peroxide

This is a good reaction for showing the effect of different catalysts. The decomposition of hydrogen peroxide is:

$$2H_2O_{2\,(aq)} \rightleftharpoons 2H_2O_{(l)} + O_{2\,(g)}$$

1) This is normally quite slow but a sprinkle of manganese(IV) oxide catalyst speeds it up no end. Other catalysts which work are found in:
a) potato peel and b) blood.

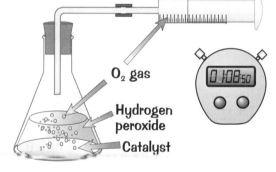

O_2 gas

Hydrogen peroxide

Catalyst

2) Oxygen gas is given off, which provides an ideal way to measure the rate of reaction using the good ol' gas syringe method.

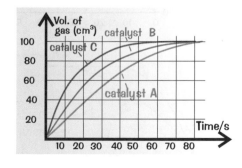

3) Same old graphs of course.

4) Better catalysts give a quicker reaction, which is shown by a steeper graph which levels off quickly.

5) This reaction can also be used to measure the effects of temperature, or of concentration of the H_2O_2 solution. The graphs will look just the same.

BLOOD is a catalyst? — eeurgh...

These pages give you enough information to be able to look at graphs showing the amount of product formed (or reactant used up) over time and comment on the reaction rates. Think of this as an early birthday present.

Rate of Reaction Data

You can learn a lot from a <u>rate of reaction</u> graph. Read on to explore this land of graphical fun...

Reaction Rate Graphs *Show* Rate of Reaction Data

(A) When marble chips are added to hydrochloric acid, CO_2 is given off. In this experiment, 5 g of marble chips were added to hydrochloric acid, and the volume of CO_2 measured every 10 seconds. The results are plotted below. Line 1 is for <u>small chips</u> and line 2 is for <u>large chips</u>.

1) Both reactions finish (the line goes flat) when 80 cm³ of CO_2 are produced.

2) The <u>reaction time</u> for Reaction 1 is about 60 s, and for Reaction 2 it's about 90 s — <u>Reaction 1 is faster</u>.

3) Another way to tell the rate of reaction is to look at the <u>slope</u> of the graph — the <u>steeper</u> the graph, the <u>faster</u> the reaction. Reaction 1 is <u>faster</u> than Reaction 2 — the <u>slope of its graph is steeper</u>.

4) <u>Reaction 1</u> is <u>faster</u> because small chips have a <u>larger surface area</u> than the same mass of large chips.

(B) In this version of the experiment the size of the chips is the same but two <u>different temperatures</u> are used.

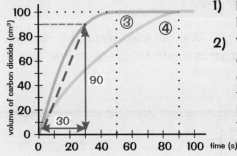

1) Both reactions finish when 100 cm³ of CO_2 have been produced. Reaction 3 is faster (about 50 s, compared to Reaction 4's 90 s or so).

2) You can calculate the <u>rate of reaction</u> by calculating the slope of the line. To find the <u>average rate</u> during the first 30 s, draw a line from the volume of CO_2 produced at the start to the volume produced at 30 s then find the slope of this line. For Reaction 3, the slope is $90 \div 30 = 3$. This means that you're getting <u>3 cm³ of CO_2 per second (3 cm³/s)</u>.

> When you're trying to work out the units of a reaction rate, take a look at the data you've got. If the data is in cm³ and seconds then the units will be cm³ per s (cm³/s). If the data is in grams and minutes then the units will be g per min (g/min).

(C) This time, a piece of magnesium has been added to hydrochloric acid. The graphs show the volume of hydrogen produced when two <u>different concentrations</u> of acid are used.

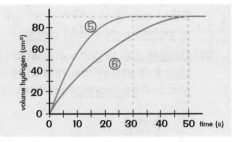

1) <u>Reaction 5</u> is <u>faster</u> than Reaction 6 — its <u>slope is steeper</u> (or use the fact that Reaction 5 takes about 30 s, and Reaction 6 about 50 s).

2) Since Reaction 5 is <u>faster</u>, it must use the <u>more concentrated</u> acid.

(D) This graph shows the effect of adding a catalyst. Line 7 is the <u>catalysed</u> reaction, line 8 is the <u>uncatalysed</u> reaction.

The graph tells you that the <u>catalyst speeds up the reaction</u> because line 7 is <u>steeper</u> than line 8 (but the <u>total volume of gas</u> produced is the <u>same</u> in each reaction).

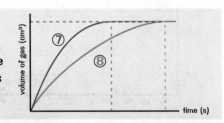

My reactions slow down when it gets hot — I get sleepy...

You can easily compare the <u>rate</u> of two reactions by comparing the <u>slopes</u> of their graphs. The <u>steeper</u> the slope, the <u>faster</u> the reaction. It's as simple as falling down a hill — the steeper the hill, the faster you'll fall.

Collision Theory

Reaction rates are explained by collision theory. It's really simple. It just says that the rate of a reaction simply depends on how often and how hard the reacting particles collide with each other. The basic idea is that particles have to collide in order to react, and they have to collide hard enough (with enough energy).

More Collisions Increases the Rate of Reaction

The effects of temperature, concentration and surface area on the rate of reaction can be explained in terms of how often the reacting particles collide successfully.

1) HIGHER TEMPERATURE increases collisions

When the temperature is increased the particles all move quicker.
If they're moving quicker, they're going to collide more often.

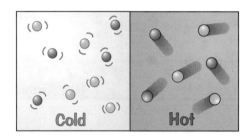

Cold   Hot

2) HIGHER CONCENTRATION (or PRESSURE) increases collisions

If a solution is made more concentrated it means there are more particles of reactant knocking about between the water molecules which makes collisions between the important particles more likely.

In a gas, increasing the pressure means the particles are more squashed up together so there will be more frequent collisions.

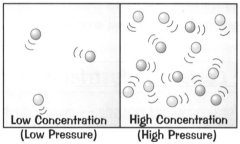

Low Concentration   High Concentration
(Low Pressure)   (High Pressure)

3) LARGER SURFACE AREA increases collisions

If one of the reactants is a solid then breaking it up into smaller pieces will increase the total surface area. This means the particles around it in the solution will have more area to work on, so there'll be more frequent collisions.

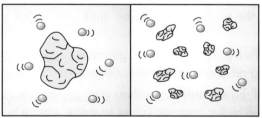

Small surface area   Big surface area

Collision theory — the lamppost ran into me...

Once you've learnt everything off this page, the rates of reaction stuff should start making a lot more sense to you. Isn't it nice when everything starts to fall into place... The concept's fairly simple — the more often particles bump into each other, and the harder they hit when they do, the faster the reaction happens.

Collision Theory and Catalysts

Without enough activation energy, it's game over before you start.

Faster Collisions Increase the Rate of Reaction

Higher temperature also increases the energy of the collisions, because it makes all the particles move faster.

Increasing the temperature causes faster collisions

Reactions only happen if the particles collide with enough energy.

The minimum amount of energy needed by the particles to react is known as the activation energy.

At a higher temperature there will be more particles colliding with enough energy to make the reaction happen.

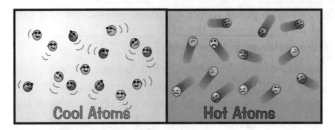

Catalysts Speed Up Reactions

Many reactions can be speeded up by adding a catalyst.

> A catalyst is a substance which speeds up a reaction, without being changed or used up in the reaction.

A solid catalyst works by giving the reacting particles a surface to stick to.
This increases the number of successful collisions (and so speeds the reaction up).

Catalysts Help Reduce Costs in Industrial Reactions

1) Catalysts are very important for commercial reasons — most industrial reactions use them.

2) Catalysts increase the rate of the reaction, which saves a lot of money simply because the plant doesn't need to operate for as long to produce the same amount of stuff.

3) Alternatively, a catalyst will allow the reaction to work at a much lower temperature. That reduces the energy used up in the reaction (the energy cost), which is good for sustainable development (see page 71) and can save a lot of money too.

4) There are disadvantages to using catalysts, though.

5) They can be very expensive to buy, and often need to be removed from the product and cleaned. They never get used up in the reaction though, so once you've got them you can use them over and over again.

6) Different reactions use different catalysts, so if you make more than one product at your plant, you'll probably need to buy different catalysts for them.

7) Catalysts can be 'poisoned' by impurities, so they stop working, e.g. sulfur impurities can poison the iron catalyst used in the Haber process (used to make ammonia for fertilisers). That means you have to keep your reaction mixture very clean.

Catalysts are like great jokes — they can be used over and over...

And they're not only used in industry... every useful chemical reaction in the human body is catalysed by a biological catalyst (an enzyme). If the reactions in the body were just left to their own devices, they'd take so long to happen, we couldn't exist. Quite handy then, these catalysts.

Energy Transfer in Reactions

Whenever chemical reactions occur <u>energy</u> is <u>transferred to</u> or <u>from</u> the <u>surroundings</u>.

In an Exothermic Reaction, Heat is Given Out

> An <u>EXOTHERMIC</u> <u>reaction</u> is one which <u>transfers energy</u> to the surroundings, usually in the form of <u>heat</u> and usually shown by a <u>rise in temperature.</u>

1) The best example of an <u>exothermic</u> reaction is <u>burning fuels</u> — also called <u>COMBUSTION</u>. This gives out a lot of heat — it's very exothermic.

2) <u>Neutralisation reactions</u> (acid + alkali) are also exothermic — see page 88.

3) Many <u>oxidation reactions</u> are exothermic. For example, adding sodium to water <u>produces heat</u>, so it must be <u>exothermic</u>. The sodium emits <u>heat</u> and moves about on the surface of the water as it is oxidised.

4) Exothermic reactions have lots of <u>everyday uses</u>. For example, some <u>hand warmers</u> use the exothermic <u>oxidation of iron</u> in air (with a salt solution catalyst) to generate <u>heat</u>. <u>Self heating cans</u> of hot chocolate and coffee also rely on exothermic reactions between <u>chemicals</u> in their bases.

In an Endothermic Reaction, Heat is Taken In

> An <u>ENDOTHERMIC</u> <u>reaction</u> is one which <u>takes in energy</u> from the surroundings, usually in the form of <u>heat</u> and is usually shown by a <u>fall in temperature.</u>

Endothermic reactions are much <u>less common</u>. <u>Thermal decompositions</u> are a good example:

> Heat must be supplied to make calcium carbonate <u>decompose</u> to make quicklime.
> $$CaCO_3 \rightarrow CaO + CO_2$$

Endothermic reactions also have everyday uses. For example, some <u>sports injury packs</u> use endothermic reactions — they <u>take in heat</u> and the pack becomes very <u>cold</u>. More <u>convenient</u> than carrying ice around.

Reversible Reactions Can Be Endothermic and Exothermic

In reversible reactions (see page 71), if the reaction is <u>endothermic</u> in <u>one direction</u>, it will be <u>exothermic</u> in the <u>other direction</u>. The <u>energy absorbed</u> by the endothermic reaction is <u>equal</u> to the <u>energy released</u> during the exothermic reaction. A good example is the <u>thermal decomposition of hydrated copper sulfate</u>.

endothermic

hydrated copper sulfate ⇌ anhydrous copper sulfate + water

exothermic

"Anhydrous" just means "without water", and "hydrated" means "with water".

1) If you <u>heat blue hydrated</u> copper(II) sulfate crystals it drives the water off and leaves <u>white anhydrous</u> copper(II) sulfate powder. This is endothermic.

Water vapour

2) If you then <u>add</u> a couple of drops of <u>water</u> to the <u>white powder</u> you get the <u>blue crystals</u> back again. This is exothermic.

Right, so burning gives out heat — really...

This whole energy transfer thing is a fairly simple idea — don't be put off by the long words. Remember, "<u>exo-</u>" = <u>exit</u>, "<u>-thermic</u>" = <u>heat</u>, so an exothermic reaction is one that <u>gives out</u> heat. And "<u>endo-</u>" = erm... the other one. Okay, so there's no easy way to remember that one. Tough.

Bonds and Energy Level Diagrams

Chemical reactions can either <u>release</u> heat energy, or <u>take in</u> heat energy.

Energy Must Always be Supplied to Break Bonds...
...and Energy is Always Released When Bonds Form

1) During a chemical reaction, <u>old bonds are broken</u> and <u>new bonds are formed</u>.

2) Energy must be <u>supplied</u> to break <u>existing bonds</u> — so bond breaking is an <u>endothermic</u> process.

3) Energy is <u>released</u> when new bonds are <u>formed</u> — so bond formation is an <u>exothermic</u> process.

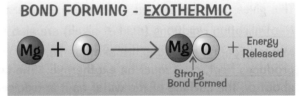

4) In an <u>exothermic</u> reaction, the energy <u>released</u> in bond formation is <u>greater</u> than the energy used in <u>breaking</u> old bonds.

5) In an <u>endothermic</u> reaction, the energy <u>required</u> to break old bonds is <u>greater</u> than the energy <u>released</u> when <u>new bonds</u> are formed.

Energy Level Diagrams Show if it's Exothermic or Endothermic

EXOTHERMIC

1) This shows an <u>exothermic reaction</u> — the products are at a <u>lower energy</u> than the reactants. The difference in <u>height</u> represents the energy <u>given out</u> in the reaction.

2) The <u>initial rise</u> in the line represents the energy needed to <u>break</u> the old bonds.

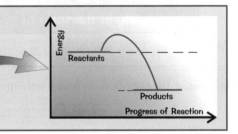

ENDOTHERMIC

1) This shows an <u>endothermic reaction</u> because the products are at a <u>higher energy</u> than the reactants.

2) The <u>difference in height</u> represents the <u>energy taken in</u> during the reaction.

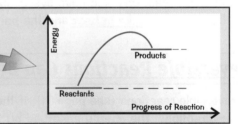

Temperature Change can be Measured

1) You can measure the amount of <u>energy produced</u> by a <u>chemical reaction</u> in solution by taking the <u>temperature of the reactants</u> (making sure they're the same), <u>mixing</u> them in a <u>polystyrene cup</u> and measuring the <u>temperature of the solution</u> at the <u>end</u> of the reaction. Easy.

2) The biggest <u>problem</u> with temperature measurements is the amount of heat <u>lost to the surroundings</u>.

3) You can reduce it a bit by putting the polystyrene cup into a beaker of <u>cotton wool</u> to give <u>more insulation</u>, and putting a <u>lid</u> on the cup to reduce energy lost by <u>evaporation</u>.

Save energy — break fewer bonds...

So now you know why reactions are exothermic or endothermic — it's all about the <u>energy</u> needed to <u>make</u> or <u>break bonds</u>. Pretty easy I'd say — endothermic reactions take in heat because there is more energy needed to make new bonds than to break old ones. And exothermic reactions do the opposite. Super. Splendid.

Revision Summary for Section 5

Well, I don't think that was too bad, was it... There are loads of methods you can use to identify substances. Chemical synthesis is used by the chemical industry to produce the chemicals that we use everyday. Four things affect the rate of reactions, there are loads of ways to measure reaction rates and it's all explained by collision theory. Reactions can be endothermic or exothermic, and quite a few of them are reversible. And so on... Easy. Ahem.

Well here are some more of those nice questions that you enjoy so much. If there are any you can't answer, go back to the appropriate page, do a bit more learning, then try again.

1) A student makes a solution of an unknown compound and adds a couple of drops of sodium hydroxide. He gets a white precipitate. He adds more sodium hydroxide and the precipitate dissolves.
   a) What positive ion is present?
   b) Write down an ionic equation for the formation of the white precipitate.

2) Iron(II) chloride forms a sludgy green precipitate with sodium hydroxide. Write down an ionic equation for this reaction.

3) Carbonates give off carbon dioxide when they're mixed with dilute acid.
   a) What's the test for carbon dioxide?
   b) Write an ionic equation for the reaction between carbonates and dilute acid.

4) What's the test for sulfates?

5) Explain how paper chromatography can be used to analyse the dyes used in a brown sweet.

6) Briefly describe how gas chromatography works.

7) Give an example of one chemical that is produced on a small scale and one chemical that is produced on a large scale.

8) What are 'batch production' and 'continuous production'?

9) Explain the advantages of using batch production to make pharmaceutical drugs. What are the disadvantages?

10) It can take 12 years and about £900 million to bring a new drug to market. Explain why.

11) What are the four factors that affect the rate of a reaction?

12) Give two reasons why it is important to control the rate of a chemical reaction in industry.

13) Describe three different ways of measuring the rate of a reaction.

14) A student carries out an experiment to measure the effect of surface area on the reaction between marble and hydrochloric acid. He measures the amount of gas given off at regular intervals.
   a) What factors must he keep constant for it to be a fair test?
   b)* He uses four samples for his experiment:
      Sample A – 10 g of powdered marble
      Sample B – 10 g of small marble chips
      Sample C – 10 g of large marble chips
      Sample D – 5 g of powdered marble
      Sketch a typical set of graphs for this experiment.

15)* A piece of magnesium is added to a dilute solution of hydrochloric acid, and hydrogen gas is produced. The experiment is repeated with a more concentrated hydrochloric acid. How can you tell from the experiment which concentration of acid produces a faster rate of reaction?

16) Explain how higher temperature, higher concentration and larger surface area increase the frequency of successful collisions between particles.

17) What is the definition of a catalyst?

18) Discuss the advantages and disadvantages of using catalysts in industrial processes.

19) What is an exothermic reaction? Give three examples.

20) The reaction to split ammonium chloride into ammonia and hydrogen chloride is endothermic. What can you say for certain about the reverse reaction?

21) Is bond breaking an exothermic or an endothermic reaction?

22) a) Draw graphs showing energy change in endothermic and exothermic reactions.
    b) Explain how bond breaking and bond forming relate to these graphs.

23) How would you measure the temperature change during a reaction?

* Answers on page 142.

Acids and Alkalis

Testing the pH of a solution means using an <u>indicator</u> — and that means pretty <u>colours</u>...

The pH Scale Goes From 0 to 14

1) The <u>pH scale</u> is a measure of how <u>acidic</u> or <u>alkaline</u> a solution is.
2) The <u>strongest acid</u> has <u>pH 0</u>. The <u>strongest alkali</u> has <u>pH 14</u>.
3) A <u>neutral</u> substance has <u>pH 7</u> (e.g. pure water).

pH 0 1 2 3 4 5 6 7 8 9 10 11 12 13 14

← ACIDS | ALKALIS →

NEUTRAL

| car battery acid, stomach acid | vinegar, lemon juice | acid rain | normal rain | pure water | washing-up liquid | pancreatic juice | soap powder | bleach | caustic soda (drain cleaner) |

Indicators and pH Meters can be Used to Determine pH

1) Indicators contain a dye that <u>changes colour</u> depending on whether it's <u>above</u> or <u>below</u> a certain pH.
2) <u>Litmus paper</u> is an easy way to find out if a solution is acidic or alkaline — it turns <u>red</u> if the solution is <u>acidic</u> and <u>blue</u> if it's <u>alkaline</u>.
3) <u>Universal indicator</u> is a very useful <u>combination of dyes</u>, which gives the colours shown above. It's useful for <u>estimating</u> the pH of a solution.
4) <u>pH meters</u> can also be used to measure the pH of a substance. These usually consist of a <u>probe</u>, which is dipped into the substance, and a <u>meter</u>, which gives a reading of the pH.
5) pH meters are <u>more accurate</u> than indicators.

Acids and Bases Neutralise Each Other

An <u>ACID</u> is a substance with a pH of less than 7. Acids form H^+ ions in <u>water</u>.
A <u>BASE</u> is a substance with a pH of greater than 7.
An <u>ALKALI</u> is a base that <u>dissolves in water</u>. Alkalis form OH^- ions in <u>water</u>.
So, <u>H^+</u> ions make solutions <u>acidic</u> and <u>OH^-</u> ions make them <u>alkaline</u>.

The reaction between acids and bases is called <u>neutralisation</u>.

$$acid + base \rightarrow salt + water$$

Neutralisation can also be seen in terms of <u>H^+</u> and <u>OH^-</u> ions like this:

$$H^+_{(aq)} + OH^-_{(aq)} \rightarrow H_2O_{(l)}$$

Hydrogen (H^+) ions react with hydroxide (OH^-) ions to produce water.

When an acid neutralises a base (or vice versa), the <u>products</u> are <u>neutral</u>, i.e. they have a <u>pH of 7</u>. An indicator can be used to show that a neutralisation reaction is over (Universal indicator will go green).

State Symbols Tell You What Physical State It's In

These are easy enough, <u>so make sure you know them</u> — especially aq (aqueous).

| (s) — Solid | (l) — Liquid | (g) — Gas | (aq) — Dissolved in water |

E.g. $2Mg_{(s)} + O_{2(g)} \rightarrow 2MgO_{(s)}$

Interesting(ish) fact — your skin is slightly acidic (pH 5.5)...

The neutralisation reaction's a great one to know. If you have <u>indigestion</u>, it's because you've got too much hydrochloric acid in your stomach. Indigestion tablets contain bases that neutralise some of the acid.

Acids Reacting With Metals

Sadly, the salts on this page aren't the sort you'd want to go putting on your fish 'n' chips.

Metals React With Acids to Give Salts

Acid + Metal → Salt + Hydrogen

That's written big 'cos it's kinda important. Here's the typical experiment:

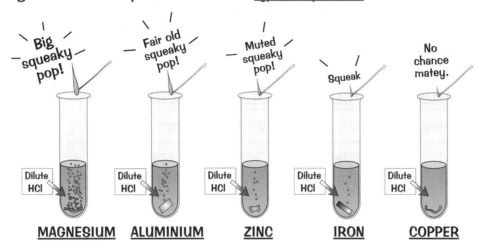

MAGNESIUM — Big squeaky pop! (Dilute HCl)
ALUMINIUM — Fair old squeaky pop! (Dilute HCl)
ZINC — Muted squeaky pop! (Dilute HCl)
IRON — Squeak (Dilute HCl)
COPPER — No chance matey. (Dilute HCl)

1) The more reactive the metal, the faster the reaction will go — very reactive metals (e.g. sodium) react explosively.

2) Copper does not react with dilute acids at all — because it's less reactive than hydrogen.

3) The speed of reaction is indicated by the rate at which the bubbles of hydrogen are given off.

4) The hydrogen is confirmed by the burning splint test giving the notorious 'squeaky pop'.

5) The name of the salt produced depends on which metal is used, and which acid is used:

Hydrochloric Acid Will Always Produce Chloride Salts:

$$2HCl + Mg \rightarrow MgCl_2 + H_2 \quad \text{(Magnesium chloride)}$$
$$6HCl + 2Al \rightarrow 2AlCl_3 + 3H_2 \quad \text{(Aluminium chloride)}$$
$$2HCl + Zn \rightarrow ZnCl_2 + H_2 \quad \text{(Zinc chloride)}$$

Sulfuric Acid Will Always Produce Sulfate Salts:

$$H_2SO_4 + Mg \rightarrow MgSO_4 + H_2 \quad \text{(Magnesium sulfate)}$$
$$3H_2SO_4 + 2Al \rightarrow Al_2(SO_4)_3 + 3H_2 \quad \text{(Aluminium sulfate)}$$
$$H_2SO_4 + Zn \rightarrow ZnSO_4 + H_2 \quad \text{(Zinc sulfate)}$$

Nitric Acid Produces Nitrate Salts When NEUTRALISED, But...

Nitric acid reacts fine with alkalis, to produce nitrates, but it can play silly devils with metals and produce nitrogen oxides instead, so we'll ignore it here. Chemistry's a real messy subject sometimes, innit.

Nitric acid, tut — there's always one...

Okay, so this stuff isn't exactly a laugh a minute, but at least it's fairly straightforward learning. Metals that are less reactive than hydrogen don't react with acid, and some metals like sodium and potassium are too reactive to mix with acid in a school lab — your beaker would explode.

Acid Reactions and Ammonia

I'm afraid there's more stuff on <u>neutralisation</u> reactions coming up...

Metal Oxides and Metal Hydroxides Are Bases

1) Some <u>metal oxides</u> and <u>metal hydroxides</u> dissolve in <u>water</u>. These soluble compounds are <u>alkalis</u>.

2) Even bases that won't dissolve in water will still react with acids.

3) So, all <u>metal oxides</u> and <u>metal hydroxides</u> react with <u>acids</u> to form a <u>salt</u> and <u>water</u>.

$$\text{Acid} + \text{Metal Oxide} \rightarrow \text{Salt} + \text{Water}$$

$$\text{Acid} + \text{Metal Hydroxide} \rightarrow \text{Salt} + \text{Water}$$

These are <u>neutralisation</u> <u>reactions</u> of course.

The Combination of Metal and Acid Decides the Salt

This isn't exactly exciting but it's pretty easy, so try and get the hang of it:

hydrochloric acid	+	copper oxide	→	copper chloride	+ water
hydrochloric acid	+	sodium hydroxide	→	sodium chloride	+ water
sulfuric acid	+	zinc oxide	→	zinc sulfate	+ water
sulfuric acid	+	calcium hydroxide	→	calcium sulfate	+ water
nitric acid	+	magnesium oxide	→	magnesium nitrate	+ water
nitric acid	+	potassium hydroxide	→	potassium nitrate	+ water

The symbol equations are all pretty much the same. Here are two of them:

$$H_2SO_{4\,(aq)} + ZnO_{(s)} \rightarrow ZnSO_{4\,(aq)} + H_2O_{(l)}$$

$$HNO_{3\,(aq)} + KOH_{(aq)} \rightarrow KNO_{3\,(aq)} + H_2O_{(l)}$$

Metal Carbonates Give Salt + Water + Carbon Dioxide

More gripping reactions involving acids. At least there are some <u>bubbles</u> involved here.

$$\text{Acid} + \text{Metal Carbonate} \rightarrow \text{Salt} + \text{Water} + \text{Carbon Dioxide}$$

The reaction is the same as the neutralisation reaction above EXCEPT that <u>carbon dioxide</u> is given off as well.

Ammonia Can Be Neutralised with HNO_3 to Make Fertiliser

<u>Ammonia</u> dissolves in water to make an <u>alkaline solution</u>.
When it reacts with <u>nitric acid</u>, you get a <u>neutral salt</u> — <u>ammonium nitrate</u>:

$$NH_{3\,(aq)} + HNO_{3\,(aq)} \rightarrow NH_4NO_{3\,(aq)}$$
$$\text{Ammonia} + \text{Nitric acid} \rightarrow \text{Ammonium nitrate}$$

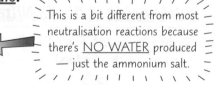

This is a bit different from most neutralisation reactions because there's <u>NO WATER</u> produced — just the ammonium salt.

<u>Ammonium nitrate</u> is an especially good fertiliser because it has <u>nitrogen</u> from <u>two sources</u>, the ammonia and the nitric acid. Kind of a <u>double dose</u>. Plants need nitrogen to make <u>proteins</u>.

There's nowt wrong wi' just spreadin' muck on it...

Not the most thrilling of pages, I'm afraid. Just loads of reactions for you to get your head around. Sad times...

Making Salts

If you're making a salt it's important to know if it's soluble or not so you know which method to use. Most chlorides, sulfates and nitrates are soluble in water (the main exceptions are lead chloride, lead sulfate and silver chloride). Most oxides and hydroxides are insoluble in water.

Making Soluble Salts Using a Metal or an Insoluble Base

1) You need to pick the right acid, plus a metal or an insoluble base (a metal oxide or metal hydroxide). E.g. if you want to make copper chloride, mix hydrochloric acid and copper oxide.

Remember some metals are unreactive and others are too reactive to use for this reaction (see page 89).

E.g. $$CuO_{(s)} + 2HCl_{(aq)} \longrightarrow CuCl_{2\,(aq)} + H_2O_{(l)}$$

filter paper
filter funnel

2) You add the metal, metal oxide or hydroxide to the acid — the solid will dissolve in the acid as it reacts. You will know when all the acid has been neutralised because the excess solid will just sink to the bottom of the flask.

3) Then filter out the excess metal, metal oxide or metal hydroxide to get the salt solution. To get pure, solid crystals of the salt, evaporate some of the water (to make the solution more concentrated) and then leave the rest to evaporate very slowly. This is called crystallisation.

Making Soluble Salts Using an Alkali

1) You can't use the method above with alkalis (soluble bases) like sodium, potassium or ammonium hydroxides, because you can't tell whether the reaction has finished — you can't just add an excess to the acid and filter out what's left.

2) You have to add exactly the right amount of alkali to just neutralise the acid — you need to use an indicator (see page 88) to show when the reaction's finished. Then repeat using exactly the same volumes of alkali and acid so the salt isn't contaminated with indicator.

3) Then just evaporate off the water to crystallise the salt as normal.

Making Insoluble Salts — Precipitation Reactions

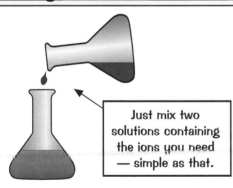

Just mix two solutions containing the ions you need — simple as that.

1) If the salt you want to make is insoluble, you can use a precipitation reaction.

2) You just need to pick two solutions that contain the ions you need. E.g. to make lead chloride you need a solution which contains lead ions and one which contains chloride ions. So you can mix lead nitrate solution (most nitrates are soluble) with sodium chloride solution (all group 1 compounds are soluble).

E.g. $$Pb(NO_3)_{2\,(aq)} + 2NaCl_{(aq)} \longrightarrow PbCl_{2\,(s)} + 2NaNO_{3\,(aq)}$$

3) Once the salt has precipitated out (and is lying at the bottom of your flask), all you have to do is filter it from the solution, wash it and then dry it on filter paper.

4) Precipitation reactions can be used to remove poisonous ions (e.g. lead) from drinking water. Calcium and magnesium ions can also be removed from water this way — they make water "hard", which stops soap lathering properly. Another use of precipitation is in treating effluent (sewage) — again, unwanted ions can be removed.

Get two beakers, mix 'em together — job's a good'n...

To make a particular soluble or insoluble salt, you need to think carefully about what chemicals you'd need to use to get the salt you want and what method you'd use. Blimey, this stuff isn't easy, is it.

Electrolysis

Hmm, electrolysis. A not-very-catchy title for quite a <u>sparky</u> subject...

Electrolysis Means "Splitting Up with Electricity"

1) If you pass an <u>electric current</u> through an <u>ionic substance</u> that's <u>molten</u> or in <u>solution</u>, it breaks down into the <u>elements</u> it's made of. This is called <u>electrolysis</u>.

2) It requires a <u>liquid</u> to <u>conduct</u> the <u>electricity</u>, called the <u>electrolyte</u>.

3) Electrolytes contain <u>free ions</u> — they're usually the <u>molten</u> or <u>dissolved ionic substance</u>.

4) In either case it's the <u>free ions</u> which <u>conduct</u> the electricity and allow the whole thing to work.

5) For an electrical circuit to be complete, there's got to be a <u>flow of electrons</u>. <u>Electrons</u> are taken <u>away from</u> ions at the <u>positive electrode</u> and <u>given to</u> other ions at the <u>negative electrode</u>. As ions gain or lose electrons they become atoms or molecules and are released.

NaCl dissolved
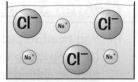

Molten NaCl
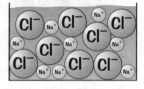

Electrolysis Reactions Involve Oxidation and Reduction

1) In Core Science you learnt about <u>reduction</u> involving the <u>loss of oxygen</u>. However...

2) <u>Reduction</u> is also a <u>gain of electrons</u>.

3) On the other hand, <u>oxidation</u> is a gain of oxygen or a <u>loss of electrons</u>.

4) So "reduction" and "oxidation" don't have to involve <u>oxygen</u>.

5) Electrolysis <u>ALWAYS</u> involves an oxidation and a reduction.

<u>Oxidation</u>
<u>Is</u>
<u>Loss</u>

<u>Reduction</u>
<u>Is</u>
<u>Gain</u>

Remember it as OIL RIG.

The Electrolysis of Molten Lead Bromide

When a salt (e.g. lead bromide) is molten it will conduct electricity.

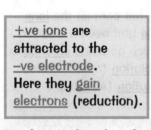

+ve ions are attracted to the <u>−ve electrode</u>. Here they <u>gain electrons</u> (reduction).

<u>Lead</u> is produced at the <u>−ve electrode</u>.

Electrode (-ve)

Electrode (+ve)

Molten lead bromide

HEAT

−ve ions are attracted to the <u>+ve electrode</u>. Here they <u>lose electrons</u> (oxidation).

<u>Bromine</u> is produced at the <u>+ve electrode</u>.

1) At the <u>−ve electrode</u>, one lead ion <u>accepts</u> two electrons to become <u>one lead atom</u>.

2) At the <u>+ve electrode</u>, two bromide ions <u>lose</u> one electron each and become <u>one bromine molecule</u>.

Faster shopping at Tesco — use Electrolleys...

Electrolysis is used lots in <u>real life</u>. For example, it's used to extract metals like aluminium from their ores (see page 94) and it can be used to make fuel for hydrogen powered cars. Isn't it nice to know how these things work?

Electrolysis of Sodium Chloride Solution

As well as <u>molten substances</u> you can also electrolyse <u>solutions</u>. But first, a bit more about the <u>products</u>...

Reactivity Affects the Products Formed By Electrolysis

1) Sometimes there are <u>more than two free ions</u> in the electrolyte.
   For example, if a salt is <u>dissolved in water</u> there will also be some <u>H</u> and <u>OH[−] ions</u>.

2) At the <u>negative electrode</u>, if <u>metal ions</u> and <u>H$^+$ ions</u> are present, the metal ions will <u>stay in solution</u> if the metal is <u>more reactive</u> than hydrogen. This is because the more reactive an element, the keener it is to stay as ions. So, <u>hydrogen</u> will be produced unless the metal is <u>less reactive</u> than it.

3) At the <u>positive electrode</u>, if <u>OH$^−$</u> and <u>halide ions</u> (Cl$^−$, Br$^−$, I$^−$) are present then molecules of chlorine, bromine or iodine will be formed. If <u>no halide</u> is present, then <u>oxygen</u> will be formed.

The Electrolysis of Sodium Chloride Solution

When common salt (sodium chloride) is dissolved in water and electrolysed,
it produces three useful products — <u>hydrogen</u>, <u>chlorine</u> and <u>sodium hydroxide</u>.

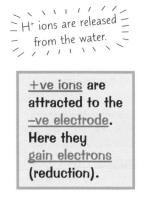
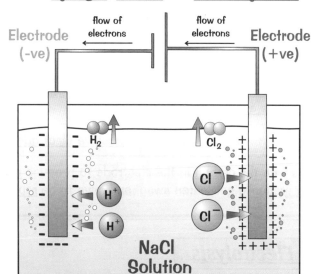

1) At the <u>negative electrode</u>, two hydrogen ions accept two electrons to become <u>one hydrogen molecule</u>.
2) At the <u>positive electrode</u>, two chloride (Cl$^−$) ions lose their electrons and become <u>one chlorine molecule</u>.
3) The <u>sodium ions</u> stay in solution because they're <u>more reactive</u> than hydrogen. <u>Hydroxide ions</u> from water are also left behind. This means that <u>sodium hydroxide</u> (NaOH) is left in the solution.

The Half-Equations — Make Sure the Electrons Balance

Half equations show the reactions at the electrodes. The main thing is to make sure the <u>number of electrons</u> is the <u>same</u> for <u>both half-equations</u>. For the electrolysis of sodium chloride the half-equations are:

You need to make sure the atoms are balanced too.

<u>Negative Electrode</u>: $2H^+ + 2e^- \rightarrow H_2$
<u>Positive Electrode</u>: $2Cl^- \rightarrow Cl_2 + 2e^-$
or $2Cl^- - 2e^- \rightarrow Cl_2$

For the electrolysis of molten lead bromide (previous page) the half equations would be:
$Pb^{2+} + 2e^- \rightarrow Pb$
and $2Br^- \rightarrow Br_2 + 2e^-$

Useful Products from the Electrolysis of Sodium Chloride Solution

The products of the electrolysis of sodium chloride solution are pretty useful in <u>industry</u>.
1) Chlorine has many uses, e.g. in the production of <u>bleach</u> and <u>plastics</u>.
2) Sodium hydroxide is a very strong <u>alkali</u> and is used <u>widely</u> in the <u>chemical industry</u>, e.g. to make <u>soap</u>.

Extraction of Aluminium and Electroplating

I bet you never thought there was so much to know about electrolysis — but sadly there is.
So get reading this lot...

Electrolysis is Used to Remove Aluminium from Its Ore

1) Aluminium's a very abundant metal, but it is always found naturally in compounds.

2) Its main ore is bauxite, and after mining and purifying, a white powder is left.

3) This is pure aluminium oxide, Al_2O_3.

4) The aluminium has to be extracted from this using electrolysis.

Cryolite is Used to Lower the Temperature (and Costs)

1) Al_2O_3 has a very high melting point of over 2000 °C
— so melting it would be very expensive.

2) Instead the aluminium oxide is dissolved in molten cryolite (a less common ore of aluminium).

3) This brings the temperature down to about 900 °C, which makes it much cheaper and easier.

4) The electrodes are made of carbon (graphite), a good conductor of electricity (see page 63).

5) Aluminium forms at the negative electrode and oxygen forms at the positive electrode.

crust

carbon positive electrode (graphite)

carbon lining (graphite) for negative electrode

bauxite in molten cryolite

molten aluminium

Negative Electrode: $Al^{3+} + 3e^- \rightarrow Al$ Positive Electrode: $2O^{2-} \rightarrow O_2 + 4e^-$

6) The oxygen then reacts with the carbon in the electrode to produce carbon dioxide. This means that the positive electrodes gradually get 'eaten away' and have to be replaced every now and again.

Electroplating Uses Electrolysis

1) Electroplating uses electrolysis to coat the surface of one metal with another metal,
e.g. you might want to electroplate silver onto a brass cup to make it look nice.

2) The negative electrode is the metal object you want to plate and the positive electrode is the
pure metal you want it to be plated with. You also need the electrolyte to contain
ions of the plating metal. (The ions that plate the metal object come from
the solution, while the positive electrode keeps the solution 'topped up'.)

Example: To electroplate silver onto a brass cup, you'd make
the brass cup the negative electrode (to attract the positive
silver ions), a lump of pure silver the positive electrode and
dip them in a solution of silver ions, e.g. silver nitrate.

pure silver strip

silver nitrate solution

object to be plated

3) There are lots of different uses for electroplating:

• Decoration: Silver is attractive, but very expensive. It's much cheaper to plate a boring brass cup
with silver, than it is to make the cup out of solid silver — but it looks just as pretty.

• Conduction: Metals like copper conduct electricity well — because of this they're
often used to plate metals for electronic circuits and computers.

Silver electroplated text is worth a fortune...

There are loads of metals you can use for electroplating, but the common ones are silver and copper.
The tricky bit is remembering that the metal object you want to plate is the negative electrode and the metal
you're plating it with is the positive electrode. Oh, and don't forget to check out aluminium electrolysis too.

Revision Summary for Section 6

Bleeuurgh... Who decided to make a section covering acids and bases <u>and</u> electrolysis — not the two nicest topics in chemistry in my view. Saying that, you still need to make sure that you can answer all of these fiendishly tricky* revision summary questions before you move on. You wouldn't want to lose marks in the exam just coz you didn't fancy learning about acids now, would you...

1) What does the pH scale show?

2) Name two ways of measuring the pH of a substance.

3) What type of ions are always present in a) acids and   b) alkalis?

4) What is neutralisation? Write down the general equation for neutralisation in terms of ions.

5) Write down the state symbol that means 'dissolved in water'.

6) What is the general equation for reacting an acid with a metal?

7) Name a metal that doesn't react at all with dilute acids.

8) What type of salts do hydrochloric acid and sulfuric acid produce?

9) What type of reaction is "acid + metal oxide", or "acid + metal hydroxide"?

10) Write a balanced symbol equation for the reaction between ammonia and nitric acid. What is the product of this reaction useful for?

11) Suggest a suitable acid and a suitable metal oxide/hydroxide to mix to form the following salts.
    a) copper chloride   b) calcium nitrate   c) zinc sulfate
    d) magnesium nitrate   e) sodium sulfate   f) potassium chloride

12) Iron chloride can made by mixing iron hydroxide (an insoluble base) with hydrochloric acid. Describe the method you would use to produce pure, solid iron chloride in the lab.

13) How can you tell when a neutralisation reaction is complete if both the base and the salt are soluble in water?

14) Give a practical use of precipitation reactions.

15) What is electrolysis? Explain why only liquids can be electrolysed.

16) Draw a detailed diagram with half equations showing the electrolysis of sodium chloride.

17) Give one industrial use of sodium hydroxide and two uses of chlorine.

18) Why is cryolite used during the electrolysis of aluminium oxide?

19) Give two different uses of electroplating.

*Disclaimer: These revision summary questions are not really fiendishly tricky, more like a mild irritant.

Section 6 — Acid Reactions, Salts and Electrolysis

Velocity and Acceleration

If you've ever felt out of your depth when talk at the dinner table turns to the <u>difference</u> between speed and velocity, then this is the page for you...

Speed <u>and</u> Velocity <u>are Both</u> HOW FAST <u>YOU'RE GOING</u>

<u>Speed and velocity</u> are both measured in <u>m/s</u> (or km/h or mph). They both simply say <u>how fast</u> you're going, but there's <u>a subtle difference</u> between them:

> <u>SPEED</u> is just <u>how fast</u> you're going (e.g. 30 mph or 20 m/s) with no regard to the direction.
>
> <u>VELOCITY</u> however must <u>also</u> have the <u>DIRECTION</u> specified, e.g. 30 mph north or 20 m/s, 060°. The distance in a particular direction is called the <u>DISPLACEMENT</u>.

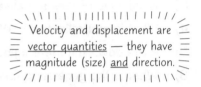
Velocity and displacement are <u>vector quantities</u> — they have magnitude (size) <u>and</u> direction.

Speed, Distance and Time — the <u>Formula:</u>

You really ought to get <u>pretty slick</u> with this <u>very easy equation</u>...

$$\text{Speed} = \frac{\text{Distance}}{\text{Time}}$$

<u>EXAMPLE:</u> A cat skulks 20 m in 35 s. Find: a) its speed, b) how long it takes to skulk 75 m.
<u>ANSWER:</u> Using the formula triangle: a) s = d/t = 20/35 = <u>0.57 m/s</u>
b) t = d/s = 75/0.57 = 132 s = <u>2 min 12 s</u>

A lot of the time we tend to use the words "speed" and "velocity" interchangeably. But if you're talking about velocity, don't forget to state a <u>direction</u>.

Acceleration <u>is</u> How Quickly Velocity <u>is</u> Changing

Acceleration is <u>definitely not</u> the same as <u>velocity</u> or <u>speed</u>.

1) Acceleration is <u>how quickly</u> the velocity is <u>changing</u>.
2) This change in velocity can be a <u>CHANGE IN SPEED</u> or a <u>CHANGE IN DIRECTION</u> or both. (You only have to worry about the change in speed bit for calculations.)
3) <u>Deceleration</u> is just negative <u>acceleration</u> (if something slows down, the change in velocity is negative).

BUT, acceleration is a <u>vector quantity</u> like velocity — it has <u>magnitude</u> and <u>direction</u>.

Acceleration — The <u>Formula:</u>

$$\text{Acceleration} = \frac{\text{Change in Velocity}}{\text{Time taken}}$$

Here, u is the <u>initial velocity</u> of the object and v is its <u>final velocity</u>.

The change in velocity can also be written as Δv.

There are <u>two tricky things</u> with this equation. First there's the '(v – u)', which means working out the '<u>change in velocity</u>', as shown in the example below, rather than just putting a <u>simple value</u> for velocity or speed in. Secondly there's the <u>unit</u> of acceleration, which is <u>m/s²</u>. (Don't get confused with the units for <u>velocity</u>, <u>m/s</u>.)

<u>EXAMPLE:</u> A skulking cat accelerates from 2 m/s to 6 m/s in 5.6 s. Find its acceleration.
<u>ANSWER:</u> Using the formula triangle: a = (v – u) / t = (6 – 2) / 5.6 = 4 ÷ 5.6 = <u>0.71 m/s²</u>

They say a change in velocity is as good as a rest...

Lots of facts on this page, but it's all useful stuff. Make sure you understand what speed and acceleration are and how to calculate them both before you move on. You'll meet speed and acceleration again on the next page.

D-T and V-T Graphs

Distance-time and velocity-time graphs are very different...

Distance-Time Graphs

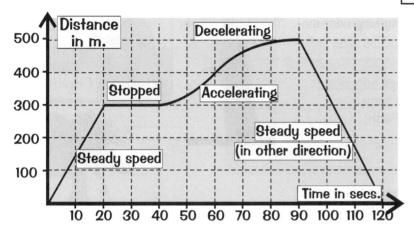

Very Important Notes:

1) Gradient = speed.
2) Flat sections are where it's stopped.
3) The steeper the graph, the faster it's going.
4) Downhill sections mean it's going back toward its starting point.
5) Curves represent acceleration or deceleration.
6) A steepening curve means it's speeding up (increasing gradient).
7) A levelling off curve means it's slowing down (decreasing gradient).

Calculating Speed from a Distance-Time Graph — It's Just the Gradient

For example, the speed of the return section of the graph is:

$$\text{Speed} = \text{gradient} = \frac{\text{vertical}}{\text{horizontal}} = \frac{500}{30} = 16.7 \text{ m/s}$$

This is just the speed equation (p.96).

Don't forget that you have to use the scales of the axes to work out the gradient. Don't measure in cm!

Velocity-Time Graphs

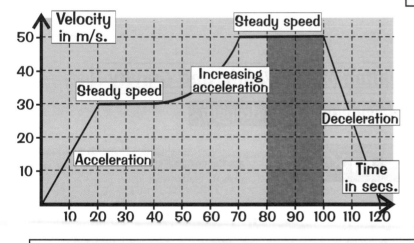

Very Important Notes:

1) Gradient = acceleration.
2) Flat sections represent steady speed.
3) The steeper the graph, the greater the acceleration or deceleration.
4) Uphill sections (/) are acceleration.
5) Downhill sections (\) are deceleration.
6) The area under any section of the graph (or all of it) is equal to the distance travelled in that time interval.
7) A curve means changing acceleration.

Calculating Acceleration and Distance from a Velocity-Time Graph

1) The acceleration represented by the first section of the graph is:

$$\text{Acceleration} = \text{gradient} = \frac{\text{vertical}}{\text{horizontal}} = \frac{30}{20} = 1.5 \text{ m/s}^2$$

This is the just the equation for acceleration (p.96).

2) The distance travelled in any time interval is equal to the area under the graph. For example, the distance travelled between $t = 80$ s and $t = 100$ s is equal to the shaded area which is equal to 1000 m. (But we can only use the method for uniform (constant or steady) acceleration.)

Understanding motion graphs — it can be a real uphill struggle...

The tricky thing about these two types of graph is that they can look pretty much the same but represent totally different kinds of motion. On a distance-time graph a straight uphill line means that the object is travelling at a steady speed, the same line on a velocity-time graph means the object is accelerating. Don't get caught out.

Weight, Mass and Gravity

Now for something a bit more attractive — the force of <u>gravity</u>. Enjoy...

Gravitational Force *is the* Force of Attraction *Between* All Masses

<u>Gravity</u> attracts <u>all</u> masses, but you only notice it when one of the masses is <u>really really big</u>, e.g. a planet. Anything near a planet or star is <u>attracted</u> to it <u>very strongly</u>.

This has <u>two</u> important effects:

1) On the surface of a planet, it makes all things <u>accelerate</u> (see p.96) towards the <u>ground</u> (all with the <u>same</u> acceleration, g, which is about <u>10 m/s^2</u> on Earth).

2) It gives everything a <u>weight</u>.

 Gravity

Weight *and* Mass *are* Not the Same

1) <u>Mass</u> is just the <u>amount of 'stuff'</u> in an object. For any given object this will have the same value <u>anywhere</u> in the universe.

2) <u>Weight</u> is caused by the <u>pull</u> of the <u>gravitational force</u>. In most questions the <u>weight</u> of an object is just the <u>force</u> of gravity pulling it towards the centre of the <u>Earth</u>.

3) An object has the <u>same</u> mass whether it's on <u>Earth</u> or on the <u>Moon</u> — but its <u>weight</u> will be <u>different</u>. A 1 kg mass will <u>weigh less</u> on the Moon (about 1.6 N) than it does on Earth (about 10 N), simply because the <u>gravitational force</u> pulling on it is <u>less</u>.

4) Weight is a <u>force</u> measured in <u>newtons</u>. It's measured using a <u>spring</u> balance or <u>newton meter</u>. Mass is <u>not</u> a force. It's measured in <u>kilograms</u> with a <u>mass</u> balance (an old-fashioned pair of balancing scales).

The Very Important Formula *Relating* Mass, Weight *and* Gravity

weight = mass × gravitational field strength

$$W = m \times g$$

The acceleration due to gravity and the gravitational field strength are always the same value, no matter what planet or moon you're on.

1) Remember, weight and mass are <u>not the same</u>. Mass is in <u>kg</u>, weight is in <u>newtons</u>.

2) The letter "g" represents the <u>strength</u> of the gravity and its value is <u>different</u> for <u>different planets</u>. On Earth g ≈ 10 N/kg. On the Moon, where the gravity is weaker, g is only about 1.6 N/kg.

3) This formula is <u>hideously easy</u> to use:

<u>Example:</u> What is the weight, in newtons, of a 5 kg mass, both on Earth and on the Moon?
<u>Answer:</u> "W = m × g". On Earth: W = 5 × 10 = <u>50 N</u> (The weight of the 5 kg mass is 50 N.)
On the Moon: W = 5 × 1.6 = <u>8 N</u> (The weight of the 5 kg mass is 8 N.)

See what I mean. Hideously easy — as long as you know what all the letters mean.

I don't think you understand the gravity of this situation...

The difference between <u>weight</u> and <u>mass</u> can be tricky to get your head around, but it's useful to know. Weight is the <u>force of gravity</u> acting on a mass, and mass is the <u>amount of stuff</u>, measured in kg. The mass of an object will always be the same no matter where it is, but its weight will change depending on <u>where</u> it is in the universe.

Resultant Forces

Gravity isn't the only force in town — there are other forces such as <u>driving forces</u> or <u>air resistance</u>. What's useful to be able to work out is how all these forces <u>add up together</u>.

Resultant Force _is the_ Overall Force _on a Point or Object_

The notion of <u>resultant force</u> is a bit tricky to get your head round:

1) In most <u>real</u> situations there are at least <u>two forces</u> acting on an object along any direction.

2) The <u>overall</u> effect of these forces will decide the <u>motion</u> of the object
— whether it will <u>accelerate</u>, <u>decelerate</u> or stay at a <u>steady speed</u>.

3) If you have a <u>number of forces</u> acting at a single point, you can replace them with a <u>single force</u>
(so long as the single force has the <u>same effect on the motion</u> as the original forces acting all together).

4) If the forces all act along the same line (they're all parallel and act in the same or the opposite direction), the <u>overall effect</u> is found by just <u>adding or subtracting</u> them.

5) The overall force you get is called the <u>resultant force</u>.

6) You can show the forces acting on an object in a force diagram. There are three rules to using them:

  • The <u>length</u> of the arrow shows the <u>size</u> of the force.

  • The <u>direction</u> of the arrow shows the <u>direction</u> of the force (didn't see that one coming, did you...).

  • If the arrows come in <u>opposite pairs</u>, and they're all the same <u>size</u>, then the <u>forces</u> are <u>balanced</u>.

Example: _Stationary Teapot — All Forces_ Balance

1) The force of <u>GRAVITY</u> (or weight) is acting <u>downwards</u>.

2) This causes a <u>REACTION FORCE</u> (see p.101) from the surface <u>pushing up</u> on the object.

3) This is the <u>only way</u> it can be in <u>BALANCE</u>.

4) <u>Without</u> a reaction force, it would <u>accelerate downwards</u> due to the pull of gravity.

5) The <u>resultant</u> force on the teapot is zero: 10 N – 10 N = 0 N.

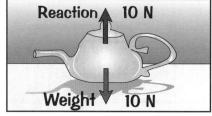

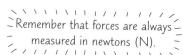

Remember that forces are always measured in newtons (N).

A Resultant Force _Means a_ Change in Velocity

1) If there is a resultant force acting on an object, then the object will <u>change its state of rest or motion</u>.

2) In other words it causes a <u>change in the object's velocity</u>.

You Can _Find the Resultant Force_ Acting in a _Straight Line_

EXAMPLE: Benny is driving along to Las Vegas in his vintage sports car.
He applies a driving force of <u>1000 N</u>, but has to overcome air resistance of <u>600 N</u>.
What is the <u>resultant force</u>? Will the car's velocity <u>change</u>?

Driving Force:
1000 N

Air Resistance:
600 N

Resultant Force:
400 N

ANSWER: Say that the forces pointing to the <u>left</u> are pointing in the <u>positive direction</u>.
The resultant force = 1000 N – 600 N = <u>400 N to the left</u>. If there is a resultant force then there is always an acceleration, so Benny's velocity <u>will</u> change. Viva Las Vegas.

And you're moving forward — what a result...

Resultant forces are just about <u>adding</u> and <u>subtracting</u> really — the trick is to make sure you've <u>accounted for everything</u>. Next up, some of the <u>thrilling physics</u> you can understand once you have resultant forces figured out.

Forces and Acceleration

Around about the time of the Great Plague in the 1660s, a chap called <u>Isaac Newton</u> worked out his <u>Laws of Motion</u>. At first they might seem kind of obscure or irrelevant, but to be perfectly blunt, if you can't understand this page then you'll never understand <u>forces and motion</u>.

An Object Needs a Force to Start Moving

If the resultant force on a <u>stationary</u> object is <u>zero</u>, the object will <u>remain stationary</u>.

Things <u>don't just start moving</u> on their own, there has to be a <u>resultant force</u> (see previous page) to get them started.

No Resultant Force Means No Change in Velocity

If there is <u>no resultant force</u> on a <u>moving</u> object it'll just carry on moving at the <u>same velocity</u>.

1) When a train or car or bus or anything else is <u>moving</u> at a <u>constant velocity</u> then the <u>forces</u> on it must all be <u>balanced</u>.

2) Never let yourself entertain the <u>ridiculous idea</u> that things need a constant overall force to <u>keep</u> them moving — NO NO NO NO NO NO!

3) To keep going at a <u>steady speed</u>, there must be <u>zero resultant force</u> — and don't you forget it.

A Resultant Force Means Acceleration

If there is a <u>non-zero resultant force</u>, then the object will <u>accelerate</u> in the direction of the force.

1) A non-zero <u>resultant</u> force will always produce <u>acceleration</u> (or deceleration).

2) This "<u>acceleration</u>" can take <u>five</u> different forms: <u>Starting</u>, <u>stopping</u>, <u>speeding up</u>, <u>slowing down</u> and <u>changing direction</u>.

3) On a force diagram, the <u>arrows</u> will be <u>unequal</u>:

<u>Don't ever say</u>: "If something's moving there must be an overall resultant force acting on it".
Not so. If there's an <u>overall</u> force it will always <u>accelerate</u>.
You get <u>steady</u> speed when there is <u>zero</u> resultant force.
I wonder how many times I need to say that same thing before you remember it?

Steady Speed Bus Tours Ltd. — providing consistent service since 1926...

<u>Objects in space</u> don't need a driving force to keep travelling at a steady speed — it's only because of <u>air resistance</u> and <u>friction</u> that we do. A steady speed means that there is <u>zero resultant force</u>.

Forces and Acceleration

More fun stuff on forces and acceleration here. The big equation on this page is <u>F = ma</u> — it's a really useful one. Remember that the F is always the <u>resultant force</u>...

A <u>Non-Zero</u> <u>Resultant Force Produces an</u> <u>Acceleration</u>

Any <u>resultant force</u> will produce <u>acceleration</u>, and this is the <u>formula</u> for it:

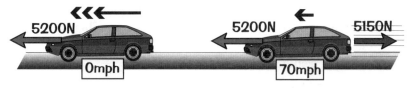

$$F = ma \qquad \text{or} \qquad a = F/m$$

m = mass in kilograms (kg)
a = acceleration in metres per second squared (m/s²)
F is the <u>resultant force</u> in newtons (**N**)

<u>EXAMPLE</u>: A car of mass of 1750 kg has an engine which provides a driving force of 5200 N.
At 70 mph the drag force acting on the car is 5150 N.
Find its acceleration a) when first setting off from rest b) at 70 mph.

<u>ANSWER</u>: 1) First draw a force diagram for both cases (no need to show the vertical forces):

5200N   **0mph**   **5200N**   **5150N**   **70mph**

2) Work out the resultant force and acceleration of the car in each case.

Resultant force = 5200 N   Resultant force = 5200 – 5150 = 50 N
a = F/m = 5200 ÷ 1750 = <u>3.0 m/s²</u>   a = F/m = 50 ÷ 1750 = <u>0.03 m/s²</u>

<u>Reaction Forces</u> <u>are</u> <u>Equal</u> <u>and</u> <u>Opposite</u>

> When <u>two objects interact</u>, the forces they
> exert on each other are <u>equal and opposite</u>.

1) That means if you <u>push</u> something, say a shopping trolley,
the trolley will <u>push back</u> against you, <u>just as hard</u>.

2) And as soon as you <u>stop</u> pushing, <u>so does the trolley</u>. Kinda clever really.

3) So far so good. The slightly tricky thing to get your head round is this — if the forces are always equal, <u>how does anything ever go anywhere</u>? The important thing to remember is that the two forces are acting on <u>different objects</u>. Think about a pair of ice skaters:

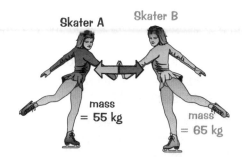

Skater A   Skater B

mass = 55 kg   mass = 65 kg

When skater A pushes on skater B (the '<u>action</u>' force), she feels an equal and opposite force from skater B's hand (the '<u>reaction</u>' force). Both skaters feel the <u>same sized force</u>, in <u>opposite directions</u>, and so accelerate away from each other.

Skater A will be <u>accelerated</u> more than skater B, though, because she has a smaller mass — remember <u>a = F/m</u>.

4) It's the same sort of thing when you go <u>swimming</u>. You <u>push</u> back against the <u>water</u> with your arms and legs, and the water pushes you forwards with an <u>equal-sized force</u> in the <u>opposite direction</u>.

<u>I have a reaction to forces — they bring me out in a rash...</u>

This is the real deal. Like... proper Physics. It was <u>pretty fantastic</u> at the time it was discovered — suddenly people understood how forces and motion worked, they could work out the <u>orbits of planets</u> and everything. Inspired? No? Shame. And I thought you were gonna turn out to be the next Newton.

Frictional Force and Terminal Velocity

Ever wondered why it's so hard to run into a hurricane whilst wearing a sandwich board? Read on to find out...

Friction Will Slow Things Down

1) When an object is moving (or trying to move) friction acts in the direction that opposes movement.

2) The frictional force will match the size of the force trying to move it, up to a point
— after this the friction will be less than the other force and the object will move.

3) Friction will act to make the moving object slow down and stop.

4) So to travel at a steady speed, things always need a driving force to overcome the friction.

5) Friction occurs in three main ways:

a) FRICTION BETWEEN SOLID SURFACES WHICH ARE GRIPPING (static friction)

b) FRICTION BETWEEN SOLID SURFACES WHICH ARE SLIDING PAST EACH OTHER

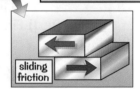

c) RESISTANCE OR "DRAG" FROM FLUIDS (LIQUIDS OR GASES, e.g. AIR)

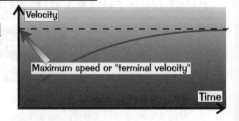

The larger the area of the object, the greater the drag. So, to reduce drag, the area and shape should be streamlined and reduced, like wedge-shaped sports cars. Roof boxes on cars spoil this shape and so slow them down. Driving with the windows open also increases drag.

Something that's designed to reduce your speed, e.g. a parachute, often has a large area to give a high drag to slow you down. For a given thrust, the higher the drag, the lower the top speed (see below). In a fluid: FRICTION (DRAG) ALWAYS INCREASES AS THE SPEED INCREASES — and don't forget it.

Objects Falling Through Fluids Reach a Terminal Velocity

When falling objects first set off, the force of gravity is much more than the frictional force slowing them down, so they accelerate. As the speed increases the friction builds up. This gradually reduces the acceleration until eventually the frictional force is equal to the accelerating force and then it won't accelerate any more. It will have reached its maximum speed or terminal velocity and will fall at a steady speed.

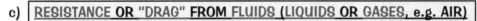

The Terminal Velocity of Falling Objects Depends on their Shape and Area

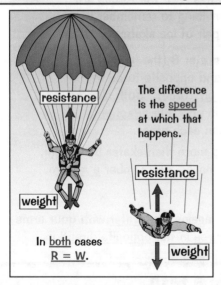

The difference is the speed at which that happens.

In both cases R = W.

The accelerating force acting on all falling objects is gravity and it would make them all fall at the same rate, if it wasn't for air resistance. This means that on the Moon, where there's no air, hamsters and feathers dropped simultaneously will hit the ground together. However, on Earth, air resistance causes things to fall at different speeds, and the terminal velocity of any object is determined by its drag in comparison to its weight. The frictional force depends on its shape and area.

The most important example is the human skydiver. Without his parachute open he has quite a small area and a force of "W = mg" pulling him down. He reaches a terminal velocity of about 120 mph. But with the parachute open, there's much more air resistance (at any given speed) and still only the same force "W = mg" pulling him down. This means his terminal velocity comes right down to about 15 mph, which is a safe speed to hit the ground at.

Air resistance — it can be a real drag...

Without friction, you wouldn't be able to walk or run or skip or write... hmm, not all bad then.

Stopping Distances

And now a page on stopping distances. This may seem a bit out of kilter with the rest of the section, but it's a <u>real world application</u> of the physics of forces. See, I told you it was useful... and fun... right?

Many Factors **Affect Your Total** Stopping Distance

1) Looking at things simply — if you <u>need to stop</u> in a <u>given distance</u>, then the <u>faster</u> a vehicle's going, the <u>bigger braking force</u> it'll need.

2) Likewise, for any given braking force, the <u>faster</u> you're going, the <u>greater your stopping distance</u>. But in real life it's not quite that simple — if your maximum braking force isn't enough, you'll go further before you stop.

3) The total <u>stopping distance</u> of a vehicle is the distance covered in the time between the driver <u>first spotting</u> a hazard and the vehicle coming to a <u>complete stop</u>.

4) The <u>stopping distance</u> is <u>the sum</u> of the <u>thinking distance</u> and the <u>braking distance</u>.

The reaction time is the time between the driver spotting a hazard and taking action.

1) Thinking Distance

"The distance the vehicle travels during the driver's reaction time".

It's affected by <u>two main factors</u>:

a) How fast you're going — Obviously. Whatever your reaction time, the <u>faster</u> you're going, the <u>further</u> you'll go.

b) How dopey you are — This is affected by <u>tiredness</u>, <u>drugs</u>, <u>alcohol</u> and a <u>careless</u> blasé attitude.

<u>Bad visibility</u> and <u>distractions</u> can also be a major factor in accidents — lashing rain, messing about with the radio, bright oncoming lights, etc. might mean that a driver <u>doesn't notice</u> a hazard until they're quite close to it. It <u>doesn't</u> affect your thinking distance, but you <u>start thinking</u> about stopping <u>nearer</u> to the hazard, and so you're <u>more likely</u> to crash.

The figures below for typical stopping distances are from the Highway Code. It's frightening to see just how far it takes to stop when you're going at 70 mph.

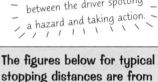

2) Braking Distance

"The distance the car travels under the breaking force".

It's affected by <u>five main factors</u>:

a) How fast you're going — The <u>faster</u> you're going, the <u>further</u> it takes to stop.

b) The MASS of your vehicle — With the <u>same</u> brakes, <u>a heavily laden</u> vehicle takes <u>longer to stop</u>. A car won't stop as quickly when it's full of people and luggage and towing a caravan.

c) How good your brakes are — All brakes must be checked and maintained <u>regularly</u>. Worn or faulty brakes will let you down <u>catastrophically</u> just when you need them the <u>most</u>, i.e. in an <u>emergency</u>.

d) How good the tyres are — Tyres should have a minimum <u>tread depth</u> of <u>1.6 mm</u> in order to be able to get rid of the <u>water</u> in wet conditions. Leaves, diesel spills and muck on the road can <u>greatly increase</u> the braking distance, and cause the car to <u>skid</u> too.

e) How good the grip is — This depends on <u>three things</u>: 1) <u>road surface</u>, 2) <u>weather</u> conditions, 3) <u>tyres</u>.

<u>Wet</u> or <u>icy roads</u> are always much more <u>slippy</u> than dry roads, but often you only discover this when you try to <u>brake</u> hard. You don't have as much grip, so you travel further before stopping.

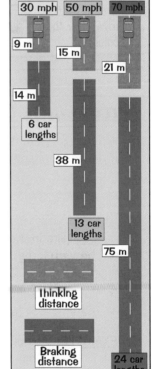

30 mph	50 mph	70 mph
9 m	15 m	21 m
14 m		
6 car lengths		
	38 m	
	13 car lengths	
		75 m

Thinking distance

Braking distance

24 car lengths

Stop right now — thank you very much...

Without <u>tread</u>, a tyre will simply <u>ride</u> on a <u>layer of water</u> and skid <u>very easily</u>. This is called "<u>aquaplaning</u>" and isn't nearly as cool as it sounds. <u>Snow and ice</u> are also very hazardous because it is difficult for the tyres to <u>get a grip</u>.

Momentum

A <u>large</u> rhino running very <u>fast</u> at you is going to be a lot harder to stop than a scrawny one out for a Sunday afternoon stroll — that's momentum for you.

Momentum = Mass × Velocity

1) Momentum (p) is a <u>property</u> of <u>moving objects</u>.

2) The <u>greater</u> the <u>mass</u> of an object and the <u>greater</u> its <u>velocity</u> (see p.96) the <u>more momentum</u> the object has.

3) Momentum is a <u>vector</u> quantity — it has size <u>and</u> direction (like <u>velocity</u>, but not speed).

Momentum (kg m/s) = Mass (kg) × Velocity (m/s)

Momentum Before = Momentum After

In a <u>closed system</u>, the total momentum <u>before</u> an event (e.g. a collision) is the same as <u>after</u> the event. This is called <u>Conservation of Momentum</u>.

A <u>closed system</u> is just a fancy way of saying that no external forces act.

Example

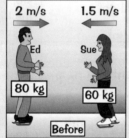

Two skaters approach each other, collide and move off together as shown. At what velocity do they move after the collision?

2 m/s Ed 80 kg — 1.5 m/s Sue 60 kg
Before

Velocity (v) = (80+60) kg
After

1) Choose which direction is <u>positive</u>.
   I'll say "<u>positive</u>" means "<u>to the right</u>".

2) <u>Total momentum before</u> collision
   = momentum of Ed + momentum of Sue
   = {80 × 2} + {60 × (−1.5)} = <u>70 kg m/s</u>

3) <u>Total momentum after</u> collision
   = momentum of Ed and Sue together = <u>140 × v</u>

4) So 140v = 70, i.e. <u>v = 0.5 m/s to the right</u>

Forces Cause Changes in Momentum

1) When a <u>force</u> acts on an object, it causes a <u>change</u> in momentum.

2) A <u>larger</u> force means a <u>faster</u> change of momentum (and so a greater <u>acceleration</u>, see p.96).

3) Likewise, if someone's momentum changes <u>very quickly</u> (like in a <u>car crash</u>), the <u>forces</u> on the body will be very <u>large</u>, and more likely to cause <u>injury</u>.

4) This is why <u>cars</u> are designed with <u>protective features</u> to slow people down over a <u>longer time</u> when they have a crash — the <u>longer</u> it takes for a <u>change in momentum</u>, the <u>smaller</u> the <u>force</u> (more on page 108).

$$\text{Force (N)} = \frac{\text{Change in momentum (kg m/s)}}{\text{Time (s)}}$$

$$F = \frac{mv - mu}{t}$$

Here, 'v' is the final velocity, 'u' is the initial velocity and m is the mass.

'mv−mu' can also be written 'ΔM'.

<u>EXAMPLE:</u> A rock with mass <u>1 kg</u> is travelling through space at <u>15 m/s</u>. A comet hits the rock, giving it a resultant force of <u>2500 N</u> for <u>0.7 seconds</u>. Calculate a) the rock's <u>initial momentum</u>, and b) the <u>change</u> in its momentum resulting from the impact.

<u>ANSWER:</u> a) Momentum = mass × velocity = 1 × 15 = <u>15 kg m/s</u>
b) Rearranging the formula,
Change of momentum = force × time = 2500 × 0.7 = <u>1750 kg m/s</u>.

Learning this stuff will only take a moment... um...

Momentum's a pretty fundamental bit of Physics — so make sure you understand it. Right then, momentum is always <u>conserved</u> in collisions and explosions when there are no external forces acting. Job's a good 'un.

Work and Power

> When a <u>force</u> moves an <u>object</u> through a <u>distance</u>,
> **ENERGY IS TRANSFERRED** and **WORK IS DONE**.

That statement sounds far more complicated than it needs to. Try this:

1) Whenever something <u>moves</u>, something else is providing some sort of '<u>effort</u>' to move it.
2) The thing putting the <u>effort</u> in needs a <u>supply</u> of energy (like <u>fuel</u> or <u>food</u> or <u>electricity</u> etc.).
3) It then does '<u>work</u>' by <u>moving</u> the object — and one way or another it <u>transfers</u> the energy it receives (as fuel) into <u>other forms</u>.
4) Whether this energy is transferred '<u>usefully</u>' (e.g. by <u>lifting a load</u>) or is '<u>wasted</u>' (e.g. lost as <u>heat</u> through <u>friction</u>), you can still say that '<u>work is done</u>'. Just like Batman and Bruce Wayne, '<u>work done</u>' and '<u>energy transferred</u>' are indeed '<u>one and the same</u>'. (And they're both given in <u>joules</u>.)

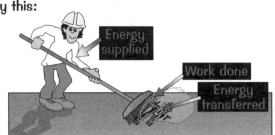

It's Just Another Trivial Formula:

$$\text{Work Done} = \text{Force} \times \text{Distance}$$

Whether the force is <u>friction</u> or <u>weight</u> or <u>tension in a rope</u>, it's always the same. To find how much <u>energy</u> has been <u>transferred</u> (in joules), you just multiply the <u>force in N</u> by the <u>distance moved in m</u>. Easy as that. I'll show you...

<u>EXAMPLE:</u> Some hooligan kids drag an old tractor tyre <u>5 m</u> over rough ground. They pull with a total force of <u>340 N</u>. Find the energy transferred.
<u>ANSWER:</u> W = F×d = 340 × 5 = <u>1700 J</u>.   Phew — easy peasy isn't it?

Power **is the "Rate of Doing Work"** — i.e. How Much per Second

<u>Power</u> is <u>not</u> the same thing as <u>force</u>, nor <u>energy</u>. A <u>powerful</u> machine is not necessarily one which can exert a strong <u>force</u> (though it usually ends up that way). A <u>powerful</u> machine is one which transfers <u>a lot of energy in a short space of time</u>. This is the <u>very easy formula</u> for power:

$$\text{Power} = \frac{\text{Work done (energy transferred)}}{\text{Time taken}}$$

<u>EXAMPLE:</u> A motor transfers 4.8 kJ of useful energy in 2 minutes. Find its power output.
<u>ANSWER:</u> P = E / t = 4800/120 = 40 W (or 40 J/s)
(Note that the kJ had to be turned into J, and the minutes into seconds.)

1 kJ = 1000 J

4.8 kJ of useful energy in 2 minutes

Power **is Measured in Watts (or J/s)**

The proper unit of power is the <u>watt</u> (W). <u>One watt = 1 joule of energy transferred per second</u>. <u>Power</u> means "how much energy <u>per second</u>", so <u>watts</u> are the same as "<u>joules per second</u>" (J/s). Don't ever say "watts per second" — it's <u>nonsense</u>.

Revise work done — what else...

Remember "<u>energy transferred</u>" and "<u>work done</u>" are the same thing. By lifting something up you do work by transferring <u>chemical energy</u> to <u>gravitational potential energy</u>. Think about that next time you're bench-pressing sheep.

Kinetic Energy

Anything that's <u>moving</u> has <u>kinetic energy</u>. There's a slightly <u>tricky formula</u> for it, so you have to concentrate a little bit <u>harder</u> for this one. But hey, that's life — it can be real tough sometimes.

Kinetic Energy *is Energy of* Movement

1) The <u>kinetic energy</u> (<u>K.E.</u>) of something is the energy it has when <u>moving</u>.

2) The <u>kinetic energy</u> of something depends on both its <u>mass</u> and <u>speed</u>.

3) The <u>greater its mass</u> and the <u>faster it's going</u>, the <u>bigger</u> its kinetic energy will be.

Sometimes kinetic energy is written as E_k.

4) For example, a <u>high-speed train</u>, or a <u>speedboat</u>, will have <u>lots of kinetic energy</u> — but your gran doing the weekly shop on her <u>little scooter</u> will only have a <u>little bit</u>.

5) You need to know how to use the <u>formula</u>:

$$\text{Kinetic Energy} = \tfrac{1}{2} \times \text{mass} \times \text{speed}^2$$

K.E.
$$\frac{\text{K.E.}}{\tfrac{1}{2} \times m \times v^2}$$

<u>EXAMPLE:</u>   A car of mass <u>1450 kg</u> is travelling at <u>28 m/s</u>. Calculate its kinetic energy.

<u>ANSWER:</u>   It's pretty easy. You just plug the numbers into the formula — but watch the 'v^2'!
K.E. $= \tfrac{1}{2}mv^2 = \tfrac{1}{2} \times 1450 \times 28^2 = $ <u>568 400 J</u>. (<u>Joules</u> because it's <u>energy</u>.)

6) If you <u>double the mass</u>, the <u>K.E. doubles</u>. If you <u>double the speed</u>, though, the <u>K.E. quadruples</u> (increases by a factor of <u>4</u>) — it's because of the 'v^2' in the formula.

small mass, not fast
low kinetic energy

big fast
lorries Ltd

big mass, real fast
high kinetic energy

Stopping Distances Increase Alarmingly *with* Extra Speed
— Mainly Because of the v^2 *Bit in the* K.E. Formula

1) To stop a car, the <u>kinetic energy</u>, $\tfrac{1}{2}mv^2$, has to be <u>converted to heat energy</u> at the <u>brakes and tyres</u>:

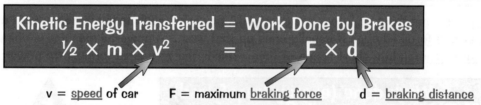

Kinetic Energy Transferred = Work Done by Brakes
$$\tfrac{1}{2} \times m \times v^2 \qquad = \qquad F \times d$$

v = <u>speed</u> of car   F = maximum <u>braking force</u>   d = <u>braking distance</u>

2) The <u>braking distance</u> (d) increases as <u>speed squared</u> (v^2) increases — it's a <u>squared relationship</u>.

3) This means if you <u>double the speed</u>, you double the value of <u>v</u>, but the v^2 means that the <u>K.E.</u> is then increased by a factor of <u>four</u>.

4) Because 'F' is always the <u>maximum possible</u> braking force (which <u>can't</u> be increased), <u>d</u> must increase by a factor of <u>four</u> to make the equation <u>balance</u>.

5) In other words, if you go <u>twice as fast</u>, the <u>braking distance</u> must increase by a <u>factor of four</u> to convert the <u>extra K.E.</u>

Look back at page 103 for more on braking distances.

6) Increasing the speed by a <u>factor of 3</u> increases the K.E. by a factor of $\underline{3}^2$ (= <u>9</u>), so the braking distance becomes <u>9 times as long</u>.

7) <u>Doubling the mass</u> of the object <u>doubles the K.E.</u> it has — which will <u>double the braking distance</u>. So a big heavy lorry will need <u>more space to stop</u> than a small car.

Stopping distance — I can carry on for miles...

So <u>that's</u> why braking distance goes up so much with speed. This stuff is really <u>scary</u> when you start thinking about it. If you're in a car travelling at <u>30 mph</u> you'll stop in about <u>23 metres</u>, but if you're travelling at <u>60 mph</u> in the same car it'll take you over <u>90 metres</u> to stop... You have been warned.

Gravitational Potential Energy

Anything that's <u>raised</u> above the ground has <u>gravitational potential energy</u> (G.P.E. or E_p).

Gravitational Potential Energy is Energy Due to Height

Gravitational Potential Energy = mass × g × height

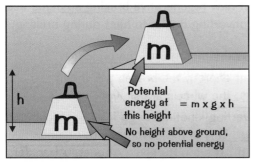

Potential energy at this height = m × g × h

No height above ground, so no potential energy

Gravitational potential energy (measured in joules) is the energy that an object has by virtue of (because of) its <u>vertical position</u> in a <u>gravitational field</u>. When an object is raised vertically, <u>work is done</u> against the <u>force of gravity</u> (it takes effort to lift it up) and the object gains gravitational potential energy. On <u>Earth</u> the gravitational field strength (g) is approximately <u>10 N/kg</u>.

<u>EXAMPLE:</u> A sheep of mass 47 kg is slowly raised through 6.3 m. Find the gain in potential energy.
<u>ANSWER:</u> Just plug the numbers into the formula:
G.P.E. = m × g × h = 47 × 10 × 6.3 = <u>2961 J</u> (<u>Joules</u> because it's <u>energy</u>.)

Falling Objects Convert G.P.E. into K.E.

1) When something <u>falls</u>, its <u>gravitational potential energy</u> is <u>converted</u> into <u>kinetic energy</u> (K.E.). So the <u>further</u> it falls, the <u>faster</u> it goes.

2) In practice, some of the G.P.E. will be <u>dissipated</u> as <u>heat</u> due to <u>air resistance</u>, but in exam questions they'll likely say you can <u>ignore</u> air resistance, in which case you can use this <u>simple</u> and <u>really quite obvious</u> formula:

K.E. <u>gained</u> = G.P.E. <u>lost</u>

3) For example, the roller coaster to the right will <u>lose G.P.E.</u> and <u>gain K.E.</u> as it falls between points <u>A and C</u>.

4) If you <u>ignore friction</u> (between the tracks and the wheels) and <u>air resistance</u>, the amount of <u>K.E.</u> it gains will be <u>the same</u> as the amount of <u>G.P.E.</u> it loses.

5) Between <u>C and D</u>, it's <u>gaining height</u>, so some of that K.E. is <u>converted back</u> to G.P.E. again.

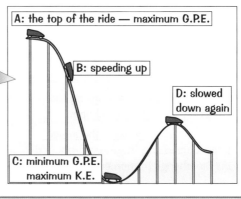

A: the top of the ride — maximum G.P.E.
B: speeding up
D: slowed down again
C: minimum G.P.E. maximum K.E.

<u>EXAMPLE:</u> The carriage in the diagram above has a weight of <u>5000 N</u> (mass about 500 kg), and the vertical height difference between A and C is <u>20 m</u>.

a) Ignoring friction and air resistance, how much <u>K.E.</u> is gained by the carriage in moving from A to C?

b) The roller coaster was stationary at A. Calculate its <u>speed</u> at C.

Weight is the <u>force</u> due to an object's <u>mass</u> and <u>gravity</u>. Weight = mass × acceleration due to <u>gravity</u> (about 10 m/s²).

<u>ANSWER:</u> a) K.E. gained = G.P.E. lost = weight × vertical height difference = 5000 × 20 = <u>100 000 J</u>

b) At C it has 100 000 J of K.E. You know that K.E. = ½mv² (see previous page), so...

If you know how much K.E. something's gained you can calculate it's speed. Handy.

½mv² = 100 000
v² = 100 000 ÷ ½m = 100 000 ÷ (½ × 500) = 400
v = √400 = <u>20 m/s</u>

Revise roller coasters — don't let your thoughts wander off into oblivion...

In reality, energy will be lost due to friction, air resistance and even as sound. But you can usually ignore these.

Car Design and Safety

A lot of the physics from the last few pages can be applied in the real world to designing safe, efficient cars.

Brakes do Work Against the Kinetic Energy of the Car

When you apply the brakes to slow down a car, work is done (see p.105).
The brakes reduce the kinetic energy of the car by transferring it into heat (and sound) energy.
In traditional braking systems that would be the end of the story, but new regenerative braking systems used in some electric or hybrid cars make use of the energy, instead of converting it all into heat during braking.

1) Regenerative brakes use the system that drives the vehicle to do the majority of the braking.

2) Rather than converting the kinetic energy of the vehicle into heat energy, the brakes put the vehicle's motor into reverse. With the motor running backwards, the wheels are slowed.

3) At the same time, the motor acts as an electric generator, converting kinetic energy into electrical energy that is stored as chemical energy in the vehicle's battery. This is the advantage of regenerative brakes — they store the energy of braking rather than wasting it. It's a nifty chain of energy transfer.

ABS (anti-lock braking system) brakes help drivers keep control of the car's steering when braking hard. They automatically pump on and off to stop the wheels locking and prevent skidding.

Cars are Designed to Convert Kinetic Energy Safely in a Crash

1) If a car crashes it will slow down very quickly — this means that a lot of kinetic energy is converted into other forms of energy in a short amount of time, which can be dangerous for the people inside.

2) In a crash, there'll be a big change in momentum (see p.104) over a very short time, so the people inside the car experience huge forces that could be fatal.

3) Cars are designed to convert the kinetic energy of the car and its passengers in a way that is safest for the car's occupants. They often do this by increasing the time over which momentum changes happen, which lessens the forces on the passengers.

airbag

seat belt

CRUMPLE ZONES at the front and back of the car crumple up on impact.

- The car's kinetic energy is converted into other forms of energy by the car body as it changes shape.
- Crumple zones increase the impact time, decreasing the force produced by the change in momentum.

SIDE IMPACT BARS are strong metal tubes fitted into car door panels. They help direct the kinetic energy of the crash away from the passengers to other areas of the car, such as the crumple zones.

SEAT BELTS stretch slightly, increasing the time taken for the wearer to stop. This reduces the forces acting in the chest. Some of the kinetic energy of the wearer is absorbed by the seat belt stretching.

AIR BAGS also slow you down more gradually and prevent you from hitting hard surfaces inside the car.

Cars Have Different Power Ratings

1) The size and design of car engines determine how powerful they are.

2) The more powerful an engine is, the more energy it transfers from its fuel every second, and so the faster its top speed can be.

3) E.g. the power output of a typical small car will be around 50 kW and a sports car will be about 100 kW (some are much higher).

Sports car power = 100 kW

Small car power = 50 kW

4) Cars are also designed to be aerodynamic. This means that they are shaped in such a way that air flows very easily and smoothly past them, so minimising their air resistance.

5) Cars reach their top speed when the resistive force equals the driving force provided by the engine (see p.102). So, with less air resistance to overcome, the car can reach a higher speed before this happens. Aerodynamic cars therefore have higher top speeds.

Don't let all this revising drive you crazy...

A car's safety features are tested using crash test dummies to make sure it's safe. The dummies have sensors at different places on their 'bodies' to show where a real person would be injured, and how bad the injury would be.

Forces and Elasticity

Forces aren't just important for cars and falling sheep — you can <u>stretch things</u> with them as well.
It can sound quite tricky at first, but it's not as hard as it looks.

Work Done to an <u>Elastic Object</u> is <u>Stored</u> as <u>Elastic Potential Energy</u>

1) When you apply a force to an object you may
cause it to <u>stretch</u> and <u>change in shape</u>.

2) Any object that can <u>go back</u> to its <u>original shape</u>
after the force has been removed is an <u>elastic object</u>.

3) <u>Work is done</u> to an elastic object to <u>change</u> its shape.
This energy is not lost but is <u>stored</u> by the object as <u>elastic potential energy</u>.

4) The elastic potential energy is then <u>converted to kinetic energy</u>
when the <u>force is removed</u> and the object returns to its original
shape, e.g. when a spring or an elastic band bounces back.

Elastic potential energy — useful
for passing exams and scaring
small children

<u>Extension</u> of an Elastic Object is <u>Directly Proportional</u> to Force...

If a spring is supported at the top and then a weight attached to the bottom, it <u>stretches</u>.

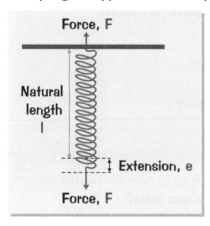

Force, F

Natural
length
l

Extension, e

Force, F

1) The <u>extension</u>, <u>e</u>, of a stretched spring
(or other elastic object) is <u>directly proportional</u>
to the load or <u>force</u> applied, <u>F</u>.
The extension is measured in metres,
and the force is measured in newtons.

2) This is the <u>equation</u> that links the force
applied and the extension of the spring:

$$F = k \times e$$

3) k is the <u>spring constant</u>. Its value
depends on the <u>material</u> that you are
stretching and it's measured in newtons
per metre (N/m).

...but this <u>Stops Working</u> when the <u>Force</u> is <u>Great Enough</u>

There's a <u>limit</u> to the amount of force you can apply to an object
for the extension to keep on increasing <u>proportionally</u>.

1) The graph shows <u>force against
extension</u> for an elastic object.

2) For small forces, force and extension are
<u>proportional</u>. So the first part of the graph shows a
straight-line relationship between force and extension.

3) There is a <u>maximum</u> force that the elastic
object can take and still extend proportionally.
This is known as the <u>limit of proportionality</u> and
is shown on the graph at the point marked P.

4) If you increase the force <u>past</u> the limit of
proportionality, the material will be <u>permanently
stretched</u>. When the force is <u>removed</u>, the
material will be <u>longer</u> than at the start.

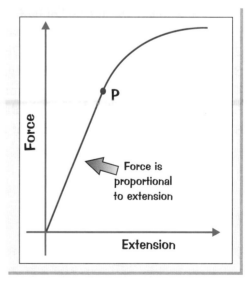

P

Force

Force is
proportional
to extension

Extension

I could make a joke, but I don't want to stretch myself...

Scaring small children aside, elastic potential is really <u>quite a useful</u> form of energy. Think of all the things we rely on
that use it — catapults, trampolines, scrunchies... Ah, elastic potential energy — thank you for enriching our lives.

Revision Summary for Section 7

Well done — you've made it to the end of another section. There are loads of bits and bobs about forces, motion and fast cars which you have to learn. The best way to find out what you know is to get stuck into these lovely revision questions, which you're going to really enjoy (honest)...

1) What's the difference between speed and velocity?
2) What is acceleration? What are its units?
3)* Write down the formula for acceleration. What's the acceleration of a soggy pea flicked from rest to a speed of 14 m/s in 0.4 seconds?
4) Sketch a typical distance-time graph and point out all the important parts of it.
5) Explain how to calculate speed from a distance-time graph.
6) Sketch a typical velocity-time graph and point out all the important parts of it.
7) Explain how to find speed, distance and acceleration from a velocity-time graph.
8) Explain the difference between mass and weight. What units are they measured in?
9) Explain what is meant by a "resultant force".
10) If an object has zero resultant force on it, can it be moving? Can it be accelerating?
11)* Write down the formula relating resultant force and acceleration.
A resultant force of 30 N pushes a trolley of mass 4 kg. What will be its acceleration?
12)* A skydiver has a mass of 75 kg. At 80 mph, the drag force on the skydiver is 650 N.
Find the acceleration of the skydiver at 80 mph (take g = 10 N/kg).
13)* A yeti pushes a tree with a force of 120 N. What is the size of the reaction force that the Yeti feels pushing back at him?
14) What is "terminal velocity"?
15) What are the two different parts of the overall stopping distance of a car?
16) Write down the formula for momentum.
17) If the total momentum of a system before a collision is zero, what is the total momentum of the system after the collision?
18)* Write down the formula for work done. A crazy dog drags a big branch 12 m over the next-door neighbour's front lawn, pulling with a force of 535 N. How much work was done?
19)* What's the formula for kinetic energy? Find the kinetic energy of a 78 kg sheep moving at 23 m/s.
20)* A car of mass 1000 kg is travelling at a velocity of 2 m/s when a dazed and confused sheep runs out 5 m in front. If the driver immediately applies the maximum braking force of 395 N, can he avoid hitting it?
21)* A 4 kg cheese is taken 30 m up a hill before being rolled back down again. If g = 10 N/kg:
a) how much gravitational potential energy does the cheese have at the top of the hill?
b) how much gravitational potential energy does it have when it gets half way down?
22)* Calculate the kinetic energy of a 78 kg sheep just as she hits the floor after falling through 20 m.
23) What is the advantage of using regenerative braking systems?
24) Explain how seat belts, crumple zones, side impact bars and air bags are useful in a crash.
25) Write down the equation that relates the force on a spring and its extension.
26) What happens to an elastic object that is stretched beyond its limit of proportionality?

* Answers on page 142.

Static Electricity

Static electricity's all about <u>charges</u> which are <u>not free to move</u>. This causes them to build up in one place, and lead to <u>sparks</u> or <u>shocks</u> when they finally do move — <u>crackling</u> when you take a jumper off, say...

Build-up of Static is Caused by Friction

1) When two <u>insulating</u> materials are <u>rubbed</u> together, negatively charged electrons will be <u>scraped off one</u> and <u>dumped</u> on the other.

2) This'll leave a <u>positive</u> static charge on one and a <u>negative</u> static charge on the other.

3) <u>Which way</u> the electrons are transferred <u>depends</u> on the <u>two materials</u> involved.

4) Electrically charged objects <u>attract</u> small objects placed near them.

5) The classic examples are <u>polythene</u> and <u>acetate</u> rods being rubbed with a <u>cloth duster</u>, as shown in the diagrams.

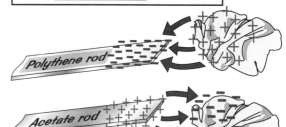

With the <u>polythene rod</u>, electrons move <u>from the duster</u> to the rod.

With the <u>acetate rod</u>, electrons move <u>from the rod</u> to the duster.

Only Electrons Move — Never the Positive Charges

Both +ve and −ve electrostatic charges are only ever produced by the movement of <u>electrons</u>. The positive charges <u>definitely do not move</u>! A positive static charge is always caused by electrons <u>moving</u> away elsewhere. The material that <u>loses</u> the electrons loses some negative charge, and is <u>left with an equal positive charge</u>, as shown above. Don't forget!

Like Charges Repel, Opposite Charges Attract

Two things with <u>opposite</u> electric charges are <u>attracted</u> to each other. Two things with the <u>same</u> electric charge will <u>repel</u> each other.

When you rub two <u>insulating</u> materials together a whole load of <u>electrons</u> get dumped <u>together</u> on one of the insulators, which becomes <u>negatively charged</u>. They try to <u>repel</u> each other, but <u>can't move</u> apart because their positions are fixed. The patch of charge that results is called <u>static electricity</u> because it can't move.

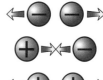

Static Electricity can be a Little Joker

Static electricity is responsible for some of life's little <u>annoyances</u>...

1) Attracting Dust

<u>Dust particles</u> are really tiny and lightweight and are easily <u>attracted</u> to anything that's <u>charged</u>. Unfortunately, many objects around the house are made of <u>insulating</u> materials (e.g. glass, wood, plastic) that get <u>easily charged</u> and attract the dust particles — this makes cleaning a <u>nightmare</u>. (Have a look at how dusty your TV screen is.)

2) Clinging Clothes and Crackles

When <u>synthetic clothes</u> are <u>dragged</u> over each other (like in a <u>tumble drier</u>) or over your <u>head</u>, electrons get scraped off, leaving <u>static charges</u> on both parts, and that leads to the inevitable — <u>attraction</u> (they stick together and cling to you) and little <u>sparks</u> or <u>shocks</u> as the charges <u>rearrange themselves</u>.

3) Bad Hair Days

Static builds up on your hair, giving each <u>strand</u> the same <u>charge</u> — so they <u>repel</u> each other.

Static caravans — where electrons go on holiday...

Static electricity's great fun. You must have tried it — rubbing a <u>balloon</u> against your <u>jumper</u> and trying to get it to stick to the ceiling. It really works... well, sometimes, and if at first you don't succeed, try, try again...

Dangers and Uses of Static Electricity

Static Electricity Can be Dangerous...

1) A Lot of Charge Can Build Up on Clothes

1) A large amount of static charge can build up on clothes made out of synthetic materials if they rub against other synthetic fabrics (see p.111).

2) Eventually, this charge can become large enough to make a spark — which is really bad news if it happens near any inflammable gases or fuel fumes... KABOOM!

2) Grain Chutes, Paper Rollers and the Fuel Filling Nightmare

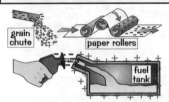

grain chute   paper rollers   fuel tank

1) As fuel flows out of a filler pipe, or paper drags over rollers, or grain shoots out of pipes, then static can build up.

2) This can easily lead to a spark and might cause an explosion in dusty or fumey places — like when filling up a car with fuel at a petrol station.

3) All these problems with sparks can be solved by earthing charged objects.

Objects Can be Earthed or Insulated to Prevent Sparks

1) Dangerous sparks can be prevented by connecting a charged object to the ground using a conductor (e.g. a copper wire) — this is called earthing and it provides an easy route for the static charges to travel into the ground. This means no charge can build up to give you a shock or make a spark.

2) Static charges are a big problem in places where sparks could ignite inflammable gases, or where there are high concentrations of oxygen (e.g. in a hospital operating theatre).

3) Fuel tankers must be earthed to prevent any sparks that might cause the fuel to explode — refuelling aircraft are bonded to their fuel tankers using an earthing cable to prevent sparks.

4) Anti-static sprays and liquids work by making the surface of a charged object conductive — this provides an easy path for the charges to move away and not cause a problem.

5) Anti-static cloths are conductive, so they can carry charge away from objects they're used to wipe.

6) Insulating mats and shoes with insulating soles prevent static electricity from moving through them, so they stop you from getting a shock.

...But it can also be Pretty Useful

1) Bikes and cars are painted using electrostatic paint sprayers. The spray gun is charged, which charges up the small drops of paint. Each paint drop repels all the others, since they've all got the same charge, so you get a very fine spray. The object to be painted is given an opposite charge to the gun and attracts the fine spray of paint. This method gives an even coat, hardly any paint is wasted and parts of the object pointing away from the spray gun still receive paint too — there are no paint shadows.

2) Dust precipitators use static electricity to clean up emissions from factories and power stations. Dust particles become negatively charged as they pass through a charged wire grid in the chimney. The negatively charged dust particles then stick to earthed metal plates and eventually fall to the bottom of the chimney where they can be removed.

Chimney

Earthed metal plates

Negatively charged grid

3) An electric shock from a defibrillator can restart a stopped heart. The defibrillator consists of two paddles connected to a power supply which are placed firmly on the patient's chest. The defibrillator operator holds insulated handles — so only the patient gets a shock. The charge passes through the paddles to the patient to make the heart contract.

Static electricity — it's really shocking stuff...

Lightning is an extreme case of a static electricity spark. It always chooses the easiest path between the sky and the ground — that's the nearest, tallest thing. That's why it's never a good idea to fly a kite in a thunderstorm...

Current and Potential Difference

Isn't <u>electricity</u> great. Mind you it's pretty bad news if the <u>words</u> don't mean anything to you...

1) **Current** is the <u>flow</u> of electric charge round the circuit. Current will <u>only flow</u> through a component if there is a <u>potential difference</u> across that component. Unit: ampere, A.

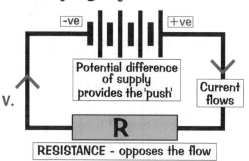

2) **Potential Difference** is the <u>driving force</u> that pushes the current round. It's also called the <u>voltage</u> Unit: volt, V.

3) **Resistance** is anything in the circuit which <u>slows the flow down</u>. Unit: ohm, Ω.

4) There's a <u>balance</u>: the <u>voltage</u> is trying to <u>push</u> the current round the circuit, and the <u>resistance</u> is <u>opposing</u> it — the <u>relative sizes</u> of the voltage and resistance decide <u>how big</u> the current will be:

> If you <u>increase the VOLTAGE</u> — then **MORE CURRENT** will flow.
> If you <u>increase the RESISTANCE</u> — then **LESS CURRENT** will flow
> (or **MORE VOLTAGE** will be needed to keep the **SAME CURRENT** flowing).

Total Charge Through a Circuit Depends on Current and Time

1) <u>Current</u> is the <u>rate of flow</u> of <u>charge</u>. When <u>current</u> (I) flows past a point in a circuit for a length of <u>time</u> (t) then the <u>charge</u> (Q) that has passed is given by this formula:

2) <u>Current</u> is measured in <u>amperes</u> (A), <u>charge</u> is measured in <u>coulombs</u> (C), <u>time</u> is measured in <u>seconds</u> (s).

$$\text{Current} = \frac{\text{Charge}}{\text{Time}} \qquad I = \frac{Q}{t}$$

3) In the <u>metal wires</u> of a circuit, this charge is carried by <u>electrons</u>. Metals are <u>good conductors</u> as they have <u>free electrons</u> which are able to move.

4) <u>More charge</u> passes around the circuit when a <u>bigger current</u> flows.

Potential Difference (P. D.) is the Work Done Per Unit Charge

1) The potential difference is the <u>work done</u> (the energy transferred, measured in joules, J) <u>per coulomb of charge</u> that passes between <u>two points</u> in an electrical circuit. It's given by this formula:

2) So, the potential difference across an electrical component is the <u>amount of energy</u> that is transferred by that electrical component (e.g. to light and heat energy by a bulb) <u>per unit of charge</u>.

$$\text{P.D.} = \frac{\text{Work done}}{\text{Charge}}$$

A Voltmeter Measures Potential Difference Between Two Points

1) A <u>battery</u> transfers energy <u>to</u> the charge as it passes — that's the "<u>push</u>" that moves the charge round the circuit.

2) <u>Components</u> transfer energy <u>away from</u> the charge as it passes — e.g. to use as <u>light</u> in a lamp or <u>sound</u> in a buzzer.

3) The voltage of a battery shows <u>how much</u> work the battery will do to charge that passes <u>through it</u> (how big a "<u>push</u>" it gives it).

4) A <u>voltmeter</u> is used to measure the <u>potential difference</u> between <u>two points</u>.

The battery <u>transfers energy to</u> the charge as it passes.

direction that current is moving

The lamp transfers the same amount of <u>energy from</u> the charge as it passes (and converts it to light and heat).

5) A voltmeter must be placed in <u>parallel</u> (see p.118) with a component so it can <u>compare</u> the energy the charge has <u>before</u> and <u>after</u> passing through the component (as in the diagram).

I think it's about time you took charge...

An interesting fact — the volt is named after Count Alessandro Volta, an Italian physicist. Ooooooh...

Circuits — The Basics

Formulas are mighty pretty and all, but you might have to design some <u>electrical circuits</u> as well one day. For that you're gonna need <u>circuit symbols</u>. Well, would you look at that... they're on this page.

Each Component Has a Circuit Symbol

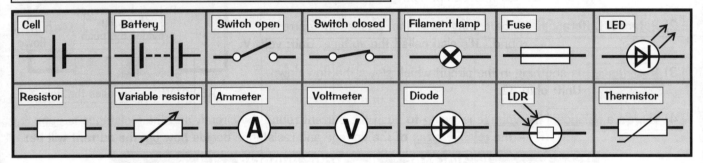

The Standard Test Circuit

This is the circuit you use if you want to know the <u>resistance of a component</u>. You find the resistance by measuring the <u>current through</u> and the <u>potential difference across</u> the component. It is absolutely the most <u>bog standard</u> circuit you could know.

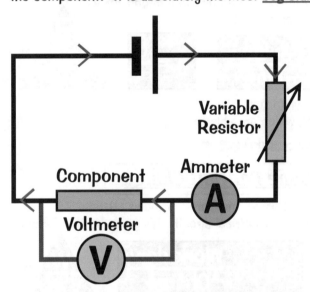

The Ammeter

1) Measures the <u>current</u> (in <u>amps</u>) flowing through the component.
2) Must be placed <u>in series</u> (see p.117).
3) Can be put <u>anywhere</u> in series in the <u>main circuit</u>, but <u>never</u> in parallel like the voltmeter.

The Voltmeter

1) Measures the <u>potential difference</u> (in <u>volts</u>) across the component.
2) Must be placed <u>in parallel</u> (see p.118) around the <u>component</u> under test — <u>NOT</u> around the variable resistor or the battery!

Five Important Points

1) This <u>very basic</u> circuit is used for testing <u>components</u>, and for getting <u>V-I graphs</u> from them (see next page).
2) The <u>component</u>, the <u>ammeter</u> and the <u>variable resistor</u> are all in <u>series</u>, which means they can be put in <u>any order</u> in the main circuit. The <u>voltmeter</u>, on the other hand, can only be placed <u>in parallel</u> around the <u>component under test</u>, as shown. Anywhere else is a definite <u>no-no</u>.
3) As you <u>vary</u> the <u>variable resistor</u> it alters the <u>current</u> flowing through the circuit.
4) This allows you to take several <u>pairs of readings</u> from the <u>ammeter</u> and <u>voltmeter</u>.
5) You can then <u>plot</u> these values for <u>current</u> and <u>voltage</u> on a <u>V-I graph</u> and find the <u>resistance</u>.

Measure gymnastics — use a vaultmeter...

The funny thing is — the <u>electrons</u> in circuits actually move from <u>−ve to +ve</u>... but scientists always think of <u>current</u> as flowing from <u>+ve to −ve</u>. Basically it's just because that's how the <u>early physicists</u> thought of it (before they found out about the electrons), and now it's become <u>convention</u>.

Resistance and V = I × R

With your current and your potential difference measured, you can now make some <u>sweet</u> graphs...

Three Potential Difference-Current Graphs

V-I graphs show how the <u>current</u> varies as you <u>change</u> the <u>potential difference</u> (P.D.).

Different Resistors	Filament Lamp	Diode
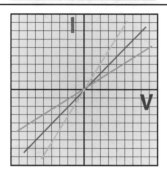	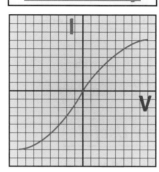	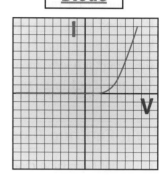

The current through a <u>resistor</u> (at constant temperature) is <u>directly proportional</u> to P.D. <u>Different resistors</u> have different resistances, hence the different <u>slopes</u>.

As the <u>temperature</u> of the filament <u>increases</u>, the <u>resistance increases</u>, hence the <u>curve</u>.

Current will only flow through a diode <u>in one direction</u>, as shown. The diode has very <u>high resistance</u> in the opposite direction.

Resistance <u>Increases</u> <u>with</u> Temperature

1) When an electrical charge flows through a resistor, some of the electrical energy is <u>transferred to heat energy</u> and the resistor gets <u>hot</u>.

2) This heat energy causes the <u>ions</u> in the conductor to <u>vibrate more</u>. With the ions jiggling around it's <u>more difficult</u> for the charge-carrying electrons to get through the resistor — the <u>current can't flow</u> as easily and the <u>resistance increases</u>.

3) A <u>filament lamp</u> contains a piece of wire with a really <u>high</u> resistance. When current passes through it, its <u>temperature increases</u> so much that it <u>glows</u> — which is the <u>light</u> you see.

4) For most resistors there is a <u>limit</u> to the amount of current that can flow. More current means an <u>increase</u> in <u>temperature</u>, which means an <u>increase</u> in <u>resistance</u>, which means the <u>current decreases</u> again.

5) This is why the graph for the filament lamp <u>levels off</u> at high currents.

Resistance, Potential Difference <u>and</u> Current: V = I × R

Potential Difference = Current × Resistance

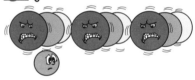

For the <u>straight-line graphs</u> above, the resistance of the component is <u>steady</u> and is equal to the <u>inverse</u> of the <u>gradient</u> of the line, or "<u>1/gradient</u>". In other words, the <u>steeper</u> the graph the <u>lower</u> the resistance.

If the graph <u>curves</u>, it means the resistance is <u>changing</u>. In that case R can be found for any point by taking the <u>pair of values</u> (V, I) from the graph and sticking them in the formula <u>R = V/I</u>. Easy.

EXAMPLE: Voltmeter V reads 6 V and resistor R is 4 Ω. What is the current through Ammeter A?

ANSWER: Use the formula triangle for V = I × R. We need to find I, so the version we need is I = V/R. The answer is then: I = 6 ÷ 4 = 1.5 A.

<u>In the end you'll have to start revising — resistance is futile...</u>

When <u>interpreting</u> potential difference-current graphs, remember the <u>steeper</u> the <u>slope</u>, the <u>lower</u> the <u>resistance</u>. A bit like rollerblading down a steep, icy footpath on a hill. Painful memories. Very painful memories.

Circuit Devices

You might consider yourself a bit of an <u>expert</u> in circuit components — you're enlightened about bulbs, you're switched on to switches... But take a look at these ones as well — they're a <u>little bit trickier</u>.

Current Only Flows in One Direction through a Diode

1) A diode is a special device made from <u>semiconductor</u> material such as <u>silicon</u>.

2) It is used to <u>regulate</u> the <u>potential difference</u> in circuits.

3) It lets current flow freely through it in <u>one direction</u>, but <u>not</u> in the other (i.e. there's a very high resistance in the <u>reverse</u> direction).

4) This turns out to be real useful in various <u>electronic circuits</u>.

Light-Emitting Diodes are Very Useful

1) A <u>light-emitting diode</u> (LED) emits light when a current flows through it in the <u>forward direction</u>.

2) LEDs are being used more and more as lighting, as they use a much <u>smaller current</u> than other forms of lighting.

3) LEDs indicate the presence of current in a circuit. They're often used in appliances (e.g. TVs) to show that they are <u>switched on</u>.

4) They're also used for the numbers on <u>digital clocks</u>, in <u>traffic lights</u> and in <u>remote controls</u>.

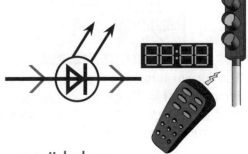

A Light-Dependent Resistor or "LDR" to You

1) An LDR is a resistor that is <u>dependent</u> on the <u>intensity</u> of <u>light</u>. Simple really.

2) In <u>bright light</u>, the resistance <u>falls</u>.

3) In <u>darkness</u>, the resistance is <u>highest</u>.

4) They have lots of applications including <u>automatic night lights</u>, outdoor lighting and <u>burglar detectors</u>.

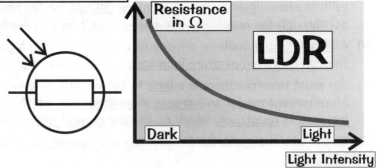

The Resistance of a Thermistor Decreases as Temperature Increases

1) A <u>thermistor</u> is a <u>temperature dependent</u> resistor.

2) In <u>hot</u> conditions, the resistance <u>drops</u>.

3) In <u>cool</u> conditions, the resistance goes <u>up</u>.

4) Thermistors make useful <u>temperature detectors</u>, e.g. <u>car engine</u> temperature sensors and electronic <u>thermostats</u>.

LDRs — Light-Dependent Rabbits...

LDRs are good triggers in security systems, because they can detect when the <u>light intensity</u> changes. So if a robber walks in front of a <u>beam of light</u> pointed at the LDR, the <u>resistance shoots up</u> and an alarm goes off.

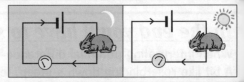

Series Circuits

You can tell the difference between series and parallel circuits <u>just by looking at them</u>.

Series Circuits — Everything in a Line

In <u>series circuits</u>, the different components are connected <u>in a line</u>, <u>end to end</u>, between the +ve and –ve of the power supply (except for <u>voltmeters</u>, which are always connected <u>in parallel</u>, but they don't count).

Potential Difference is Shared:

1) In series circuits, the <u>total</u> <u>potential difference</u> (P.D.) of the <u>supply</u> is <u>shared</u> between the various <u>components</u>. So the <u>P.D.s</u> round a series circuit always <u>add up</u> to equal the P.D. across the <u>battery</u>: $\boxed{V = V_1 + V_2}$

2) This is because the total <u>work done</u> <u>on</u> the charge by the <u>battery</u> must equal the total <u>work done</u> <u>by</u> the charge on the <u>components</u>.

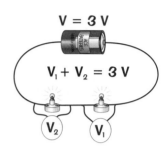

V = 3 V

$V_1 + V_2 = 3\ V$

V_2 V_1

Current is the Same Everywhere:

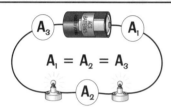

$A_1 = A_2 = A_3$

1) In series circuits the <u>same current</u> flows through <u>all parts</u> of the circuit: $\boxed{A_1 = A_2 = A_3}$

2) The <u>size</u> of the current is determined by the <u>total P.D.</u> of the cells and the <u>total resistance</u> of the circuit: i.e. $I = V/R$. This means <u>all</u> the components get the same <u>current</u>.

Resistance Adds Up:

1) In series circuits, the <u>total resistance</u> is just the <u>sum</u> of the individual resistances: $\boxed{R = R_1 + R_2 + R_3}$

2) The resistance of <u>two</u> (or more) resistors in <u>series</u> is <u>bigger</u> than the resistance of just one of the resistors on its own because the <u>battery</u> has to <u>push charge</u> through <u>all</u> of them.

3) The <u>bigger</u> the resistance of a component, the bigger its <u>share</u> of the <u>total P.D.</u> because more <u>work is done</u> by the charge when moving through a <u>large</u> resistance, than through a <u>small</u> one.

4) If the resistance of <u>one</u> component <u>changes</u> (e.g. if it's a variable resistor, light-dependent resistor or thermistor) then the <u>potential difference</u> across <u>all</u> the components will change too.

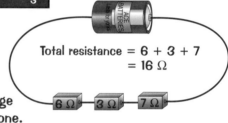

Total resistance = 6 + 3 + 7
= 16 Ω

6 Ω   3 Ω   7 Ω

Cell Voltages Add Up:

1) If you connect <u>several cells in series</u>, <u>all the same way</u> (+ to –) you get a <u>bigger total voltage</u> — because each charge in the circuit passes though all the cells and gets a 'push' from each cell in turn.

2) So <u>two 1.5 V cells</u> <u>in series</u> would supply <u>3 V in total</u>.

3) Cell voltages <u>don't</u> add up like that for cells connected <u>in parallel</u>. Each charge only goes through <u>one cell</u>.

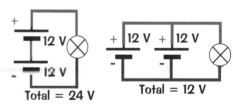

Total = 24 V   Total = 12 V

Cell Current Doesn't Add Up:

1) Adding cells in <u>series</u> <u>doesn't increase the current</u> in a circuit. The <u>maximum current</u> in the circuit will just be the <u>same</u> as if you had <u>one cell</u> in the circuit.

2) Cells connected in <u>parallel</u> <u>increase the total current</u> in the circuit. However, the current through <u>each cell</u> is <u>less</u> than in the rest of the circuit because they <u>join together</u> to make the total current.

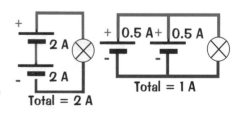

Total = 2 A   Total = 1 A

Series circuits — they're no laughing matter...

If you connect some <u>lamps</u> in <u>series</u> and one of them <u>breaks</u> then <u>all</u> of them stop working. This is <u>unhelpful</u>.

Parallel Circuits

Parallel circuits are much more sensible than series circuits and so they're much more common in real life. All the electrics in your house will be wired in parallel circuits.

Parallel Circuits — Independence and Isolation

1) In parallel circuits, each component is separately connected to the +ve and –ve of the supply.

2) If you remove or disconnect one of them, it will hardly affect the others at all.

3) This is obviously how most things must be connected, for example in cars and in household electrics. You have to be able to switch everything on and off separately.

1) P.D. is the Same Across All Components:

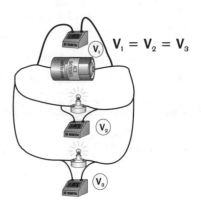

$V_1 = V_2 = V_3$

1) In parallel circuits all components get the full source P.D., so the voltage is the same across all components:

$$V_1 = V_2 = V_3$$

2) This means that identical bulbs connected in parallel will all be at the same brightness.

2) Current is Shared Between Branches:

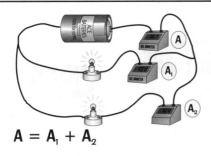

$A = A_1 + A_2$

1) In parallel circuits the total current flowing around the circuit is equal to the total of all the currents through the separate components.

$$A = A_1 + A_2 + \ldots$$

2) In a parallel circuit, there are junctions where the current either splits or rejoins. The total current going into a junction has to equal the total current leaving.

3) If two identical components are connected in parallel then the same current will flow through each component.

3) Resistance Is Tricky:

1) The total resistance of a parallel circuit is tricky to work out, but it's always less than that of the branch with the smallest resistance.

Total R < R_1
and
Total R < R_2

2) The resistance is lower because the charge has more than one branch to take — only some of the charge will flow along each branch.

3) A circuit with two resistors in parallel will have a lower resistance than a circuit with either of the resistors by themselves — which means the parallel circuit will have a higher current.

Voltmeters and Ammeters Are Exceptions to the Rule:

1) Ammeters and voltmeters are exceptions to the series and parallel rules.

2) Ammeters are always connected in series even in a parallel circuit.

3) Voltmeters are always connected in parallel with a component even in a series circuit.

A current shared — is a current halved...

Parallel circuits might look a bit scarier than series ones, but they're much more useful. Remember: each branch has the same voltage across it, and the total current is equal to the sum of the currents through each of the branches.

Mains Electricity

Electric current is the movement of charge carriers. To transfer energy, it doesn't matter which way the charge carriers are going. That's why an alternating current works. Read on to find out more...

Mains Supply is AC, Battery Supply is DC

1) The UK mains supply is approximately 230 volts.

2) It is an AC supply (alternating current), which means the current is constantly changing direction.

3) The frequency of the AC mains supply is 50 cycles per second or 50 Hz (hertz).

4) By contrast, cells and batteries supply direct current (DC). This just means that the current always keeps flowing in the same direction.

Electricity Supplies Can Be Shown on an Oscilloscope Screen

1) A cathode ray oscilloscope (CRO) is basically a snazzy voltmeter.

2) If you plug an AC supply into an oscilloscope, you get a 'trace' on the screen that shows how the voltage of the supply changes with time. The trace goes up and down in a regular pattern — some of the time it's positive and some of the time it's negative.

3) If you plug in a DC supply, the trace you get is just a straight line.

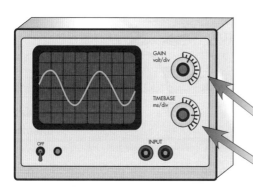

4) The vertical height of the AC trace at any point shows the input voltage at that point. By measuring the height of the trace you can find the potential difference of the AC supply.

5) For DC it's a lot simpler — the voltage is just the distance from the straight line trace to the centre line.

> The GAIN dial controls how many volts each centimetre division represents on the vertical axis.

> The TIMEBASE dial controls how many milliseconds (1 ms = 0.001 s) each division represents on the horizontal axis.

It's Pretty Easy to Read an Oscilloscope Trace

DC supply

A DC source is always at the same voltage, so you get a straight line.

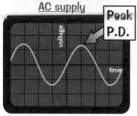

AC supply

Peak P.D.

An AC source gives a regularly repeating wave. From that, you can work out the period and the frequency of the supply.

You work out the frequency using:

$$\text{Frequency (Hz)} = \frac{1}{\text{Time period (s)}}$$

EXAMPLE: The trace below comes from an oscilloscope with the timebase set to 5 ms/div. Find: a) the time period, and b) the frequency of the AC supply.

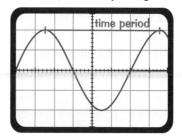

time period

> Time period = the time to complete one cycle.
> 1 ms = 0.001 s.

ANSWER: a) To find the time period, measure the horizontal distance between two peaks. The time period of the signal is 6 divisions. Multiply by the timebase:
Time period = 5 ms × 6 = 0.03 s

b) Using the frequency formula on the left:
Frequency = 1/0.03 = 33 Hz

I wish my bank account had a gain dial...

Because mains power is AC, its current can be increased or decreased using a device called a transformer. The lower the current in power transmission lines, the less energy is wasted as heat.

Electricity in the Home

Now then, did you know... electricity is <u>dangerous</u>. It can kill you. Well just watch out for it, that's all.

Hazards *in the* <u>Home</u> — *Eliminate Them Before They* <u>Eliminate You</u>

Sometimes examiners like to show you a picture of domestic bliss but with various <u>electrical hazards</u> in the picture, such as kids shoving their fingers into sockets and stuff like that, and they'll ask you to <u>list all the hazards</u>. This should be mostly <u>common sense</u>, but it won't half help if you already know some of the likely hazards. Here are 9 examples:

1) <u>Long cables</u>.
2) <u>Frayed cables</u>.
3) <u>Cables</u> in contact with something <u>hot</u> or <u>wet</u>.
4) <u>Water near sockets</u>.
5) <u>Shoving</u> things into sockets.

6) <u>Damaged plugs</u>.
7) <u>Too many</u> plugs into one socket.
8) Lighting sockets <u>without bulbs in</u>.
9) Appliances without their <u>covers</u> on.

Most <u>Cables</u> *Have* <u>Three</u> *Separate* <u>Wires</u>

1) Most electrical appliances are connected to the mains supply by <u>three-core</u> cables. This means that they have <u>three wires</u> inside them, each with a <u>core of copper</u> and a <u>coloured plastic coating</u>.
2) The brown <u>LIVE WIRE</u> in a mains supply alternates between a <u>HIGH +VE AND −VE VOLTAGE</u>.
3) The blue <u>NEUTRAL WIRE</u> is always at <u>0V</u>. Electricity normally flows in and out through the live and neutral wires only.
4) The green and yellow <u>EARTH WIRE</u> is for protecting the wiring, and for safety — it works together with a fuse to prevent fire and shocks. It is attached to the metal casing of the plug and <u>carries the electricity to earth</u> (and away from you) should something go wrong and the live or neutral wires touch the metal case.

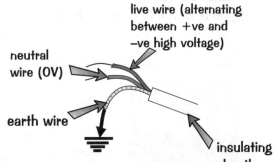

live wire (alternating between +ve and −ve high voltage)

neutral wire (0V)

earth wire

insulating sheath

<u>Three-Pin Plugs</u> *and Cables* <u>Have</u> *Safety Features*

<u>The Wiring Needs</u> *to be Right*

1) The <u>right coloured wire</u> is connected to each pin, and <u>firmly screwed</u> in.
2) <u>No bare wires</u> showing inside the plug.
3) <u>Cable grip</u> tightly fastened over the cable <u>outer layer</u>.
4) Different appliances need <u>different</u> amounts of electrical energy. <u>Thicker</u> cables have <u>less resistance</u>, so they carry <u>more current</u>.

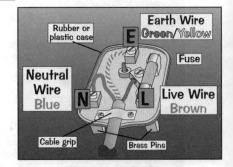

Rubber or plastic case

Earth Wire Green/Yellow

E

Fuse

Neutral Wire Blue

N L

Live Wire Brown

Cable grip

Brass Pins

<u>Plug</u> *Features*

1) The <u>metal parts</u> are made of copper or brass because these are <u>very good conductors</u>.
2) The case, cable grip and cable insulation are made of <u>rubber</u> or <u>plastic</u> because they're really good <u>insulators</u>, and <u>flexible</u> too.
3) This all keeps the electricity flowing <u>where it should</u>.

<u>CGP books are ACE — well, I had to get a plug in somewhere...</u>

Pure water doesn't conduct electricity, but water (usually) has mineral salts dissolved in it. These carry the charge around really well, making it a <u>very good conductor</u>. So don't blow dry your hair in the bath, OK?

Fuses and Earthing

Learning about fuses involves a whole barrel of fun — electrical current, resistance, energy transfers and electrical safety... Read on, read on.

Earthing and Fuses Prevent Electrical Overloads

The earth wire and fuse (or circuit breaker) are included in electrical appliances for safety and work together like this:

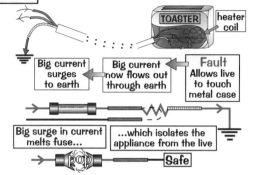

1) If a fault develops in which the live wire somehow touches the metal case, then because the case is earthed, too great a current flows in through the live wire, through the case and out down the earth wire.

2) This surge in current melts the fuse (or trips the circuit breaker in the live wire) when the amount of current is greater than the fuse rating. This cuts off the live supply and breaks the circuit.

3) This isolates the whole appliance, making it impossible to get an electric shock from the case. It also prevents the risk of fire caused by the heating effect of a large current.

4) As well as people, fuses and earthing are there to protect the circuits and wiring in your appliances from getting fried if there is a current surge.

5) Fuses should be rated as near as possible but just higher than the normal operating current.

6) The larger the current, the thicker the cable you need to carry it.
That's why the fuse rating needed for cables usually increases with cable thickness.

Insulating Materials Make Appliances "Double Insulated"

All appliances with metal cases are usually "earthed" to reduce the danger of electric shock. "Earthing" just means the case must be attached to an earth wire. An earthed conductor can never become live. If the appliance has a plastic casing and no metal parts showing then it's said to be double insulated.

Anything with double insulation like that doesn't need an earth wire — just a live and neutral. Cables that only carry the live and neutral wires are known as two-core cables.

Circuit Breakers Have Some Advantages Over Fuses

1) Circuit breakers are an electrical safety device used in some circuits.
Like fuses, they protect the circuit from damage if too much current flows.

2) When circuit breakers detect a surge in current in a circuit, they break the circuit by opening a switch.

3) A circuit breaker (and the circuit they're in) can easily be reset by flicking a switch on the device. This makes them more convenient than fuses — which have to be replaced once they've melted.

4) They are, however, a lot more expensive to buy than fuses.

5) One type of circuit breaker used instead of a fuse and an earth wire is a Residual Current Circuit Breaker (RCCB):

   a) Normally exactly the same current flows through the live and neutral wires. If somebody touches the live wire, a small but deadly current will flow through them to the earth. This means the neutral wire carries less current than the live wire. The RCCB detects this difference in current and quickly cuts off the power by opening a switch.

   b) They also operate much faster than fuses — they break the circuit as soon as there is a current surge — no time is wasted waiting for the current to melt a fuse. This makes them safer.

   c) RCCBs even work for small current changes that might not be large enough to melt a fuse. Since even small current changes could be fatal, this means RCCBs are more effective at protecting against electrocution.

Why are earth wires green and yellow — when mud is brown..?

All these safety precautions mean it's pretty difficult to get electrocuted on modern appliances. But that's only so long as they are in good condition and you're not doing something really stupid. Watch out for frayed wires, don't overload plugs, and for goodness sake don't use a knife to get toast out of a toaster when it is switched on.

Energy and Power in Circuits

Electricity is just another form of <u>energy</u> — which means that it is always <u>conserved</u>.

Energy is Transferred from Cells and Other Sources

Anything which <u>supplies electricity</u> is also supplying <u>energy</u>.

So cells, batteries, generators, etc. all <u>transfer energy</u> to components in the circuit:

| <u>Motion</u>: motors | <u>Light</u>: light bulbs | <u>Heat</u>: Hair dryers/kettles | <u>Sound</u>: speakers |

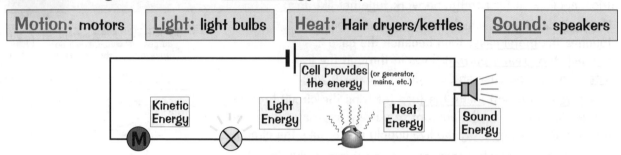

All Resistors Produce Heat When a Current Flows Through Them

1) Whenever a <u>current</u> flows through anything with <u>electrical resistance</u> (which is pretty much everything) then <u>electrical energy</u> is converted into <u>heat energy</u>.

2) The <u>more current</u> that flows, the more heat is produced.

3) A <u>bigger voltage</u> means more heating because it pushes more current through.

4) <u>Filament bulbs</u> work by passing a current through a very <u>thin wire</u>, heating it up so much that it glows. Rather obviously, they waste a lot of energy as <u>heat</u>.

If an Appliance is Efficient it Wastes Less Energy

All this energy wasted as heat can get a little <u>depressing</u> — but there is a solution.

1) When you buy electrical appliances you can choose to buy ones that are more <u>energy efficient</u>.

2) These appliances transfer more of their <u>total electrical energy output to useful energy</u>.

Not an energy efficient lamp.

3) For example, less energy is wasted as heat in power-saving lamps such as <u>compact fluorescent lamps</u> (CFLs) and <u>light emitting diodes</u> (p.116) than in ordinary filament bulbs.

4) Unfortunately, they do <u>cost more to buy</u>, but over time the money you <u>save</u> on your electricity bills pays you back for the initial investment.

Power Ratings of Appliances

The total energy transferred by an appliance depends on <u>how long</u> the appliance is on and its <u>power rating</u>.
The power of an appliance is the <u>energy</u> that it uses <u>per second</u>.

Energy Transferred = Power rating × time

$$\frac{E}{P \times t}$$

For example, if a 2.5 kW kettle is on for 5 minutes, the energy transferred by the kettle in this time is $300 \times 2500 = 750\,000$ J $= 750$ kJ. (5 minutes $= 300$ s).

Ohm's girlfriend was a vixen — he couldn't resistor...

Remember: power is energy transferred per second. Power is energy transferred per second. Power is energy transferred per second....

Power and Energy Change

You can think about electrical circuits in terms of energy transfer — the charge carriers take charge around the circuit, and when they go through an electrical component energy is transferred to make the component work.

Electrical Power and Fuse Ratings

1) The formula for electrical power is:

POWER = CURRENT × POTENTIAL DIFFERENCE

$$P = I \times V$$

2) Most electrical goods show their power rating and voltage rating. To work out the size of the fuse needed, you need to work out the current that the item will normally use:

> EXAMPLE: A hair dryer is rated at 230 V, 1 kW. Find the fuse needed.
>
> ANSWER: I = P/V = 1000/230 = 4.3 A. Normally, the fuse should be rated just a little higher than the normal current, so a 5 amp fuse is ideal for this one.

The Potential Difference is the Energy Transferred per Charge Passed

1) When an electrical charge (Q) goes through a change in potential difference (V), then energy (E) is transferred.

2) Energy is supplied to the charge at the power source to 'raise' it through a potential.

3) The charge gives up this energy when it 'falls' through any potential drop in components elsewhere in the circuit.

The formula is real simple:

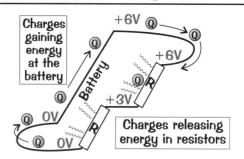

Energy transformed = Charge × Potential difference

4) The bigger the change in P.D. (or voltage), the more energy is transferred for a given amount of charge passing through the circuit.

5) That means that a battery with a bigger voltage will supply more energy to the circuit for every coulomb of charge which flows round it, because the charge is raised up "higher" at the start (see above diagram) — and as the diagram shows, more energy will be dissipated in the circuit too.

> EXAMPLE: The motor in an electric toothbrush is attached to a 3 V battery. If a current of 0.8 A flows through the motor for 3 minutes:
>
> a) Calculate the total charge passed.
>
> b) Calculate the energy transformed by the motor.
>
> c) Explain why the kinetic energy output of the motor will be less than your answer to b).
>
> ANSWER: a) Use the formula (p.113) Q = I × t = 0.8 × (3 × 60) = 144 C
>
> b) Use E = Q × V = 144 × 3 = 432 J
>
> c) The motor won't be 100% efficient. Some of the energy will be transformed into sound and heat.

You have the power — now use your potential...

Ok, another two formulas. By this point you're probably experiencing a little bit of formula fatigue, but trust me, you will be glad that you can use them all. Try to think about exactly what each one means and how they work together — things are a lot easier to memorise if you have a real understanding of why they are there.

Generating Electricity

It's difficult to imagine a world without electricity — it would be hard to bake cakes at night, for a start.

Moving a Magnet _into_ a Coil of Wire Induces a Voltage

1) You can create a voltage, and maybe a current, in a conductor by moving a magnet in or near a coil of wire. This is called electromagnetic induction.

2) As you move the magnet, the magnetic field through the coil changes — this change in the magnetic field induces (creates) a voltage across the ends of the coil.

3) If the ends of the wire are connected to make a closed circuit then a current will flow in the wire.

4) The direction of the voltage depends on which way you move the magnet:

If you move the magnet into the coil the voltage is induced in the opposite direction from when you move it out of the coil.	If you reverse the magnet's North-South polarity — so that the opposite pole points into the coil, the voltage is induced in the opposite direction.

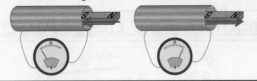
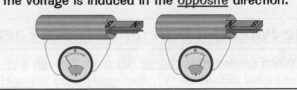

AC Generators — _Just Turn the Magnet_ and There's a Current

1) In a generator, a magnet (or an electromagnet) rotates in a coil of wire. As the magnet turns, the magnetic field through the coil changes — this change in the magnetic field induces a voltage, which makes a current flow in the coil.

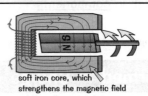

soft iron core, which strengthens the magnetic field

2) When the magnet is turned through half a turn, the direction of the magnetic field through the coil reverses. When this happens, the voltage reverses, so the current flows in the opposite direction around the coil of wire.

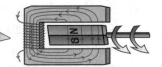

3) If the magnet keeps turning in the same direction — clockwise, say — then the voltage keeps on reversing every half turn and you get an AC current.

Four Factors _Affect the Size_ of the Induced Voltage

1) If you want a bigger peak voltage (and current) you could do one or more of these four things...

> 1) Add an IRON CORE inside the coil
> 2) Increase the STRENGTH of the MAGNETIC FIELD
> 3) Increase the SPEED of ROTATION
> 4) Increase the number of TURNS on the COIL

2) To reduce the voltage, you would reduce one of the factors or take the iron core out.

So THAT's how they make electricity — I always wondered...

Generators are mostly powered by burning things to make steam, to turn a turbine, to rotate the magnet. You can get portable generators too, to use in places without mains electricity — like at music festivals.

Transformers

So you've generated your electricity, but it's not at the right <u>voltage</u> — what do you need? A <u>transformer</u>.

Transformers <u>Change the</u> Voltage — <u>but Only</u> AC <u>Voltages</u>

<u>Transformers</u> are used to change the <u>size</u> of the <u>voltage</u> — they use <u>electromagnetic induction</u> to 'step up' or 'step down' the <u>voltage</u>. They have two coils of wire, the <u>primary</u> and the <u>secondary</u> coils, wound around an <u>iron core</u>.

The <u>alternating current</u> in the <u>primary</u> coil causes <u>changes</u> in the iron core's <u>magnetic field</u>, which <u>induces</u> a <u>changing voltage</u> in the <u>secondary</u> coil (see below).

<u>STEP-UP TRANSFORMERS</u> step the voltage <u>up</u> (increase it). They have <u>more</u> turns on the <u>secondary</u> coil than the primary coil.

<u>STEP-DOWN TRANSFORMERS</u> step the voltage <u>down</u> (decrease it). They have <u>more</u> turns on the <u>primary</u> coil than the secondary.

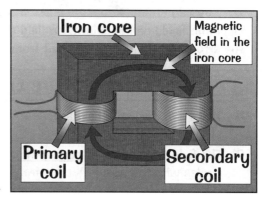

Transformers <u>Work by</u> Electromagnetic Induction

1) The primary coil <u>produces a magnetic field</u> which stays <u>within the iron core</u>.

2) Because there's an <u>alternating current</u> (AC) in the <u>primary coil</u>, the magnetic field in the iron core constantly <u>changes direction</u> (100 times a second if it's at 50 Hz) — i.e. it's a <u>changing</u> magnetic field.

3) This changing magnetic field <u>induces</u> an <u>alternating voltage</u> in the secondary coil (with the same frequency as the alternating current in the primary) — <u>electromagnetic induction</u> of a voltage in fact.

4) The <u>relative number of turns</u> on the two coils determines whether the voltage induced in the secondary coil is <u>greater</u> or <u>less</u> than the voltage in the primary coil (see equation below).

5) If you supplied <u>direct current</u> (DC) to the primary coil, you'd get <u>nothing</u> out of the secondary coil at all. Sure, there'd still be a magnetic field in the iron core, but it wouldn't be <u>constantly changing</u>, so there'd be no <u>induction</u> in the secondary coil — because you need a <u>changing field</u> to induce a voltage. So don't forget it — transformers only work with <u>AC</u>. They won't work with DC <u>at all</u>.

<u>The</u> Transformer Equation — <u>Use It</u> Either Way Up

You can calculate the <u>output voltage</u> from a transformer if you know the <u>input voltage</u> and the <u>number of turns</u> on each coil.

$$\frac{\text{Voltage across primary coil}}{\text{Voltage across secondary coil}} = \frac{\text{Number of turns in primary coil}}{\text{Number of turns in secondary coil}}$$

$$\frac{V_P}{V_S} = \frac{N_P}{N_S} \quad \text{or} \quad \frac{V_S}{V_P} = \frac{N_S}{N_P}$$

Well, it's <u>just another formula</u>. You stick in the numbers you've got and work out the one <u>that's left</u>. And you can write the formula <u>either way up</u> — you should always put the thing you're trying to find <u>on the top</u>.

<u>EXAMPLE:</u> A transformer has 40 turns on the primary coil and 800 on the secondary coil. If the input voltage is 1000 V, find the output voltage.

<u>ANSWER:</u> The question asks you to find V_S, so put it on the top: $\frac{V_S}{V_P} = \frac{N_S}{N_P}$

Substitute the values: $\frac{V_S}{1000} = \frac{800}{40}$, $V_S = 1000 \times \frac{800}{40} = \underline{20\,000\text{ V}}$

<u>Which transformer do you need to enslave the Universe — Megatron...</u>

You should practise with that tricky equation. The transformer equation is unusual because it can't be put into a formula triangle, but other than that, the method is the same — stick in the numbers. Just <u>practise</u>.

Magnetic Fields

Loads of electrical appliances use <u>magnetic fields</u> generated by <u>electric currents</u>.

> A <u>MAGNETIC FIELD</u> is a region where <u>MAGNETIC MATERIALS</u> (like iron and steel) and also <u>WIRES CARRYING CURRENTS</u> experience a <u>FORCE</u> acting on them.

Magnetic fields can be shown on <u>field diagrams</u>.
The arrows on the <u>field lines</u> point from the <u>North</u> pole of the magnet to the <u>South</u> pole.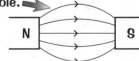

A Current-Carrying Wire Creates a Magnetic Field

1) There is a magnetic field around a <u>straight</u>, <u>current-carrying wire</u>.

2) The field is made up of <u>concentric circles</u> with the wire in the centre.

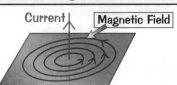

A Rectangular Coil Reinforces the Magnetic Field

1) If you <u>bend</u> the current-carrying wire round into a <u>coil</u>, the magnetic field looks like this.

2) The circular magnetic fields around the sides of the loop <u>reinforce</u> each other at the centre.

3) If the coil has <u>lots of turns</u>, the magnetic fields from all the individual loops reinforce each other <u>even more</u>.

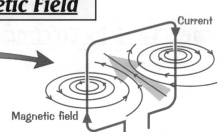

A Current in a Magnetic Field Experiences a Force

1) Because of its magnetic field, a <u>current-carrying wire</u> or <u>coil</u> can exert a <u>force</u> on <u>another</u> current-carrying wire or coil, or on a <u>permanent magnet</u>.

2) When a current-carrying wire is put in a <u>different</u> magnetic field, the <u>two</u> magnetic fields <u>affect one another</u>. The result is a <u>force</u> on the <u>wire</u>.

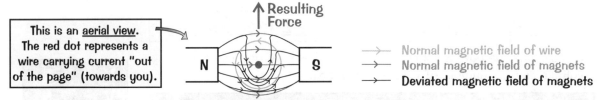

3) To feel the <u>full force</u>, the <u>wire</u> has to be at <u>right-angles</u> (<u>90°</u>) to the <u>lines of force</u> of the <u>magnetic field</u> it's placed in. (As it is in the diagram above.)

4) If the wire runs <u>parallel</u> to the lines of force of the magnetic field, it won't experience <u>any force at all</u>. And at angles <u>in between</u> 0° and 90° it'll feel <u>some</u> force.

5) When the wire is at right-angles to the magnetic field, the <u>force</u> always acts at <u>right-angles</u> to <u>both</u> the lines of force of the magnetic field <u>and</u> the direction of the current.

Fleming's Left-Hand Rule Tells You Which Way the Force Acts

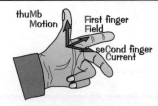

1) Using your <u>left hand</u>, point your <u>First finger</u> in the direction of the <u>Field</u> and your <u>seCond finger</u> in the direction of the <u>Current</u>.

2) Your <u>thuMb</u> will then point in the direction of the <u>force</u> (<u>Motion</u>).
(Give it a try with the diagram of the wire and the magnet field above.)

Use the force — at right-angles to the magnetic field...

When I'm <u>parallel</u> to my bed I don't feel any force pulling me out of it. Just like wires and magnets... Sort of.

The Motor Effect

The _motor effect_ — that's how _electric motors_ work. Should be _easy_ to remember that.

Magnetic Fields _Make Current-Carrying Coils Turn_

If a _rectangular coil_ of wire carrying a _current_ is placed in a _uniform_ magnetic field, the _force_ will cause it to _turn_. This is called the _motor effect_. You can use Fleming's _left-hand rule_ (_LHR_), from the previous page, to work out which _way_ the coil will turn:

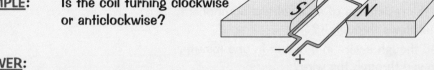

A _uniform_ magnetic field has the _same strength_ _everywhere_ in the field.

EXAMPLE: Is the coil turning clockwise or anticlockwise?

ANSWER:

1) Draw in current arrows (+ve to –ve) and magnetic field lines, which always run from North to South.

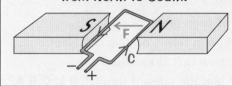

2) Use LHR on one side of the coil (I've used the right-hand side).

SeCond finger Current

First finger Field

thuMb Motion

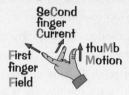

3) Draw in direction of motion (force).

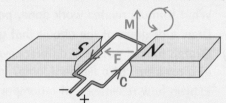

So — the coil is turning _anticlockwise_.

The Simple _Electric Motor_

1) The diagram shows the _forces_ acting on the two _side arms_ of a _coil_.

2) These forces are just the _usual forces_ which act on _any_ current-carrying wire in a _magnetic field_.

3) Because the coil is on a _spindle_ and the forces act _one up_ and _one down_, it _rotates_.

4) The _split-ring commutator_ is a clever way of _swapping_ the contacts _every half turn_.

5) This reverses the direction of the _current_ every half-turn to keep the coil rotating _continuously_ in the _same direction_.

6) Otherwise, the direction of the _force_ would _reverse_ every half turn and the coil would _change direction_ every half turn instead of fully _rotating_.

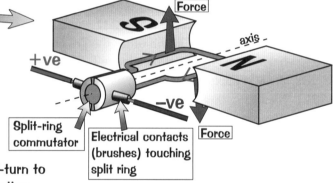

Force

axis

+ve

–ve

Split-ring commutator

Electrical contacts (brushes) touching split ring

Force

Anything That _Uses Rotation_ can be _Powered_ by an _Electric Motor_

Lots of devices use _rotation_. They all work by using an _electric motor_ in a similar way.

1) Link the coil to an _axle_, and the axle _spins round_.

2) In the diagram there's a _fan_ attached to the axle, but you can stick _almost anything_ on a motor axle and make it spin round.

3) For example:

- In a _DVD player_, the axle's attached to the bit _the DVD sits on_ to make it spin.
- Electric _cars_ and _trains_ have their _wheels_ attached to axles.
- Electric motors spin the _platters_ (the bits where information is stored) of a computer _hard disc drive_.
- _Domestic appliances_, such as washing machines, fridges and vacuum cleaners all use electric motors.

axle

fan

coil

Hello Motor...

Loudspeakers demonstrate the _motor effect_. _AC_ electrical signals from the amplifier are fed to the _speaker coil_ (shown red). These make the coil move back and forth over the poles of the _magnet_. These movements make the cardboard cone _vibrate_ and this creates _sounds_.

Revision Summary for Section 8

There's some pretty heavy physics in this section. But just take it one page at a time and it's not so bad. You're even allowed to go back through the pages for a sneaky peak if you get stuck on these questions.

1) What causes the build-up of static electricity? Which particles move when static builds up?

2) Describe the forces between objects with: a) like charges,   b) opposite charges.

3) Explain how static electricity can make synthetic clothes crackle when you take them off.

4) Describe the dangers associated with static electricity when refuelling a vehicle. What can be done to make refuelling safer?

5) True or false: the greater the resistance of an electrical component, the smaller the current that flows through it?

6)* 240 C of charge is carried though a wire in a circuit in one minute. How much current has flowed through the wire?

7) What is another name for potential difference?

8) What formula relates work done, potential difference and charge?

9) Draw a diagram of the circuit that you would use to find the resistance of a motor.

10) Sketch typical potential difference-current graphs for: a) a resistor, b) a filament lamp, c) a diode. Explain the shape of each graph.

11) Explain how resistance of a component changes with its temperature in terms of ions and electrons.

12)* What potential difference is required to push 2 A of current through a 0.6 Ω resistor?

13)* Calculate the resistance of a wire if the potential across it is 12 V and the current through it is 2.5 A.

14) Give three applications of LEDs.

15) Describe how the resistance of an LDR varies with light intensity. Give an application of an LDR.

16) Explain, in terms of energy, why P.D. is shared out in a series circuit.

17) Two circuits each contain a 2 Ω and a 4 Ω resistor — in one circuit they're in series, in the other they're in parallel. Which circuit will have the higher total resistance? Why?

18)* An AC supply of electricity has a time period of 0.08s. What is its frequency?

19) Name the three wires in a three-core cable.

20) Sketch and label a properly wired three-pin plug.

21) Explain fully how a fuse and earth wire work together.

22) How does an RCCB stop you from getting electrocuted?

23) What does the power of an appliance measure?

24)*Which uses more energy, a 45 W pair of hair straighteners used for 5 minutes, or a 105 W hair dryer used for 2 minutes?

25)*Calculate the energy transformed by a torch using a 6 V battery when 530 C of charge pass through.

26) Define electromagnetic induction.

27) Explain how a generator works — use a sketch if it helps.

28) What are the four factors that affect the size of the induced voltage produced by a generator?

29) Write down the transformer equation.

30)*A transformer has 500 turns on the primary coil and 20 on the secondary coil. If the output voltage is 9 V, find the input voltage.

31) A current-carrying wire runs parallel to the lines of force of a magnetic field. Does the wire feel a force?

32) Draw a field diagram to show the resulting force on a current-carrying wire placed at right-angles to the lines of force of a magnetic field.

33) What part of an electric motor reverses the direction of the current? Why is this important?

34) Briefly describe three uses of electric motors.

* Answers on page 142.

Atomic Structure

Ernest Rutherford didn't just pick the nuclear model of the atom out of thin air. It all started with a Greek fella called Democritus in the 5th Century BC. He thought that all matter, whatever it was, was made up of identical lumps called "atomos". And that's about as far as the theory got until the 1800s...

Rutherford Scattering and the Demise of the Plum Pudding

1) In 1804 John Dalton agreed with Democritus that matter was made up of tiny spheres ("atoms") that couldn't be broken up, but he reckoned that each element was made up of a different type of "atom".

2) Nearly 100 years later, J J Thomson discovered that electrons could be removed from atoms. So Dalton's theory wasn't quite right (atoms could be broken up). Thomson suggested that atoms were spheres of positive charge with tiny negative electrons stuck in them like plums in a plum pudding.

3) That "plum pudding" theory didn't last very long though. In 1909 Rutherford and Marsden tried firing a beam of alpha particles (see p.131) at thin gold foil. They expected that the positively charged alpha particles would be slightly deflected by the electrons in the plum pudding model.

4) However, most of the alpha particles just went straight through, but the odd one came straight back at them, which was frankly a bit of a shocker for Rutherford and his pal.

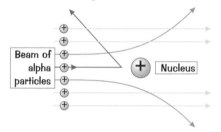

5) Being pretty clued-up guys, Rutherford and Marsden realised this meant that most of the mass of the atom was concentrated at the centre in a tiny nucleus. They also realised that the nucleus must have a positive charge, since it repelled the positive alpha particles.

6) It also showed that most of an atom is just empty space, which is also a bit of a shocker when you think about it.

Rutherford and Marsden Came Up with the Nuclear Model of the Atom

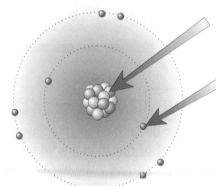

The nucleus is tiny but it makes up most of the mass of the atom. It contains protons (which are positively charged) and neutrons (which are neutral) — which gives it an overall positive charge.

The rest of the atom is mostly empty space. The negative electrons whizz round the outside of the nucleus really fast. They give the atom its overall size — the radius of the atom's nucleus is about 10 000 times smaller than the radius of the atom. Crikey.

Here are the relative charges and masses of each particle:

PARTICLE	MASS	CHARGE
Proton	1	+1
Neutron	1	0
Electron	1/2000	-1

Number of Protons Equals Number of Electrons

1) Atoms have no charge overall.
2) The charge on an electron is the same size as the charge on a proton — but opposite.
3) This means the number of protons always equals the number of electrons in a neutral atom.
4) If some electrons are added or removed, the atom becomes a charged particle called an ion.

And I always thought Kate Moss was the best model...

The nuclear model is just one way of thinking about the atom. It works really well for explaining a lot of physical properties of different elements, but it's certainly not the whole story. Other bits of science are explained using different models of the atom. The beauty of it though is that no one model is more right than the others.

Atoms and Radiation

You have just entered the <u>subatomic</u> realm — now stuff starts to get real interesting...

Isotopes are Different Forms of the Same Element

1) <u>Isotopes</u> are atoms with the <u>same</u> number of <u>protons</u> but a <u>different</u> number of <u>neutrons</u>.

2) Hence they have the <u>same atomic number</u>, but <u>different mass numbers</u>.

3) Atomic (proton) number is the <u>number of protons</u> in an atom. Mass (nucleon) number is the <u>number of protons</u> + the <u>number of neutrons</u> in an atom.

4) <u>Carbon-12</u> and <u>carbon-14</u> are good examples of isotopes:

5) <u>Most elements</u> have different isotopes, but there are usually only one or two <u>stable</u> ones (like carbon-12).

6) The other isotopes tend to be <u>radioactive</u> (like carbon-14) which means they <u>decay</u> into <u>other elements</u> and <u>give out radiation</u>.

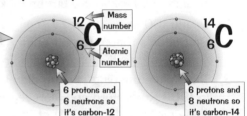

Radioactivity is a Totally Random Process

1) <u>Radioactive substances</u> give out radiation from the nuclei of their atoms — <u>no matter what is done to them</u>.

2) This process is entirely <u>random</u>. This means that if you have 1000 unstable nuclei, you can't say when <u>any one of them</u> is going to decay, and neither can you do anything at all <u>to make a decay happen</u>. It's completely unaffected by <u>physical</u> conditions like <u>temperature</u> or by any sort of <u>chemical bonding</u> etc.

3) Radioactive substances <u>spit out</u> one or more of the three types of radiation, <u>alpha</u>, <u>beta</u> or <u>gamma</u> (see next page). In the process, the nucleus will often change into a new element.

Background Radiation Comes from Many Sources

<u>Background radiation</u> is radiation that is present at all times, all around us, wherever you go. The background radiation we receive comes from:

1) Radioactivity of naturally occurring <u>unstable isotopes</u> which are <u>all around us</u> — in the <u>air</u>, in <u>food</u>, in <u>building materials</u> and in the <u>rocks</u> under our feet.

2) Radiation from <u>space</u>, which is known as <u>cosmic rays</u>. These come mostly from the <u>Sun</u>.

3) Radiation due to <u>man-made sources</u>, e.g. <u>fallout</u> from <u>nuclear weapons tests</u>, <u>nuclear accidents</u> (such as Chernobyl) or <u>dumped nuclear waste</u>.

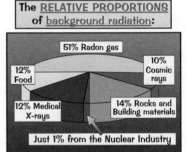

The <u>RELATIVE PROPORTIONS</u> of <u>background radiation</u>:

51% Radon gas
10% Cosmic rays
12% Food
14% Rocks and Building materials
12% Medical X-rays
Just 1% from the Nuclear Industry

Radiation Dose Depends on Location and Occupation

How likely you are to <u>suffer damage</u> if you're exposed to nuclear radiation depends on the <u>radiation dose</u>. Radiation dose is measured in <u>sieverts</u> (<u>Sv</u>) and depends on the <u>type</u> and <u>amount of radiation</u> you've been exposed to. The <u>higher</u> the radiation dose, the <u>more at risk</u> you are of <u>developing cancer</u>. The amount of radiation you're exposed to (and hence your radiation dose) can be affected by your <u>location</u> and <u>occupation</u>.

1) Certain <u>underground rocks</u> (e.g. granite) can cause higher levels at the <u>surface</u>, especially if they release <u>radioactive radon gas</u>, which tends to get <u>trapped inside people's houses</u>.

2) At <u>high altitudes</u> (e.g. in <u>jet planes</u>) the background radiation <u>increases</u> because of more exposure to <u>cosmic rays</u>. That means <u>commercial pilots</u> have an increased risk of getting some types of cancer.

3) <u>Underground</u> (e.g. in <u>mines</u>, etc.) it increases because of the <u>rocks</u> all around, posing a risk to <u>miners</u>.

4) <u>Nuclear industry</u> workers and <u>uranium miners</u> are typically exposed to <u>10 times</u> the normal amount of radiation. They wear <u>protective clothing</u> and <u>face masks</u> to stop them from <u>touching</u> or <u>inhaling</u> the radioactive material, and <u>monitor</u> their radiation doses with <u>special radiation badges</u> and <u>regular check-ups</u>.

5) <u>Radiographers</u> work in hospitals using ionising radiation and so have a higher risk of radiation exposure. They wear <u>lead aprons</u> and stand behind <u>lead screens</u> to protect them from <u>prolonged exposure</u> to radiation.

Completely random — just like your revision shouldn't be...

The number of <u>protons</u> decides what <u>element</u> something is and the number of <u>neutrons</u> decides what <u>isotope</u> it is.

Ionising Radiation

Alpha (α) Beta (β) Gamma (γ) — there's a short alphabet of radiation for you to learn here. And it's all ionising.

Alpha Particles are Helium Nuclei

1) An alpha particle is two neutrons and two protons.

2) They are relatively big and heavy and slow moving.

3) They therefore don't penetrate very far into materials and are stopped quickly, even when travelling through air.

4) They are strongly ionising (they bash into a lot of atoms and knock electrons off them before they slow down, which creates lots of ions — hence the term "ionising").

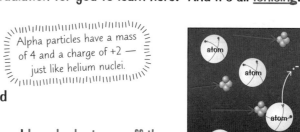
Alpha particles have a mass of 4 and a charge of +2 — just like helium nuclei.

Beta Particles are Electrons

1) Beta particles are in between alpha and gamma in terms of their properties.

2) They move quite fast and they are quite small (they're electrons).

3) They penetrate moderately into materials before colliding, have a long range in air, and are moderately ionising too.

4) For every β-particle emitted, a neutron turns to a proton in the nucleus.

5) A β-particle is simply an electron, with virtually no mass and a charge of –1.

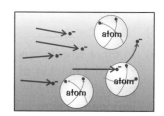

Nuclear Equations need to Balance

You can write alpha and beta decays as nuclear equations. Watch out for the mass and atomic numbers — they have to balance up on both sides.

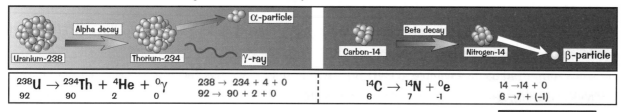
Uranium-238 — Alpha decay → Thorium-234, γ-ray, α-particle   Carbon-14 — Beta decay → Nitrogen-14, β-particle

$$^{238}_{92}\text{U} \rightarrow \,^{234}_{90}\text{Th} + \,^{4}_{2}\text{He} + \,^{0}_{0}\gamma$$
$$238 \rightarrow 234 + 4 + 0$$
$$92 \rightarrow 90 + 2 + 0$$

$$^{14}_{6}\text{C} \rightarrow \,^{14}_{7}\text{N} + \,^{0}_{-1}\text{e}$$
$$14 \rightarrow 14 + 0$$
$$6 \rightarrow 7 + (-1)$$

Gamma Rays are Very Short Wavelength EM Waves

1) If nuclei need to get rid of some extra energy they can emit gamma rays.

2) Gamma rays are just energy (they have no mass and no charge) so they don't change the element of the nucleus that emits it.

3) They can penetrate a long way into materials without being stopped and pass straight through air.

4) This means they are weakly ionising because they tend to pass through rather than collide with atoms. Eventually they hit something and do damage.

Alpha and Beta Particles are Deflected by Electric and Magnetic Fields

1) Alpha particles have a positive charge, beta particles have a negative charge.

2) When travelling through a magnetic or electric field, both alpha and beta particles will be deflected. They're deflected in opposite directions because of their opposite charge.

3) Alpha particles have a larger charge than beta particles, and feel a greater force in magnetic and electric fields. But they're deflected less because they have a much greater mass.

4) Gamma radiation is an electromagnetic (EM) wave and has no charge, so it doesn't get deflected by electric or magnetic fields.

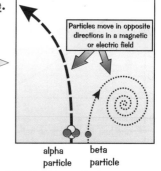
Particles move in opposite directions in a magnetic or electric field

alpha particle   beta particle

I once beta particle — it cried for ages...

So, when a nucleus decays by alpha emission, its atomic number goes down by two and its mass number goes down by four. Beta emission increases the atomic number by one (the mass number doesn't change).

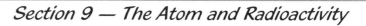

Half-Life

The <u>unit</u> for measuring <u>radioactivity</u> is the <u>becquerel</u> (Bq). 1 Bq means <u>one nucleus decaying per second</u>.

The Radioactivity of a Sample Always Decreases Over Time

1) Each time a <u>decay</u> happens and an alpha, beta or gamma is given out, it means one more <u>radioactive nucleus</u> has <u>disappeared</u>.

2) Obviously, as the <u>unstable nuclei</u> disappear, the <u>activity</u> (the number of nuclei that decay per second) will <u>decrease</u>. So the <u>older</u> a sample becomes, the <u>less radiation</u> it will emit.

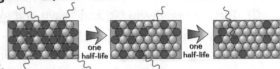

3) <u>How quickly</u> the activity <u>drops off</u> varies a lot. For <u>some</u> substances it takes <u>just a few microseconds</u> before nearly all the unstable nuclei have <u>decayed</u>, whilst for others it can take <u>millions of years</u>.

4) The problem with trying to <u>measure</u> this is that <u>the activity never reaches zero</u>, which is why we have to use the idea of <u>half-life</u> to measure how quickly the activity <u>drops off</u>.

5) Here's the <u>definition</u> of <u>half-life</u>:

6) In other words, it is the <u>time it takes</u> for the <u>count rate</u> (the number of radioactive emissions detected per unit of time) from a sample containing the isotope to <u>fall to half its initial level</u>.

> **HALF-LIFE is the AVERAGE TIME it takes for the NUMBER OF NUCLEI in a RADIOACTIVE ISOTOPE SAMPLE to HALVE.**

7) A <u>short half-life</u> means the <u>activity falls quickly</u>, because <u>lots</u> of the nuclei decay <u>quickly</u>.

8) A <u>long half-life</u> means the activity <u>falls more slowly</u> because <u>most</u> of the nuclei don't decay <u>for a long time</u> — they just sit there, <u>basically unstable</u>, but kind of <u>biding their time</u>.

Do Half-Life Questions Step by Step

Half-life can be confusing, but the calculations are <u>straightforward</u> so long as you do them <u>STEP BY STEP</u>:

A VERY SIMPLE EXAMPLE:

The activity of a radioactive sample is 640 Bq. Two hours later it has fallen to 40 Bq. Find its half-life.

<u>ANSWER:</u> Go through it in <u>short simple steps</u> like this:

INITIAL		after ONE		after TWO		after THREE		after FOUR
count:	(÷2) →	half-life:	(÷2) →	half-lives:	(÷2) →	half-lives:	(÷2) →	half-lives:
640		320		160		80		40

This careful <u>step-by-step method</u> shows that it takes <u>four half-lives</u> for the activity to fall from 640 to 40. So <u>two hours</u> represents <u>four half-lives</u> — so the half-life is 2 hours ÷ 4 = <u>30 MINUTES</u>.

And here's how you calculate the half-life of a sample from a <u>graph</u>. Relax, this is (almost) <u>fun</u>.

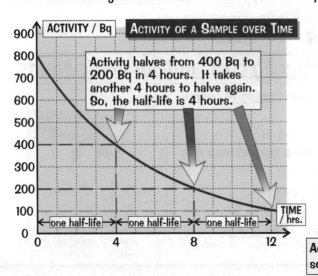

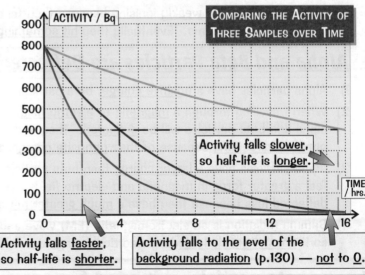

Half-life of a box of chocolates — about five minutes...

To measure half-life, you time how <u>long it takes</u> for the number of decays per second to <u>halve</u>. Simples.

Radioactive Safety

When <u>Marie Curie</u> discovered the radioactive properties of <u>radium</u> in 1898, nobody knew about its dangers. Radium was used to make glow-in-the-dark watches and many <u>watch dial painters</u> developed cancer as a result.

Ionising Radiation can Damage Living Cells

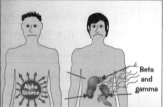

1) Alpha, beta and gamma radiation are all <u>ionising radiation</u> — they can <u>break up</u> molecules into smaller bits called <u>ions</u>. Ions can be <u>very chemically reactive</u>, so they go off and react with things and generally make <u>nuisances</u> of themselves.

2) In humans, ionisation can cause <u>serious damage</u> to the cells in the body.

3) A high dose of radiation tends to <u>kill cells</u> outright, causing <u>radiation sickness</u>. Lower doses tend to <u>damage cells</u> without killing them, which can cause <u>cancer</u>.

4) Radioactive materials put people at risk through either:

- <u>IRRADIATION</u> — being exposed to radiation <u>without</u> coming into contact with the source. The damage to your body <u>stops</u> as soon as you leave the radioactive area.

- <u>CONTAMINATION</u> — <u>picking up</u> some radioactive material, e.g. by <u>breathing it in</u>, <u>drinking</u> contaminated water or getting it on your skin. You'll <u>still</u> be exposed to the radiation once you've <u>left</u> the radioactive area.

Outside the Body, β and γ-Sources are the Most Dangerous

This is because <u>beta and gamma</u> can get <u>inside</u> to the delicate <u>organs</u>, whereas alpha is much less dangerous because it <u>can't penetrate the skin</u>.

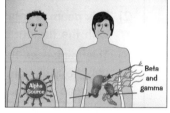

Inside the Body, an α-Source is the Most Dangerous

<u>Inside the body</u> alpha sources do all their damage in a <u>very localised area</u>. Beta and gamma sources on the other hand are <u>less dangerous</u> inside the body because they mostly <u>pass straight out</u> without doing much damage.

Here's What Blocks the Three Types of Radiation...

<u>Alpha particles</u> are blocked by <u>paper</u>. <u>Beta particles</u> are blocked by thin <u>aluminium</u>. <u>Gamma rays</u> are blocked by <u>thick lead</u>. <u>Similar</u> things will also block them, e.g. <u>skin</u> will stop <u>alpha</u>, a thin sheet of <u>any metal</u> will stop <u>beta</u>, and <u>very thick concrete</u> will stop <u>gamma</u>.

You Need to Keep Safe whilst Handling Radioactive Sources

1) When conducting experiments, use radioactive sources for as <u>short a time</u> as possible so your <u>exposure</u> is kept to a <u>minimum</u>.

2) <u>Never allow skin contact</u> with a source. Always handle with <u>tongs</u>.

3) Hold the source at <u>arm's length</u> to keep it <u>as far</u> from the body <u>as possible</u>. This will decrease the amount of radiation that hits you, especially for alpha particles as they <u>don't travel far in air</u>.

4) Keep the source <u>pointing away</u> from the body and <u>avoid looking directly at it</u>.

5) <u>Lead</u> absorbs all three types of radiation (though a lot of it is needed to stop gamma radiation completely). <u>Always</u> store radioactive sources in a <u>lead box</u> and put them away <u>as soon</u> as the experiment is <u>over</u>. Medical professionals who work with radiation <u>every day</u> (such as radiographers) wear <u>lead aprons</u> and stand behind <u>lead screens</u> for extra protection because of its radiation absorbing properties.

6) When someone needs an X-ray or radiotherapy, only the area of the body that <u>needs to be treated</u> is exposed to radiation. The rest of the body is <u>protected with lead</u> or other <u>radiation absorbing</u> materials.

Radiation sickness — well yes, it does all get a bit tedious...

In the months following the <u>atomic bombing of Japan</u> in 1945, thousands suffered from <u>radiation sickness</u> — the symptoms of which include nausea, fatigue, skin burns, hair loss and, in serious cases, death.

Uses of Radiation

Radiation gets a lot of bad press, but the fact is it's essential for things like modern medicine. Read on chaps...

Smoke Detectors — Alpha Radiation

1) A weak alpha radioactive source is placed in the detector, close to two electrodes.
2) The source causes ionisation of the air particles which allows a current to flow.
3) If there is a fire, then smoke particles are hit by the alpha particles instead.
4) This causes less ionisation of the air particles — so the current is reduced causing the alarm to sound.

Radiotherapy — the Treatment of Cancer Using Gamma Rays

1) Since high doses of gamma rays will kill all living cells, they can be used to treat cancers.
2) The gamma rays have to be directed carefully and at just the right dosage, so as to kill the cancer cells without damaging too many normal cells.
3) However, a fair bit of damage is inevitably done to normal cells, which makes the patient feel very ill. But if the cancer is successfully killed off in the end, then it's worth it.

TO TREAT CANCER:

1) The gamma rays are focused on the tumour using a wide beam.
2) This beam is rotated round the patient with the tumour at the centre.
3) This minimises the exposure of normal cells to radiation, and so reduces the chances of damaging the rest of the body.

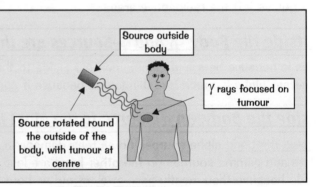

Source outside body

γ rays focused on tumour

Source rotated round the outside of the body, with tumour at centre

Tracers in Medicine — Short Half-life Gamma and Beta Emitters

1) Certain radioactive isotopes that emit gamma (and sometimes beta) radiation can be used as tracers in the body.
2) They should have a short half-life — around a few hours, so that the radioactivity inside the patient quickly disappears.
3) They can be injected inside the body, drunk or eaten or ingested.
4) They are allowed to spread through the body and their progress can be followed on the outside using a radiation detector.

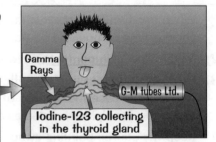

Gamma Rays

G-M tubes Ltd.

Iodine-123 collecting in the thyroid gland

Example

Iodine-123 is absorbed by the thyroid gland.
It gives out radiation which can be detected to indicate whether or not the thyroid gland is taking in the iodine as it should.

5) All isotopes which are taken into the body must be GAMMA or BETA (never alpha). This is because gamma and beta radiation can penetrate tissue and so are able to pass out of the body and be detected.
6) Alpha radiation can't penetrate tissue, so you couldn't detect the radiation on the outside of the body. Also alpha is more dangerous inside the body (see previous page).

Ionising radiation — just what the doctor ordered...

See — radiation isn't all bad. It also kills bad things, like disease-causing bacteria. Radiotherapy and chemotherapy (which uses chemicals instead of gamma rays) are commonly used to treat cancer.
They both work in the same way — by killing lots and lots of cells, and trying to target the cancerous ones...

Uses of Radiation

Ionising radiation has loads more uses, and you get to read all about them. Whoop-ti-do.

Tracers in Industry — For Finding Leaks

This is much the same technique as the medical tracers (see previous page).

1) Radioactive isotopes can be used to track the movement of waste materials, find the route of underground pipe systems or detect leaks or blockages in pipes.

2) To check a pipe, you just squirt the radioactive isotope in, then go along the outside with a detector. If the radioactivity reduces or stops after a certain point, there must be a leak or blockage there. This is really useful for concealed or underground pipes — no need to dig up the road to find the leak.

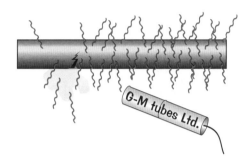

3) The isotope used must be a gamma emitter, so that the radiation can be detected even through metal or earth which may be surrounding the pipe. Alpha and beta radiation wouldn't be much use because they are easily blocked by any surrounding material.

4) It should also have a short half-life so as not to cause a hazard if it collects somewhere.

Sterilisation of Food and Surgical Instruments Using γ-Rays

1) Food can be exposed to a high dose of gamma rays which will kill all microbes, keeping the food fresh for longer.

2) Medical instruments can be sterilised in just the same way, rather than by boiling them.

3) The great advantage of irradiation over boiling is that it doesn't involve high temperatures, so things like fresh apples or plastic instruments can be totally sterilised without damaging them.

4) The food is not radioactive afterwards, so it's perfectly safe to eat.

5) The isotope used for this needs to be a very strong emitter of gamma rays with a reasonably long half-life (at least several months) so that it doesn't need replacing too often.

Beta Radiation is Used in Thickness Gauges

1) Beta radiation is used in thickness control.

2) You direct radiation through the stuff being made (e.g. paper), and put a detector on the other side, connected to a control unit.

3) When the amount of detected radiation changes, it means the paper is coming out too thick or too thin, so the control unit adjusts the rollers to give the correct thickness.

4) The radioactive source used needs to have a fairly long half-life so it doesn't decay away too quickly.

5) It also needs to be a beta source, because then the paper will partly block the radiation (see p.133). If it all goes through (or none of it does), then the reading won't change at all as the thickness changes.

Warning — Only use a thickness gauge on inanimate objects...

Nuclear radiation is used for loads more things than tracers and thickness gauges. It can be dangerous if you're not careful with it, but mostly it's really handy. Phew, there's quite a lot to take in on those last few pages but there's no rest for the wicked — I guess you must have been really bad as there are still a few pages to go...

Nuclear Fission

Unstable isotopes aren't just good for medicine — with the right set-up you can generate some serious energy.

Nuclear Fission — the Splitting Up of Big Atomic Nuclei

Nuclear power stations generate electricity using nuclear reactors.
In a nuclear reactor, a controlled chain reaction takes place in
which atomic nuclei split up and release energy in the form of heat.
This heat is then simply used to heat water to make steam, which is
used to drive a steam turbine connected to an electricity generator.
The "fuel" that's split is usually uranium-235,
though sometimes it's plutonium-239 (or both).

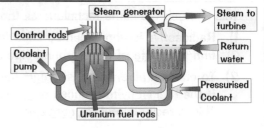

The Chain Reactions:

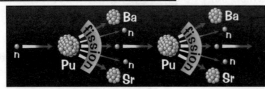 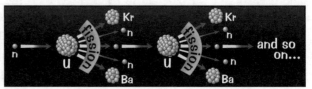

1) For nuclear fission to happen, a slow moving neutron must be absorbed into a uranium or plutonium nucleus. This addition of a neutron makes the nucleus unstable, causing it to split.

2) Each time a uranium or plutonium nucleus splits up, it spits out two or three neutrons, one of which might hit another nucleus, causing it to split also, and thus keeping the chain reaction going.

3) The chain reaction in the reactor has to be controlled, or the reactor would overheat.

4) Control rods absorb some of the neutrons and slow down the reaction.

5) When a large atom splits in two it will form two new smaller nuclei. These new nuclei are usually radioactive because they have the "wrong" number of neutrons in them.

6) A nucleus splitting (called a fission) gives out a lot of energy — lots more energy than you get from any chemical reaction. Nuclear processes release much more energy than chemical processes do. That's why nuclear bombs are so much more powerful than ordinary bombs (which rely on chemical reactions).

Nuclear Power Stations May Cause Quite a Few Problems

The main problem with nuclear power is that it produces radioactive waste.

1) Most waste from power stations (or medical use, see p.134) is 'low level' (slightly radioactive). E.g. things like paper and gloves, etc. This waste can be disposed of by burying it in secure landfill sites.

2) Intermediate level waste includes things like the metal cases of used fuel rods and some waste from hospitals. It's usually quite radioactive — and some of it will stay that way for tens of thousands of years. It's often sealed into concrete blocks then put in steel canisters for storage.

3) High level waste from nuclear power stations is so radioactive that it generates a lot of heat. This waste is sealed in glass and steel, then cooled for about 50 years before it's moved to more permanent storage.

4) The canisters of intermediate and high level wastes could then be buried deep underground. However, it's difficult to find suitable places. The site has to be geologically stable (e.g. not suffer earthquakes), since big movements in the rock could break the canisters and radioactive material could leak out.

5) Even when geologists do find suitable sites, people who live nearby often object.

6) So, at the moment, most intermediate and high level waste is kept 'on-site' at nuclear power stations.

7) Nuclear fuel is cheap but the overall cost of nuclear power is high due to the cost of the power plant and final decommissioning. Dismantling a nuclear plant safely takes decades.

8) Nuclear power also carries the risk of radiation leaks from the plant or a major catastrophe like Chernobyl.

I'm split over fissi drinks — loads of energy, but bad for your teeth...

There's enough uranium and plutonium around to provide us with energy for years, but it's difficult to deal with the waste we've already got. I bet you wouldn't want nuclear waste buried under your backyard, eh...

Nuclear Fusion

Loads of energy's released either when you break apart <u>really big nuclei</u> or join together <u>really small nuclei</u>. You can't do much with the ones in the middle, I'm afraid. (Don't ask, you don't want to know.)

Nuclear Fusion — The Joining of Small Atomic Nuclei

1) <u>Nuclear fusion</u> is the <u>opposite</u> of nuclear <u>fission</u>.

2) In nuclear fusion, two <u>light nuclei combine</u> to create a larger nucleus.

3) One example is <u>two atoms</u> of different <u>hydrogen</u> isotopes combining to form <u>helium</u>:

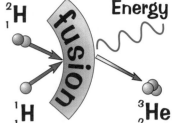

$$^1_1H + ^2_1H \rightarrow ^3_2He$$

4) Fusion releases <u>a lot</u> of energy (<u>more</u> than fission for a given mass) — all the energy released in <u>stars</u> comes from fusion at extremely <u>high temperatures</u> and <u>pressures</u>. So people are trying to develop <u>fusion reactors</u> to make <u>electricity</u>.

5) Fusion <u>doesn't</u> leave behind much radioactive <u>waste</u> and there's <u>plenty</u> of hydrogen about to use as <u>fuel</u>.

6) The <u>big problem</u> is that fusion only happens at <u>really high pressures</u> and <u>temperatures</u> (about <u>10 000 000 °C</u>). It doesn't happen at <u>low temperatures</u> and <u>pressures</u> due to the <u>electrostatic repulsion</u> of <u>protons</u> (like charges repel each other, see p.111).

7) <u>No material</u> can physically withstand that kind of temperature and pressure — so fusion reactors are <u>really hard</u> to <u>build</u>.

8) It's also hard to <u>safely control</u> the high temperatures and pressures.

9) There are a few <u>experimental</u> reactors around at the moment, the biggest one being <u>JET</u> (Joint European Torus), but <u>none</u> of them are <u>generating electricity yet</u>. It takes <u>more</u> power to get up to temperature than the reactor can produce.

10) <u>Research</u> into fusion power production is carried out by <u>international</u> groups to <u>share</u> the <u>costs</u>, <u>expertise</u>, experience and the <u>benefits</u> (when they eventually get it to work reliably).

> **FUSION BOMBS**
>
> * Fusion reactions also happen in <u>fusion bombs</u>.
> * You might have heard of them as <u>hydrogen</u>, or <u>H bombs</u>.
> * In fusion bombs, a <u>fission reaction</u> is used first to create the really <u>high temperatures</u> needed for fusion.

Cold Fusion — Hoax or Energy of the Future?

1) A new scientific theory has to go through a <u>validation</u> process before it's accepted.

2) An example of a theory which <u>hasn't</u> been accepted yet is '<u>cold fusion</u>'.

3) Cold fusion is <u>nuclear fusion</u> which occurs at around <u>room temperature</u>, rather than at millions of degrees Celsius.

4) In 1989, two scientists reported that they had succeeded in releasing energy from cold fusion, using a simple experiment. This caused a lot of <u>excitement</u> — cold fusion would make it possible to generate lots of electricity, easily and cheaply.

5) After the press conference, the experiments and data were <u>shared</u> with other scientists so they could <u>repeat</u> the experiments. But <u>few</u> managed to reproduce the results <u>reliably</u> — so it hasn't been accepted as a <u>realistic</u> method of energy production.

Pity they can't release energy by confusion...*

Fusion bombs are <u>incredibly powerful</u> — they can release a few <u>thousand</u> times more energy than the nuclear fission bombs that destroyed Hiroshima and Nagasaki in World War II.

---

*There'd be plenty of physics books to use as fuel.

The Life Cycle of Stars

Stars go through many traumatic stages in their lives — just like teenagers.

Protostar

1) Stars initially form from clouds of DUST AND GAS. The force of gravity makes the gas and dust spiral in together to form a protostar.

2) Gravitational energy is converted into heat energy, so the temperature rises. When the temperature gets high enough, hydrogen nuclei undergo nuclear fusion to form helium nuclei and give out massive amounts of heat and light. A star is born. Smaller masses of gas and dust may also pull together to make planets that orbit the star.

**Main
Sequence
Star**

3) The star immediately enters a long stable period, where the heat created by the nuclear fusion provides an outward pressure to balance the force of gravity pulling everything inwards. The star maintains its energy output for millions of years due to the massive amounts of hydrogen it consumes. In this stable period it's called a MAIN SEQUENCE STAR and it lasts several billion years. (The Sun is in the middle of this stable period — or to put it another way, the Earth has already had half its innings before the Sun engulfs it!)

**Stars much
bigger than
the Sun**

**Stars about
the same size
as the Sun**

4) Eventually the hydrogen begins to run out. Heavier elements such as iron are made by nuclear fusion of helium. The star then swells into a RED GIANT, if it's a small star, or a RED SUPER GIANT if it's a big star. It becomes red because the surface cools.

Red Giant

White Dwarf

Red Super Giant

5) A small-to-medium-sized star like the Sun then becomes unstable and ejects its outer layer of dust and gas as a PLANETARY NEBULA.

6) This leaves behind a hot, dense solid core — a WHITE DWARF, which just cools down to a BLACK DWARF and eventually disappears.

Supernova

Neutron Star...

...or Black Hole

7) Big stars, however, start to glow brightly again as they undergo more fusion and expand and contract several times, forming elements as heavy as iron in various nuclear reactions. Eventually they explode in a SUPERNOVA, forming elements heavier than iron and ejecting them into the universe to form new planets and stars.

8) The exploding supernova throws the outer layers of dust and gas into space, leaving a very dense core called a NEUTRON STAR. If the star is big enough this will become a BLACK HOLE.

Red Giants, White Dwarfs, Black Holes, Green Ghosts...

The early universe contained only hydrogen, the simplest and lightest element. It's only thanks to nuclear fusion inside stars that we have any of the other naturally occurring elements. Remember — the heaviest element produced in stable stars is iron, but it takes a supernova (or a lab) to create the rest.

Revision Summary for Section 9

Phew... what a relief — you made it to the end of the book. But don't run off to put the kettle on just yet — make sure that you really know your stuff with these revision questions.

1) Explain how the experiments of Rutherford and Marsden led to the nuclear model of the atom.

2) Draw a table stating the relative mass and charge of the three basic subatomic particles.

3) Explain what isotopes are. Give an example. Do stable or unstable isotopes undergo nuclear decay?

4) True or false: radioactive decay can be triggered by certain chemical reactions.

5) Give three sources of background radiation.

6) What are the units of radiation dose? What two things does radiation 'dose' take into account?

7) List two places where the level of background radiation is increased and explain why.

8) Name three occupations that have an increased risk of exposure to radiation.

9) What type of subatomic particle is a beta particle?

10)* Complete the following nuclear equations by working out the missing numbers shown by the dotted lines:
   a) $^{131}_{53}\text{I} \rightarrow \,^{.....}_{.....}\text{Xe} + \,^{0}_{-1}\beta$ b) $^{.....}_{.....}\text{Gd} \rightarrow \,^{144}_{62}\text{Sm} + \,^{4}_{2}\alpha$

11) Sketch the paths of an alpha particle and a beta particle travelling through an electric field.

12) Define half-life.

13)* The activity of a radioactive sample is 840 Bq. Four hours later it has fallen to 105 Bq. Find the half-life of the sample.

14) Sketch a typical graph of activity against time for a radioactive source. Show how you can find the half-life from your graph.

15) Explain what kind of damage ionising radiation causes to body cells. What are the effects of high doses? What damage can lower doses do?

16) Which is the most dangerous form of radiation if you eat it? Why?

17) What substances could be used to block:
    a) alpha radiation, b) beta radiation, c) gamma radiation?

18) Describe the precautions you should take when handling radioactive sources in the laboratory.

19) Describe in detail how radioactive sources are used in each of the following:
    a) treating cancer,   b) medical tracers,   c) sterilising food,   d) thickness gauges.

20) Draw a diagram to illustrate the fission of uranium-235 and explain how the chain reaction works.

21) What is the main environmental problem associated with nuclear power?

22) What is nuclear fusion? Why is it difficult to construct a working fusion reactor?

23) Briefly explain why cold fusion isn't accepted as a realistic method of energy production.

24) Describe the steps that lead to the formation of a main sequence star (like our Sun).

25) Why will our Sun never form a black hole?

* Answers on page 142.

Index

Index

Index and Answers

Revision Summary for Section 2 (page 42)

23) BB and bb

Example on page 64

A is simple molecular, B is giant metallic,
C is giant covalent, D is giant ionic

Bottom of page 67

1) Cu: 63.5, K: 39, Kr: 84, Cl: 35.5

2) NaOH: 40, Fe_2O_3: 160, C_6H_{14}: 86, $Mg(NO_3)_2$: 148

Bottom of page 68

1) a) 30.0% b) 88.9% c) 48.0% d) 65.3%

2) CH_4

Bottom of page 69

1) 21.4 g

2) 38.0 g

Revision Summary for Section 4 (page 72)

12) $2Li_{(s)} + Cl_{2(g)} \rightarrow 2LiCl_{(s)}$

18) a) KCl   b) $CaCl_2$

19)

29) a) 40 b) 108 c) 44 d) 84 e) 106 f) 81
    g) 56 h) 17

31) a)i) 12.0% ii) 27.3% iii) 75.0%
    b)i) 74.2% ii) 70.0% iii) 52.9%

32) $MgSO_4$

33) 80.3 g

Revision Summary for Section 5 (page 87)

14) b)

Revision Summary for Section 7 (page 110)

3) $a = (v - u) \div t$; 35 m/s^2

11) $F = ma$, so $a = F \div m$; 7.5 m/s^2

12) 1.33 m/s^2

13) 120 N

18) $E = F \times d$; 6420 J

19) $KE = \frac{1}{2} \times m \times v^2$; 20 631 J

20) The car would stop in 5.1 m, so he will hit the sheep.

21) a) 1200 J
    b) 600 J

22) 15 600 J

Revision Summary for Section 8 (page 128)

6) 4 A

12) 1.2 V

13) 4.8 W

18) 12.5 Hz

24) Hair straighteners: E = 13 500 J
    Hair dryer: E = 12 600 J
    The hair straighteners use more energy.

25) 3180 J

30) $V_p/V_s = N_p/N_s$ so
    $V_s = (500 \div 20) \times 9 = 25 \times 9 = 225$ V

Revision Summary for Section 9 (page 139)

10) a) $^{131}_{53}I \rightarrow \,^{131}_{54}Xe + \,^{0}_{-1}\beta$

    b) $^{148}_{64}Gd \rightarrow \,^{144}_{62}Sm + \,^{4}_{2}\alpha$

13) 1 hr 20 minutes

15) When using the concentrated acid it will take less time to produce the same amount of gas than when using the dilute acid — the rate of reaction is faster.
    The slope of the graph (time vs volume of gas) will be steeper for the acid which produces the faster rate of reaction.